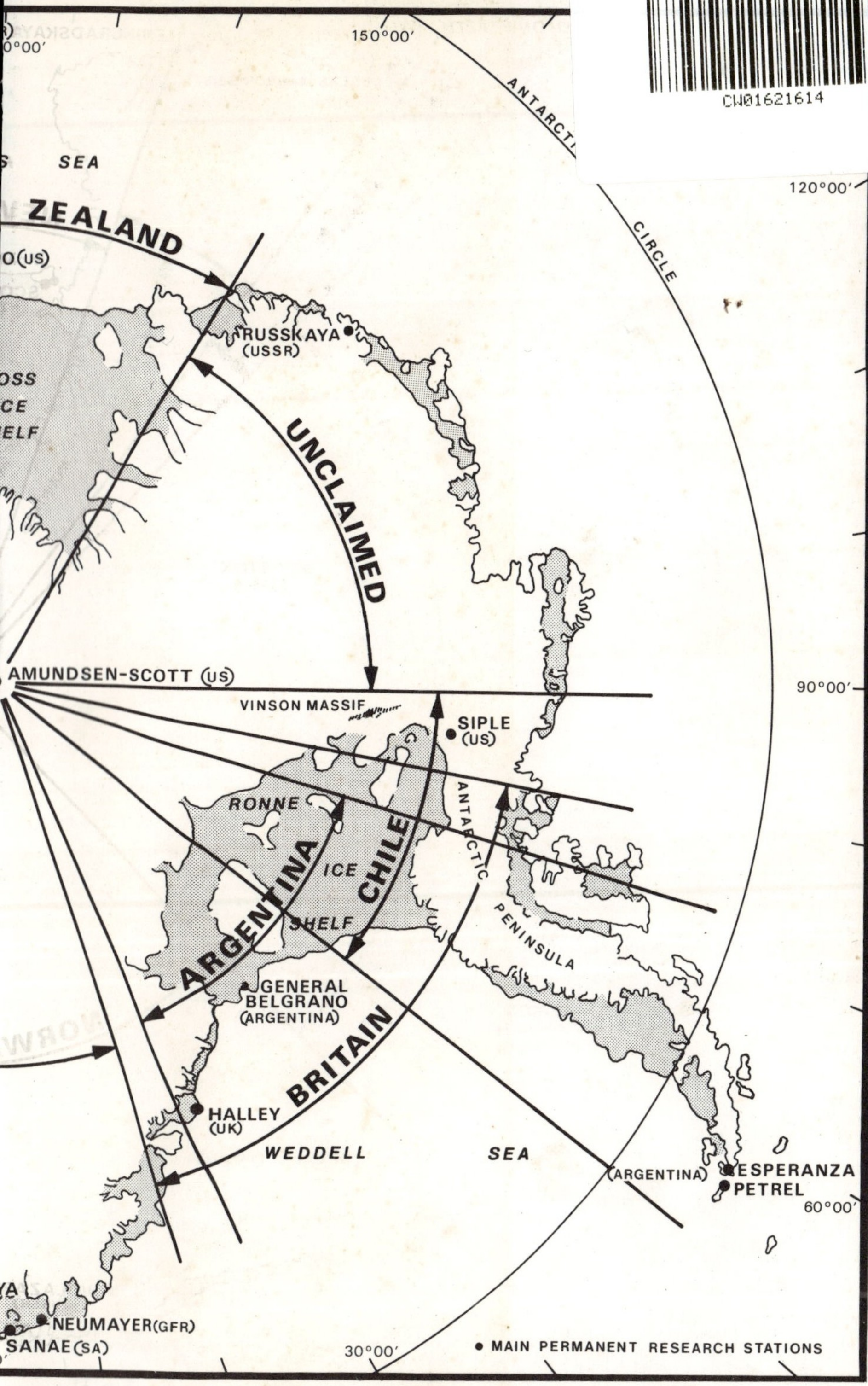
150°00′
ANTARCTIC CIRCLE
120°00′
SEA
ZEALAND
RUSSKAYA
(USSR)
UNCLAIMED
AMUNDSEN-SCOTT (US)
VINSON MASSIF
SIPLE
(US)
90°00′
RONNE
ICE
SHELF
ARGENTINA
CHILE
ANTARCTIC
PENINSULA
GENERAL
BELGRANO
(ARGENTINA)
BRITAIN
HALLEY
(UK)
WEDDELL
SEA
(ARGENTINA)
ESPERANZA
PETREL
60°00′
NEUMAYER(GFR)
SANAE(SA)
30°00′
• MAIN PERMANENT RESEARCH STATIONS

SITTING ON PENGUINS

PEOPLE AND POLITICS IN AUSTRALIAN ANTARCTICA

STEPHEN MURRAY-SMITH

Drawings by Jan Senbergs

HUTCHINSON
AUSTRALIA

CENTURY HUTCHINSON AUSTRALIA PTY LTD
89-91 ALBION STREET, SURRY HILLS, NEW SOUTH WALES 2010

SYDNEY LONDON
AUCKLAND JOHANNESBURG
AND AGENCIES THROUGHOUT THE WORLD

FIRST PUBLISHED 1988

NATIONAL LIBRARY OF AUSTRALIA
CATALOGUING-IN-PUBLICATION DATA

MURRAY-SMITH, STEPHEN, 1922– .
SITTING ON PENGUINS.

BIBLIOGRAPHY.
INCLUDES INDEX.
ISBN 0 09 169120 6.

1. ANTARCTIC REGIONS – DESCRIPTION AND TRAVEL. 2. AUSTRALIAN ANTARCTIC TERRITORY (ANTARCTIC REGIONS). I. SENBERGS, JAN, 1939– . II. TITLE.

919.8′904

DESIGNED BY GUY MIRABELLA
TYPESET IN 11/13 VLADIMIR
BY SOLO TYPESETTING, SOUTH AUSTRALIA
PRINTED IN SINGAPORE

CONTENTS

FOR

SHIRLEY AND STAN GREY

OF DEAL ISLAND

KEEPERS OF THE LIGHT

PREFACE

Sitting on Penguins has several purposes, but first among them is to present the experience of an Australian's first visit to Antarctica *according to the impressions received at the time.*

This is not, then, a study in repose, a disinterested history or any form of recollection in tranquillity. The facts here are verifiable only in the sense that they happened to me or were told to me. I believe this is a useful way of presenting an experience of this nature. Readers may note inconsistencies or contradictions in my responses. My answer is "Of course." This is the way we all work towards an understanding of what is happening to us.

Looking back at the voyage of the *Icebird* from a perspective of nearly two years leads me to a more charitable view of shortcomings than perhaps emerges from these pages. In relation to the Antarctic Division, and to the events of 1985–86, I am now inclined to give more weight than I did then to several factors: upheavals within the Antarctic Division, the efforts against opposition of a Minister and Director to change much of the philosophy of Australia in Antarctica, and above all the enormous pressures surrounding the carrying out, against appalling natural difficulties, of some of the most complex operations known to man. I have a hearty appreciation of those who meet these challenges and, time and again, overcome them. But first impressions are also important.

I of course owe special gratitude to Barry Jones, then Minister for Science, for making my voyage possible; to Jim Bleasel, Director of the Antarctic Division, for his continued friendly support of my interference in Antarctic affairs; and to Graeme Manning, my voyage leader, who did so much to make my experience fruitful. I am also in debt to those, both within and outside the Antarctic Division, who read the manuscript and made useful comments on it.

Captain Ewald Brune, and the officers and crew of the *Icebird*, were exemplary hosts and became good friends. And my friends and fellow-passengers on the *Icebird*, as well as those on the bases, all helped to turn interest into understanding, or so I hope.

Jan Senbergs' generous agreement to allow his drawings to be used in this book adds greatly to it. His visit to the Antarctic, also on the *Icebird*, followed a year after mine.

This book owes most to Elizabeth Douglas, then of these publishers, who thought of it.

S. M-S.

AUTHOR'S NOTE

Measurements in this book are given variously in metric and imperial terms, sometimes within the same paragraph. No attempt at consistency has been made in this. We are living in a period in which both forms of measurement are in common use in Australian society, and I have used the form in each case which seemed most natural to me at the time of writing. In any case, in historical contexts in particular, imperial standards are more appropriate. A conversion table follows.

S. M-S.

1d (penny)	0.83 cent
1s (shilling)	10 cents
£1 (pound)	$2
1 inch	2.54 centimetres
1 foot	0.30 metre
1 mile	1.60 kilometres
1 acre	0.40 hectare
1 oz (ounce)	28.3 grams
1 lb (pound)	0.45 kilogram
1 gallon	4.54 litres

GLOSSARY

ANARE	Australian National Antarctic Research Expeditions. The term covers those sections of the work of the Antarctic Division concerned with the establishment, operation and maintenance of Australian stations and bases in Antarctica. This includes transport, logistics and research both in Australia and in Antarctica.
Antarctic Division	The Antarctic Division of the Department of Science of the government of Australia. (Since 1987 the Division is part of the Department of the Arts, Sport, the Environment, Tourism and Territories, known variously as "Disneyland" and the "Mickey Mouse Club".)
base	Used by the Antarctic Division to mean a temporary Antarctic establishment, as distinct from a *station*.
DHC	Department of Housing and Construction, now (1988) DASCON (Department of Administrative Services (Construction Group).
dongas	Detached sleeping quarters at Antarctic stations.
jolly	An excursion for purposes of pleasure.
larc	Amphibious landing craft (Lighter Amphibious Resupply Cargo).

oic	Officer-in-charge of an Antarctic station or base. Pronounced *oik.* This traditional title has been replaced (1988) by that of Station Leader.
RTA	Return to Australia, of stores or personnel.
station	A permanent Antarctic (Casey, Davis, Mawson) or sub-Antarctic (Macquarie Island) establishment.
supercargo	Ship's officer responsible for the stowage and handling of cargo.

1

I pulled myself up out of the bunk at five in the morning to peer out of the cabin window. It was dark, and darkness at night was already something I had half-forgotten about. Indeed the ship's doctor had said to me, weeks before down in the Antarctic, "When you go back you'll welcome the dark." What he hadn't said was that I would also welcome the rain. Only a day or two before the first spatters of rain, of real, wet water, had slashed the bridge windows where I was standing, and I went outside to feel it on my skin. For I had come from a continent which is always dry, where water is almost unknown, and where rain does not exist. Even falling—as distinct from driven—snow is rare. Actual precipitation along the Antarctic coast I had visited is about three inches a year—one-tenth that of Melbourne. Antarctica, in other words, is a desert, a desert where bulldozers pulling sledges replace camel trains, and the nearest thing to an oasis is an ice-free outcrop of rock. The Russians actually called one of their stations Oasis.

I did see some water in Antarctica. At Commonwealth Bay, the site of Douglas Mawson's old hut, and the windiest place on earth, it was unseasonably warm. The day we were there the temperature was just above freezing; it was snowing, but the snow was turning to water as it hit the ground. There were runnels of water under the snow and ice, busily gurgling down into Boat Harbor. We were warned that we could fall through crusts into hidden ponds. Our 'ventiles'—jackets and trousers made of closely woven English cotton cloth—were useless; designed to ward off the wind, the great ally of cold and its sharp-edged sword, they simply absorbed the water which was never supposed to fall on them. And the water at Commonwealth Bay spelt death for thousands, as we shall see.

I had a reason for glancing out of that cabin window at five in the morning. I wanted to remind myself that I belonged somewhere. I had, six weeks before, been unrooted from my homeland. I had sailed, with sixty or seventy companions, ever southwards, almost dead southwards. I had passed through regions ever more remote, inducted day by day into new levels of mystery, hiding as the experience deepened much of my consciousness of what lay behind me. We were excited, even the old hands. Our minds were thrusting forward. The story-books of generations were coming alive. As one gate opened before us, another closed behind. Shortly we were enmeshed in the nets of a new world, where the sun shone twenty-four hours a day, and something new was happening every one of those twenty-four hours. The news we heard was of 'fast' ice, not urban tragedy. The plans we were party to were plans of cargo-handling, not of electoral intrigue. We were in a kind of limbo.

Return from this was unexpectedly hard. We had to orient ourselves anew, from the simple but profound to the complex but superficial. We had been allowed to glimpse great beauties, unimagined beauties; and although man in Antarctica is rarely beautiful, at least his ugliness is no more than a spot of ink on a great marble edifice. We were returning to a society in which all sorts of ugliness, and not just physical ones, were inescapable. We were also, of course, returning from paternalism, at many levels and in many forms, to responsibility.

In other words, we were returning to a real world, and as our ship, homeward bound, reeled off the thousands of miles, sanity, a grasp of reality, started to prevail. "*No-one* on this ship is sane," said our doctor. "Those with us who have been away their fourteen or sixteen months are certainly not sane; but even you, by the time you've been on this ship in these waters two or three weeks, are not sane either." A curtain had been lifted for us—and it was now dropped. We were beginning to think of leaving the theatre, and of where the car was parked.

We were thinking of nice things, like families and friends, and no doubt of nasty things, like bank managers—on whom be peace—also. And I—I was starting to think of where I belonged. Part of me stayed in Antarctica—I have plenty to spare—but most of me came back.

And, in the dark far out from that cabin window, I saw what I of the Derwent, a far outer suburb of Hobart. It was a political deal by the Fraser government, designed to win Tasmanian votes. As a deal it didn't have much going for it. Melbourne had been the home of the Antarctic Division since its establishment in 1948. Melbourne was closer to political power, to contractors, to communications. Moving to Hobart lost the Division a lot of its best people, not readily replaceable.

Moving not only to Hobart, but to what people in Hobart regard as the sticks, created yet further problems. The purchase of the site at Kingston was part, it is said, of yet another political deal. Magnificent sites were offered on the waterfront in Hobart, sites which would have been suitable at least for the main administrative offices of the Division, but they were rejected. Many of those now at Kingston feel that they are doubly isolated from the stimulus of a metropolis.

Yet the move had its logic, the move to Hobart at least. Hobart looks straight south to the Antarctic. As we sailed away in the *Icebird* on 29 December 1985 and left the Derwent, feeling the ship starting to rise and fall under our feet as the westerly swells rolled at us, Peter Gormly—ship's doctor for the trip—turned to me and said: "You're very lucky, you know. On this trip we're going straight south, the way they did in the old days. Keep on this heading and you'll reach the South Pole. Our Australian stations are far to the west—normally we make a long slant down to them. This time we're going straight there." And so we did. It seemed hardly believable, looking back at it, that we crossed the Antarctic Circle and reached the continent itself within five days. Hobart is much closer to Antarctica than to Perth.

And perhaps no lover of Tasmania can begrudge its getting a slice of the Commonwealth cake. Cynics say that another advantage of the move to Tasmania is that ships take less time to load there than on the Melbourne docks. But for me there's enough justification that it feels right to sail down the Derwent to Antarctica, and it wouldn't feel right to sail down the Yarra on the same mission.

So you get a taxi and you wend way out through the hills to Kingston. The evening before you landed in Hobart with a great load of gear destined for the Antarctic venture: clothes, and

had been looking for: a spot of light which grew and exploded and then diminished, with another spot following close behind it, and then the blackness closed in before the pattern repeated itself. The light of Maatsuyker Island. Julie and Graham Heynes were there, back of that light; Julie's parents, Shirley and Stan Grey, have been on the Deal Island light-station for a number of years. Shirley and Stan are dear friends. My wife Nita and my daughter Joanna have just spent a month over there beside them, on the next-door island. Nita will be home now. She'll be wanting to know what time the ship berths, how I'll be getting back to Melbourne. How will I get a message to her?

And so the old curtain I had forgotten about rises before me, and I find myself gazing at a stage where so much is familiar, and is loved. I am, in short, home.

But not quite. Dawn breaks as we are close inshore along that magnificent south coast of Tasmania. There is Precipitous Bluff; on our starboard side Pedra Branca and the extraordinary stack of Eddystone Rock, looking as though it were erected of masonry. Soon there is Bruny light; and as we pass round and turn north into D'Entrecasteaux Channel, I think of how many weary seamen in centuries past—Tasman, Cook, Bligh among them—were grateful for the haven of Adventure Bay tucked in round the corner: furled sails, level decks, rest, wood and water.

It is high-jinks weekend in Hobart, Regatta Day coming up, and the navy's coming in. In fact a sinister black submarine tracks us up the Derwent. A pilot boards, and for the first time on the voyage we are driven off the bridge.

Lee Ranford, from the Bureau of Mineral Resources, is a big bloke with one of the ship's best senses of humor. He's been a major contributor to my morale on board. We're chatting down the blunt end with the two delightful Italian observers we have had as shipmates. Lee says to them, that wicked gleam in his eye, "You know, it's always a mistake to bring too many Australian warships together in the one place. They have a tendency to run into each other."

The banks of this beautiful river slide past us on this last hour of our long voyage. There's plenty to do. All our gear has to be brought down interminable companionways and piled on the foredeck, to be offloaded by Customs before we leave the ship. (There's much hard feeling among expeditioners about the way they are done over by Hobart Customs on their arrival. "They've so little to do they welcome the chance to get stuck into us," is the general comment. The opportunities for smuggling from the Antarctic are limited! Certainly the blokes down there can buy duty-free goods when they go down, but the Antarctic Division, worried about the grog position, discourages any follow-up orders—a paternalism that rankles. The Customs reception certainly detracts from the emotional drama of returning home, and families that may not have seen each other for well over a year are kept compulsorily apart for an hour after berthing.)

We're up into the Hobart dock area now. Our bows are swinging around to the Salamanca Place wharf. Uwe Johannssen, the rubicund chief cook, has had his beloved German military marches blasting over the loudspeakers, and over half of Hobart, for the last half-hour: a rather bizarre accompaniment to our return, but accepted in good humor. The chaps—and a few women aboard—are lining the rails, trying to pick out girlfriends and boyfriends and wives, mothers and fathers, daughters and sons. Some have come from far away to be here. The returners are happy—some have the last remaining tinnies on board in their hands—but a bit subdued. This is a serious moment.

And suddenly, watching it from above, much of the cynicism of the last weeks falls away from me. The irritations of shipboard life, the disappointments that men and women in Antarctica are as other men and women are, and no better, the gossip on manners and morals, these seem trivial things. I am caught up—not much better than an observer, it is true, but still a part of it—I am caught up in a heightening of emotion, in a rite of passage, in something that is bigger than its parts. In Australian terms, in terms of national understatement, in terms of the absence of heroics, there is suddenly a heroic element intruding itself here. Perhaps it is only I who has a lump in my throat—but I think that others do too. "I come from realms of ice and snow"—isn't that a quotation? It's true enough, at any rate: these people have crossed a great divide, and have now crossed back again.

They carry with them, my companions, memories and insights

and knowledge and feelings which they can never fully impar others, no matter how much they love them and how much t try. All travellers have this problem, but for us, whose travels h been in strange regions and by strange ways, the problen greater. It is not a problem of description, though that is a fac for what you see is really a part of the circumstance of seeing. more a problem of emotion, of attitude, of the mind. "All you have not loved her, You will not understand"—that's a par another half-remembered quotation.

Well, perhaps this all seems a bit ridiculous. We have undergone separation, but few have experienced peril. Still, feeling is there. That is why, now at the end, we suddenly see best in each other, cling in the last dying moments of the voyag the *Icebird* to those who have been worked as we have, who been changed, who will, in the common idiom, 'never be the s again'.

And then it is all over. Some are claimed by those they Some disappear to weekend billets. Some, a fortunate fe Antarctic bureaucrats, just go home. Some of us, urban cun still surviving within us, organise ourselves a lift to the airport the way Paul Butler, facing a reunion in Melbourne with a and young son he has not seen for well over a year, says to "That sudden end. That passing through the wall. It make think of other things that will happen to us." I know wha means.

The first news we heard on landing was that HMAS *Pert* Hobart for the celebratory weekend, had rammed a pie berthing, had demolished an office on the pier and very nearl people inside it, had then backed off and rammed it again. much must be said for our navy: when we passed the ship o way to the airport, an hour or so after the occurrence, they slapped a coat of paint over the battered bow of the ship.

2

The Antarctic Division of the Department of Science was 'up from Melbourne in 1981 and deposited at Kingston, on the es tobacco, a video camera, a 'steam' camera, dozens of films, clothes of all sorts (you've been told people wander around the airconditioned ship in shorts, and indeed some do), a large fruitcake baked by wife and daughter, a library of books, Antarctic and otherwise, a typewriter—and half a dozen duty-free bottles of Black Label, not actually with you and ordered to be put on the ship in advance.

You have already, that evening before, boarded the ship, and without permission. No-one seemed to mind. You went straight there from the airport, and your eyes widened a little as you saw this strange-looking, 6000-ton ship lying there at the Salamanca Place wharf, where so many have laid before her: whalers and traders and windjammers and perhaps even Roald Amundsen's *Fram* herself, for this was Amundsen's first port of call after winning the race to the South Pole, and tonight you intend to sleep—as you always sleep when you come to Hobart—in the bed at Hadley's Hotel which was Amundsen's first bed in a year or more. Or so you like to imagine.

Streaming with sweat, and with the help of two kind friends who met you at the airport, you lug your heavy gear up what seem interminable flights of stairs inside the *Icebird* to your neat cabin high up in what you learn to call the 'module'. Ulli, one of the two women stewards on board, obligingly shows you the way and unlocks the cabin for you. You dump everything inside, except what you want for the night in Amundsen's bed, and then set out ashore in quest of a cold, cold beer. Soon you will be in places where they heat beer up to melt it.

But now we are at the futuristic headquarters of the Antarctic Division at Kingston, looking more like the headquarters of a space mission than of polar explorers. Other lost-looking people are gathering. You wander around the 'display' area: old wooden sledges, stuffed penguins, a gentleman in full Antarctic gear you very nearly ask a question of until you realise he's a dummy. Gradually you are taken in hand: you are ticketed and listed. You are sent to a quartermaster's store where, if you have been in the army, you will recognise the experience of being regarded as a nuisance and issued on a hit-or-miss basis with what are supposed to be the essentials for Antarctic survival. ('Round-trippers', of whom you are one, are in any case regarded as a pretty contemptible species of Antarctic traveller.) Still on your best behavior, you do not argue.

Summoned to a meeting hall, you are given brief lectures on the nature of the operation you will be taking part in, and on health and safety. You would be more impressed by the latter if in fact you had just been issued with the proper clothes you are now told are necessary to keep you alive, but even so the pictures of horrible frost-bite lesions which are thrown up on a screen before you, and of black and burst fingers (I recognise some of these as belonging to a former neighbor of mine), do have the intended effect, even on a Hobart summer day. And, enlightened self-interest being what it is, you look carefully at the graphs which show you that it is the 'wind-chill' factor that kills, not the temperature.

Jim Bleasel is the Director of the Antarctic Division. He is an engineer, and prior to joining the Antarctic Division worked with the National Materials Handling Bureau in Sydney, where he dealt with the supply and transport problems of remote communities in Australia and in the 'developing' countries. He has been in charge of our Antarctic affairs since early 1984, being confirmed as Director in January 1985, a few days after his forty-ninth birthday.

He's a cheery fellow, quick to admit his problems, not rattled by hard questions. If he were a boxer, you feel, he'd be exceptionally quick on his feet, and perfectly capable of smiling sweetly as he landed an unexpected jab on your ribs. He hasn't had the easiest of times since he first occupied the Director's chair. His first sin, in the eyes of some, is that he's not a scientist but an engineer. Indeed this is a nice issue. Under the Antarctic Treaty our only reason for being in Antarctica is to do scientific work, and other nations' Antarctic work—that of Britain and New Zealand, for instance—is largely masterminded by scientists. On the other hand—I'll talk about it later—our main problems in Antarctica at the moment are organisational, logistical, engineering problems. (Behind these again are conceptual problems, but that's another matter.) Whether it's the complicated shipping position we are talking about (devilishly complicated, this summer) or the complete physical reconstruction of our bases which is now under way, most of our problems down south at the moment *are* physical ones.

Jim's other sin is that he is not an 'Antarctic' man: that he came in through public service channels and on the basis of his reputation as a trouble-shooter. He came into a Division which (although weakened by the move to Hobart) was intensely proud of its 'hands-on' expertise. Jim had never driven a team of huskies, he'd never fallen through the sea-ice into freezing water, he'd never spent a winter in the cold and dark on an Antarctic base. Indeed, until the summer of 1984–85, he'd never set eyes on the frozen land. He has had to fill in gaps, by imagination and study and talk, that others knew about the hard way.

Not easy. Most people like to feel that the general who is sending them into battle has, at least in his youth, heard a shot or two fired in anger. Phil Law, Jim's most famous predecessor and the founder of our present Antarctic work—his *Antarctic Odyssey*, which I read on the voyage, is a splendid and exciting account of 'early days' and the establishment of our first base at Mawson in 1954—admittedly never wintered in Antarctica either. But Phil notched up some thirty gruelling trips down south and took an active part in field work: his real contribution, overlaid by other concerns since he resigned in 1966, is only now beginning to be seen in its true perspective. I don't know if Phil Law ever hankered after as meretricious an award as a knighthood, but I do know that it was pathetic that public service and political jealousies prevented his being offered one. Few men in his time did more for Australia.

Jim Bleasel's 'handicaps', which he seems to be gamely surmounting—partly by recognising them—are interesting because they reflect wider issues. The basic issue is one which lies over our whole Antarctic endeavors—are we still running a corner-store, or are we running a supermarket? If we are running a corner-store, we need to know how to make a chocolate malted. If we're running a supermarket, we need to know a lot about market trends, local demography, delivery trucks, public relations, managerial skills.

The image of the family grocer, long white apron and pencil behind ear, is an attractive one—some of us remember them. The image of the Antarctic explorer, furred and mittened, icicles on the beard, cursing as he struggles with his sled over the sastrugi, is also an image to be held dear. And, as a matter of fact, that kind of Antarctic explorer, unlike the grocer, is still around, though you will have to travel far—to our Mawson station, in fact—to find him.

No-one would want to see the huskies removed from Mawson—almost the last place they are to be found in the Antarctic—and, in fact, it's a rare concession to the sense of history that we still have them there. (Get an accountant into the Antarctic Division as Director and they'll soon be gone.) But in some ways they hold us back. Courage, fortitude, kindness, humor, patience are characteristics that are still needed in Antarctica, and always will be. Antarctica, Australian Antarctica, is run by people, and perhaps in these days of high tech there is some danger of forgetting this. The calibre of the people we have down there, and the support we can give them, is fundamental. Things go wrong and there are many grouches. Our bases down there sometimes self-destruct. As a diesel mechanic said to me, ANTARCTICA IS A PEOPLE PROBLEM, something that should be engraved above every room in the Antarctic Division.

But the issues, political and planning, are now on a rarified level. The last English king to lead his troops into battle was George II. Douglas Mawson ran his Antarctica, when he was down there in 1912, from the hut at Commonwealth Bay. Today Australian Antarctica is run from Hobart and from Canberra. The computer and the satellite have placed the Book of All Power in the hands of 'central office'. The results of this are both good and bad, as we shall see. Given the situation, though, it is more important for a Director of the Antarctic Division to be able to chair a meeting well than for him to be able to read a sun compass.

For all that, looking at the Antarctic Division as it is in 1988 as this book goes to press, and giving credit to Jim Bleasel for much dedicated and remarkable work, it must be said that the problems of the Division remain considerable. It is one of the purposes of this book to suggest how and why this is so. Bleasel is, as I have recounted, on the surface the most open of men—or at least he has been with me. I have no doubt that he has visions for the Division, and for Australia in Antarctica. I suspect he works well at a political and at an international level. But I also suspect that his problems are more complex than can be accounted for by a simple 'new man' versus 'old guard' thesis. He feels very strongly that managerial competence is a far rarer commodity than Antarctic experience, and far more relevant in today's world, and he carries this attitude through with an entrepreneurial flair which gives not a few of his colleagues the impression that their views, their own experiences, are not rated highly. I admire Bleasel greatly, but I think this is an area he should watch, not so much for his sake as for all our sakes.

Antarctica is thirteen and a half million square kilometres, half again the size of Australia. The ice dome which rides down hard on the rocky base of the continent is up to 4800 metres thick. Vinson Massif, the highest point of the continent, is 5140 metres high. The mean annual temperature is minus 10° Celsius at sea level, minus 60° on the plateau. (Read that last figure again.) The lowest temperature recorded is minus 89.6° (at the Soviet base of Vostok, actually, on what we are pleased to call Australian Antarctic Territory). The wind may blow in excess of 150 knots (ah, at last we're back with a pre-metric measurement which Captain Scott would have recognised).

All this we learn from a noticeboard. We thought we knew a bit about Antarctica, we did, but there is food for thought there.

Jim Bleasel invites a few of us into his office. His enthusiasm masks the fact that he probably hasn't had lunch, and even turns our mind off our own stomachs. He sits us down and gives us a beer, and starts to give us some more facts and figures on Antarctica. He talks to us first about why we are going by ship, when the New Zealanders and the Americans fly blithely into McMurdo base in the Ross Sea by great aircraft out of Christchurch. Attempts to establish a safe runway on the ice near Casey have failed—and we shall hear more about this when we get to Casey. Even if there were a safe strip there, elementary arithmetic now enters the issue. From Hobart, in say a Hercules aircraft, it would only take seven and a half hours (assuming a fifty-knot headwind) to fly to Casey, the nearest Australian station, 1846 nautical miles. But how long would it *really* take to get there? First of all, we have to have thirteen extra staff, meteorologists and the like, down at Casey to handle the receiving end of the air link. (There are already complaints about too many support personnel and too few scientists on the stations.) Our loading capacity at Hobart would be limited, for any aircraft would have to carry fuel for the whole round trip plus a considerable safety margin. It can be worked out fairly accurately how often flights would have to be cancelled or, once in the air, aborted. When the sums are done we find that mathematically it would take six days to fly to Casey. A ship, sailing directly from Hobart to Casey, takes six days, perhaps seven.

So we are already being conditioned about what we will later hear spoken about as the "A-factor", the Antarctic factor, the *man proposes God disposes* factor, the sense you sometimes have in Antarctica that you are being played with, in an amused kind of way, by forces beyond your comprehension or imagination. You will learn that the A-factor breaks marriages and breaks men, that it has simple ways of humiliating those who go down there armoured with horse-power and great machines and state-of-the-art technology and what the Greeks called *hubris*, an arrogance that arises from self-confidence. The earlier explorers were more humble than we are. Their armor was very thin, and unless they learnt fast that the only way to beat Antarctica was to work *with* it, they failed or they perished.

They taught us much, but not enough. If you don't have a gun, you have to persuade people to your point of view. If you don't have a bulldozer, you think more carefully before you start digging with pick and shovel. Technology leads, not only to arrogance, but also to false security. Last year one of our tracked vehicles, out on the icecap, fell into a crevasse (a 'slot', as it's called in Antarctic parlance). The men in it were safe, and so was the machine, but it was immovable. The answer should have been simple—send a radio message to Casey on the distress frequency. But the radio room at Casey was so busy that the distress frequency was turned down low, and no-one heard the message. As a result our people had an uncomfortable night out. The best-laid plans . . .

Yet, with luck, man will also match his ingenuity to the challenge. This conversation may bear witness:

Don the 'dieso' (diesel mechanic): "My New Guinea girlfriend has too many brains for a dieso like me."

Me: "Now look, you were out there on traverse, four months away from Casey in all, living in a caravan pulled by a bulldozer. About eight weeks out and 800 kilometres from Casey the dozer snapped a link. The only normal way to replace one is with a sixty-ton press in a workshop. You got going with an ordinary vice, a piece of pipe and an oxy flame, and you managed to get a spare link fitted. The temperature at the time was minus 47° Celsius, the wind was sixty-five knots. It was a magnificent bit of improvisation. And you say that to pull that off doesn't require brains!"

Don: "You wouldn't be out there if you had any brains."

From the problems of air transport Jim Bleasel moves on to the grosser problems of institutionalisation in Australian Antarctica, the freezing of the arteries, so to speak, the great master plan we have down there which, to our surprise and embarrassment, in the last few years we have found mastering us, rather than the other way around. Since we all learn by doing, not by being told, we listen with only one ear. Later, when our noses are rubbed in the icecap, we see what Jim means, except that by that time his words have faded and we think we're making a new discovery for ourselves. But one phrase he uses will then come back to me: "We unfortunately now have the best of everything, being put together by bright young engineers who have never heard of a steady state. We don't need the best of everything."

Bleasel probably won't like those words being quoted. They were made off the cuff in a private conversation. Nor are they literally true. We haven't got the best of everything in Antarctica, even if Louis Bernacci or Douglas Mawson, Edgeworth David or Griffith Taylor would not believe the evidence of their eyes if they went down there today. It is true that, in the modern manner of government, money has been thrown at problems in the hope that they will go away; but it is also true that many problems remain, some caused by money and some—'people problems' particularly—which are not solvable by money. Jim Bleasel would wish to qualify and footnote his remark before it got into print. I'm not going to let him, partly because it gives a hint as to the character of the man, daring to be a Daniel, and partly because in its essence it contains a great deal of the truth which those of us, now boarding the *Icebird*, were on the way to finding out for ourselves.

3

Twenty-four hours out. Three hundred and fifty nautical miles south of Hobart, and for the first time there's a premonitory chill in the air—nothing much to go on yet, but it's creeping in the porthole, slightly ajar, with just that touch of a finely honed edge.

Peering out, I see the seas from the back, for they are coming at us from the prevailing western weather systems, they are right on the beam, and from our port-side spy-point, perched up on the top storey of the so-called 'module', we see them only after they have passed under us. I know enough to realise that, from this angle of vision, they look far less threatening than they would if they were coming at you over the bow. The giveaways are the breaking tops

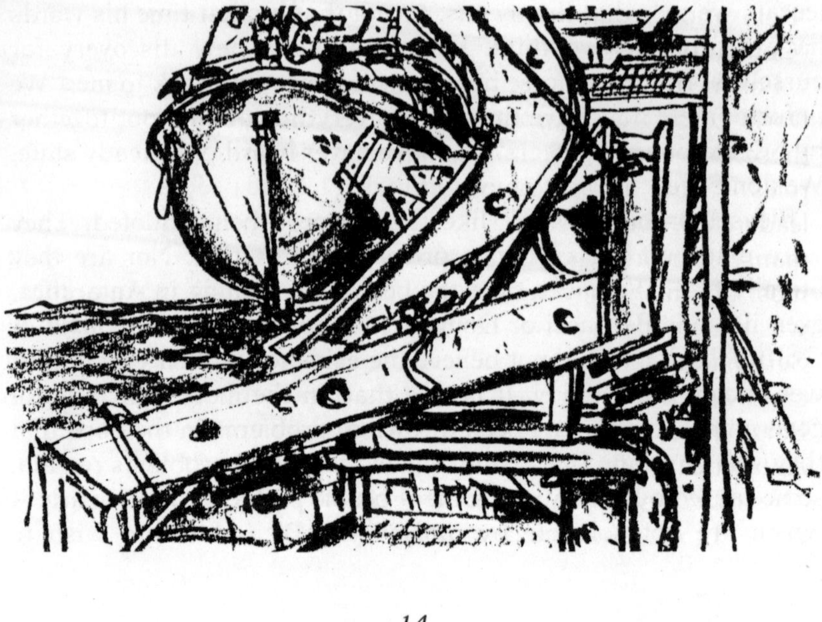

and the white slicks running down their backs, signs of trouble and anger. Grey sprays drift across from our bows.

We are on our way to Antarctica. I wonder how many have made this trip before us, to land on the last continent. Seventy or eighty thousand? Only forty years ago there would have been so few that we would have known most of the names. But since then? Over a thousand Americans a year these days, and for how many years has that been going on? Dozens of bases and more to come every year. We have Italians and a Spaniard and a Swede on board, all wanting a finger in the pie. Two or three hundred Australians alone just this very summer. They say the marks of all these grubby hands are very visible. I shall see.

4

It all started at something called a "Word Fest" in Canberra early in the year 1985. I had reluctantly and foolishly broken my personal rule not to attend conferences of any kind, and a reach-me-down mob of poetasters and politicians was edging its way into a formal dinner at University House—the place with the Henry Moore-ish figure of a reclining man outside, originally titled "Relaxation" but—so it is said—by official rescript retitled "Contemplation".

For me the dinner was notable for three reasons. I talked with Doris Lessing on my interest in remote communities and the way those that survive seem to do so by suppressing overt leadership roles—"But," Doris Lessing said, "don't some people seem to *want* leadership, whatever the social system: the Russians, the Germans?" I heard Thomas Keneally tell his audience, in one of the most optimistic statements ever made by man or woman, that it was the civilising power of the written word that had stopped the Serb hating the Croat, the Irish Protestant child the Irish Catholic child, and the Greek the Turk. And I made an impertinent aside to Barry Jones, Minister for Science and hence also Minister for Antarctica: "When are you going to send me down to Antarctica?" "Next December" came the reply before Barry disappeared in the crush. I took it as a piece of sadistic humor.

Still, a few months later I did ask Barry Jones if he meant it. In that crisp way of his he said, "Certainly." Then I asked why he would want to send me down south. "I want you to give me your views on what you think is going on." "But I must have a title—you can't send me out into the cold without a title!" Trouble here. Most titles have been grabbed by government and mean, for instance, that you have to be paid. I wasn't going to be paid and I didn't want to be. Finally it was agreed that I should be a Ministerial Observer, a fine bit of bureaucratese which may mean as little or as much as one wishes.

Later on Barry Jones, with whom I have fought shoulder to shoulder in many a doughty fight on international quiz programs against the heathen New Zealanders and British, agreed that it would be a good idea if I 'wrote for the press'—a fine old phrase—while I was a-travelling. The *Australian* said they'd be pleased if I would write for them. It was a happy association. I enjoyed taking up a journalistic pen I had dropped many years before. Shipboard life has some delights, but they quickly dull, and I had something to keep me as busy as I cared to be while afloat. And, most important of all, having to write for an audience about what I was seeing meant that I had to seek out opinions, dig for facts, and put both the opinions and the facts into my own conclusions, and then work out how best to present those conclusions in words that would be read by some hundreds of thousands of people.

It wasn't easy. In fact it was a damn sight harder than I thought it was going to be. First there was the moral question: I had to tell the truth as I saw it to my readers, but I also had a responsibility to Barry Jones, both as my 'employer' and as my friend. What if he, or Jim Bleasel, didn't like what I had to say? What if they viewed me as a snake let loose in an icy Eden? I decided that both Jones and Bleasel were big boys, sophisticated men who would see, or at any rate come to see, that writing about problems and eschewing puffery would in the long run, and probably in the short run, do them more credit than not. All writing is selection and 'heightening', and good painting 'distorts' in order to be true, as the columns on the Parthenon bulge half way up in order to appear straight. It is more important to tell the truth as you see it than to strive for some sort of gutless 'objectivity'.

There was another problem, an infinitely more frustrating one, the physical problem of transmitting press messages from a ship in the Antarctic. It would sometimes take two days to get a press story researched, written, entered into the word-processor in the radio room by the bridge, and finally transmitted.

The only place I could conveniently type was in the cramped cabin I shared with Brendan Doran. Brendan, in his thirties, works in the Antarctic section of the Department of Foreign Affairs. Bearded, spectacled, quiet, methodical, he hides a sense of humor under a diplomat's formal facade. From 1981 to 1984 he was first secretary at the Australian Embassy in Madrid, and hence he was the only man who could converse in Spanish with the Spanish observer on board, the amiable, tall and craggy-nosed Jaime Ribes-Lorda, an army major and a Catalan.

Later on in the voyage we were joined by another cabin-mate, a German biotechnician from Kiel, Andreas Kühn, who, poor fellow, spent much of his time in his bunk with a very pale face. Neither Brendan nor Andreas were smokers, and found the pipe I smoke when composing a bit ripe. They often wanted to rest when I wished to write. Even if all was well, in some seas the carriage of my typewriter, travelling downhill as I typed and the ship heeled, found the effort of coming back again too much.

Once the message was written it had to be taken up to the radio room. On the *Icebird*, owing to its peculiar configuration, most movement is in a vertical rather than a horizontal plane: to get to the bridge involved me in descending thirty-one steps and then ascending fifty-five, a tiresome process in a moving ship, repeated many times a day. The radio officer would then point out that there was some reason why I couldn't type my story into the processor: meteorological reports to go out, 'radphone' calls booked, long official satellite phone calls between Hobart and the ship, even—in rough weather—an inability to link up with the Inmarsat satellite because of the hectic rolling of the ship. Sometimes I was just ready to get stuck into it by noon, when the radio officer went off duty for two hours! All the time deadlines back in Sydney were getting closer: 3 p.m. Eastern Summer Time for features, 6 p.m. for news stories.

The point about this was that, as we gradually steamed west, starting at the longitude of Hobart and ending at the longitude of Bombay, we were falling further and further behind Eastern Summer Time! A deadline of six in Sydney therefore sometimes meant a deadline of 2 p.m. on the *Icebird*. Hours could be spent kicking one's heels outside the radio room, meals missed, tension mounting, anger rising. Then the chance to go! Sit at the processor. Try to anchor the chair, which slides backwards and forwards across the floor at each roll of the ship. A lurch, wrong keys hit, backtrack and correct copy. Finally message typed in, button pressed, hey presto! and in a matter of a minute or two the story is in the *Australian*'s computer: AUS ONLY ATTENTION PIERS AKERMAN FROM STEPHEN MURRAY-SMITH ABOARD MV ICEBIRD IN ANTARCTIC WATERS. Tomorrow the world!

When I got back to Australia I asked Piers Akerman, deputy editor of the *Australian*, why some of my stories hadn't appeared. He was puzzled. Later the explanation emerged. "They went into the computer and were lost, and now we have no way of getting them out again." I thought glumly of my heroic Antarctic endeavors in the cause of public enlightenment.

So that is why, in this book, I print a number of the stories I sent back to the *Australian*. Generously treated though my copy was, some of the stories never appeared, some were shortened, a few inaccuracies and misreadings occurred, inevitably, in the process of subediting in the *Australian*'s office. Here the stories are printed as they were written. The date of publication in the newspaper is appended, though the story as printed here may be slightly different from the story that appeared in the *Australian*, and corrections have been made.

And here is the first.

The custom-built polar vessel *Icebird*, on charter from its German owners to the Australian government, left Hobart yesterday evening on the fifth of seven Antarctic voyages mounted or planned this year under Australia's expanded $40 million high-latitude programs. The voyage is under the leadership of Graeme Manning, the Expedition and Field Operations Manager of the Antarctic Division of the Department of Science.

Among the fifty-six passengers on the *Icebird* are scientists and technicians, both for the present summer programs and in some cases for an extended stay over the winter. Special guests of the Australian

> government are representatives of Swedish, Spanish and Italian Antarctic committees. Thirty members of an Italian exploratory scientific expedition have already landed at Terra Nova Bay on the Victoria Land coast of the Ross Sea, and will remain there two months. The Italian government will establish a provisional base there next year.
>
> *Icebird* will reach Commonwealth Bay, the site of Mawson's base of 1911–13, on 5 January, to embark members of the Project Blizzard party who have been investigating the preservation of Mawson's hut, which is still standing. Two sons of C.T. Madigan, the well-known geologist and Central Australian explorer, and the man in charge of the erection of Mawson's hut in 1912, are aboard *Icebird*. They are Sir Russel Madigan, mining engineer, deputy chairman of Conzinc Rio Tinto Australia, and chairman of the Australian Antarctic Names and Polar Medals Committee, and Michael Madigan, a surgeon resident in England, who has flown out especially for this visit of family significance. The Madigans hope to lie in the bunk on which, photographs show, their father's name is carved.
>
> The major aims of this voyage are to investigate the establishment of a future summer station in the Commonwealth Bay area, to resupply Casey, one of three permanent Australian Antarctic stations, and to service bases at Davis and Mawson. An attempt is to be made while at sea to locate the exact present position of the South Magnetic Pole. The ship is proceeding in fair weather and moderate seas. A sweep is being run on the sighting of the first icebergs, expected in two or three days' time.
>
> (*Australian*, 31 December 1985)

It may serve as an illustration of the hazards of reporting at a distance that the last sentence of this story was printed in the *Australian* as "Radar sweepings are being run in anticipation of first iceberg sightings"!

5

Why call a German ship the *Icebird*? I asked. The question caused our German friends some amusement. We're a business, they said. We were built in a business-like way in the shipyard at Oldenburg—one year from laying down the keel to our first polar voyage. You Australians try that out, they said. (They like us, but they think the way we run things is for the pixies. "It costs as much to ship a container from Melbourne to Hobart as from

Hamburg to Melbourne.") We work in a business-like way. We're the ANTARKTIS-UND SPEZIALFAHRT SCHIFFAHRTSGESELLSCHAFT mbH of Hamburg. We have eleven ice-strengthened ships. We operate on contract all round the world. You charter us for 150 days for $4 million. After that you pay us $1300 an hour. We don't make much on our work down here for you. The icing on the cake is the work we do up in the Arctic in the northern summer—when we leave here we're going to take oil-drilling equipment from Japan to north of Alaska. This ship is a work-horse on the international market. We have to have an international name. *Eisvögel* wouldn't do. *Icebird* was adopted as a tribute to the scholar, navigator and author David Lewis, who made the first single-handed voyage to Antarctica, and to his yacht, *Ice Bird*.

We are a *GL + 100 A4 E4 Arc 1 GMC E4 Aut forepart Arc 2 Icebreaker*. Icebreaker? Well, yes, the *Icebird* is *ice-strengthened*, and it can charge into five-foot-thick hard ice, as we did at Davis, ride up on it with its flat sloping bow, and with luck break it, but it's not a *real* icebreaker. *Icebird* develops 5400 horse-power, the Japanese icebreaker *Shirase* 30,000! Ice which stops *Icebird* dead the *Shirase* steams through merrily, like a bay excursion steamer, while the crew play tennis on the top deck. It was the *Shirase* which went into the frozen pack for us in December 1985, and rescued the *Nella Dan* after nearly eight weeks' besetment. (No charge—everyone takes in each other's washing in Antarctica.) *Real* icebreakers like the *Shirase* cost . . . well, let's quote John D. Rockefeller when a fellow capitalist asked him how much it cost to build and run his yacht: "If you need to ask you can't afford it."

She's a rum ship in many ways, the *Icebird*. The state of the art, they say. Barry Jones went into raptures over chartering her in 1984 for a five-year stint. She's 6300 tons deadweight, 360 feet long, sixty-six feet wide, with a working speed of about thirteen knots. Red all over, with the crest of Hamburg on her bow, she has many special features, such as holds that open right up, so that there's no deck overhang. Looked at quizzically from the dock, as I did that first day in Hobart, you'd see her basic similarity to a container ship in outline—

—but you'd be puzzled by one or two things. Those four red lifeboats, for instance, are fully enclosed: you enter through hatches, and pull them to after you. (They can hold about fifty people, and if capsized can be righted by shifting those inside around.) Then there are two enormous cranes. Again, forward of the superstructure at the back of the ship there is a three-storey, square iron box with a flat roof. It is enormous (it weighs 300 tons), it is removable (though only a few cranes in the world can remove it) and it houses the ship's passengers.

This 'module' deserves a few words to itself. It provides comfortable accommodation for the passengers, fifty to a hundred. Some of the cabins indeed have their own bathrooms. The 'ground floor' includes a large mess room, a servery and a hospital. The module is completely independent from the rest of the ship: if it fell overboard the ship could carry on as before, and there would be many fewer mouths to feed. Fell overboard? You're joking! Well, the trouble is that some clever German engineers mounted the module on rubber blocks (as is the superstructure). When the *Icebird* shoves its way through the pack-ice, both the superstructure and the module vibrate backwards and forwards. It's a bit like being on a cantering horse. But worse, when the ship rolls, the module shifts from side to side on its blocks, until it is brought up against retaining devices. It's an unnerving experience, lying in your bunk and waiting for that reassuring *clunk!* It's said that the first time it happened, during the *Icebird*'s first season, the module emptied more smartly than it had ever done at a boat drill. And a song was composed about it, to the tune of "Click go the Shears": "Snap go the Bolts". I heard one expeditioner say with feeling: "I'll need an independent engineer's certificate of safetly before I board this ship again." No doubt an overreaction—but it *is* a strange feeling.

The other problem about the module are the vacuum-operated lavatories, about which I shall have more to say later. They did cause a lot of hard feelings, especially among the highly trained engineers who had to clear them every morning, so much so that one of the ship's engineers was heard to remark bitterly, on the general question of the module: "This isn't German engineering. This is *South* German engineering—and a five million mark solution to a 20 million mark problem!"

By Australian standards the *Icebird* is run, very efficiently, by a small, hard-working crew: a master and three mates, a radio operator, two engineers, an electrician, a bosun, two ABs and three Ordinary Seamen (one of whom happened to be a seawoman, a Tasmanian, actually), two cooks, three stewards and two "motormen", assistant engineers. They don't *ask* for assistance, and perhaps don't even *want* it, but the Antarctic Division believes that everyone on the ship should make at least a gesture towards working their passage, and so shipboard duties are posted every day. Some clean passageways and public rooms, such as they are. Others serve as "Mombasas", as scullions or slushies. The word Mombasa enters our language—cleaning those pots and pans can be *quite* a job. Why Mombasa? Uwe, the cook (who quietly ran me up a few of my favorite German dishes on the side) was once on the Hamburg–East Africa run. When in African ports he had African helpers in the kitchen, and they came to be called Mombasas. We had a fellow-feeling for them.

In the pack, of course, there was much to see, either from the deck or up on the bridge. Even so, there were many hours each day when those on board had to find their own amusement. There was a neatly fitted-out bar below decks, donated to the ship by the Hamburg brewery whose products (72,000 bottles at the beginning of the season, 64,800 left by the middle of January) helped to ballast the ship. The bar was open briefly in the morning, closed at the time you most felt like a drink, just before dinner, and open after dinner. Prices were not cheap: sixty cents for a small bottle of beer, $12 for a bottle of champagne, $22 for a bottle of Black Label, available duty-free at $7 and probably less to the ship. The cynics aboard ascribed the pricing policy either to the rapaciousness of the ship's owners or to the wowserish paternalism of the Antarctic Division, or to both. This didn't stop some wild parties in the bar—you didn't have to be in the bar to know about them—one of which ended up with a visit to the ship's hospital.

You could read, of course, though there wasn't much of a ship's library. You could sleep. You could spend a couple of hours a day eating, if you wanted to: there was plenty of food, a strange Australian/German mixed cuisine, and always materials for a snack left out in the servery for raids by anyone at any time, a pleasant Antarctic tradition. I often found the ship's Dagwood Bumsteads down there at two o'clock in the morning.

The main fall-back for most passengers was watching videos in the mess room. There was a large television in the corner and an enterprising collection of cassettes. During some exceptionally bad weather, when sleep was out of the question for many, I once received an invitation to "the 5 a.m. Western". When all the videos had been run through once, they went on air a second time, starting, I think, with *The Anzacs*, another example of the 'let's pat ourselves on the back' self-satisfied Oz myth-making which seems to suit our current national yearning. Yes, it was the videos that kept boredom at bay for most—or perhaps they just intensified it.

Down in the bowels of the ship, where the beer was stored, half a hold had been left clear for a volley-ball court—since the module was on top of it, it couldn't be used for ordinary cargo in any case—and there were many bitterly contested games—the Mombasas versus the German crew—until the two volley-balls disappeared. Malevolence? A drunk booting them overboard? Resentment by some that others were enjoying themselves too much? Many felt the loss of the balls deeply, and when we called at the Antarctic stations we found they didn't have any to spare. Late in the voyage one of the balls turned up again, but by then the heart had gone out of what had been a vigorous competition.

AFTERWORD

It's easy to be seduced by the affability of the *Icebird*'s officers and crew, but later on matters fall into other perspectives. Despite breezy remarks about the relative unimportance of the Australian charter, as matters stood in 1987 this charter was of fundamental importance to the ship, which has not been successful in obtaining much other work. More importantly, there is a basic contradiction between the interests of *any* chartered ship and the interests of the people, in this case the Australian people, who charter her. The Antarctic Division's objectives with shipping are to deploy and retrieve personnel, and to equip and re-supply our bases, as expeditiously and as safely as possible. The interests of any private company from which a ship is chartered are to extract the maximum profit from the contract. There are legitimate, marginally legitimate and illegitimate ways of doing this. While ships are on time contracts, as our Antarctic ships are, rather than job contracts, there will always be accusation and counter-accusation in these areas.

As Voyage 6 developed the tensions between the chartered and the charterer became increasingly visible. To an extent, of course, such tensions are to be expected. But it will be clear that for the

Icebird to accuse the Antarctic Division of being amateurish and ill-informed in shipping matters is to bolster the case for the *Icebird*'s freedom of action in its own interests. The observer has to beware of being used as a pawn in a game. Unfortunately there is evidence both of the absence of high-level shipping operations know-how in the Antarctic Division, and of the *Icebird*'s taking advantage of this. "These Germans aren't that smart, but they're smart enough to pick our weaknesses," said one astute observer.

6

Diary, 1 January 1986

The lassitude of recent days is disappearing from the ship. People are stirring. The mess, empty for days, apart from a few hardy ones, is now full again at mealtimes. The commodious and handsome bridge has its wandering population of stickybeaks and adventurers who want to know what's going on around them. Up there you can pick up all sorts of trifles of information: the sea temperature is down to 2°C; shearwaters (muttonbirds) breed on Macquarie Island; no-one has positioned themselves over the South Magnetic Pole since Mayaud in 1952, and that was only the third time it had been done—in a few days we hope to do it for the fourth time. Up on the bridge one of our Italian observers tells me that salt water freezes, not at 0°C, but at −1.8°C. An officer tastes the cup of coffee he has just made for himself, grimaces, and darts into the lavatory to dispose of it. A flurry of snow is reported. Geraldine, our cheerful and concerned deputy voyage leader, looks out over the grey seas and the grey skies and says, "It's wonderful what you can see out there if you look." She adds: "No white water today. You ought to be able to see the whales spouting." But I look in vain.

Our most stricken passenger, Michael Madigan, is again on his feet, and seems little the worse for his miseries of recent days. At four this morning a befuddled New Year reveller, stumbling upstairs from the little smoke-filled 'pub' in the bowels of the ship, tried to get into bed with Michael. The shock seems to have effected an instant cure. Nothing impresses me more about this mob of Australians that I am with than the fact that I have heard no complaints about having to drink warm German beer rather than cold Aussie cans. (Though last night the champagne flowed free as well as freely.)

The point is that everyone on board has a job to do, and is either doing it now or soon will be. They are obviously a competent lot, whether they are army larc drivers, experienced Antarctic geologists or my cabin companion, Brendan from Foreign Affairs. Brendan will arrive with two others, all but unannounced, at the door of the Frenchmen at their Dumont d'Urville base on Friday, to carry out an inspection of their station under the terms of the Antarctic Treaty—the first inspection carried out by Australians of another nation's base since 1963, and a mark of our determination to employ our rights rather than, Brendan says, to assert them.

What could they be doing wrong? I ask. Well, in theory they could be disposing of nuclear wastes, or setting up rocket bases, or laying waste the environment. (Actually, there has been criticism of the airstrip the French are building at Dumont d'Urville, which is said to have obliterated penguin colonies, but I don't think our inspectors will be looking for trouble. The Antarctic Treaty is fragile enough without members of it going out of their way to annoy each other.) Will the rest of us get ashore? We don't know yet. First of all, we're in a hurry. Then the French would have to invite us. But in any case, they say, the anchorage is spectacular.

Our friends are tight-lipped about it, but I suspect we would have liked to have dropped in on a Russian base, on this trip, to give them a *dobryi den* and the once-over. The chance of doing that has been put paid to by the bloody *Nella Dan* incident: as we left Hobart she came in, fifty-four days beset in the ice, and rescued by that Japanese icebreaker. So that's put everything back. It's really a count-back job. Traditional Antarctic wisdom says that all ships should be well out of the place by the beginning of March. This year the *Icebird*, as plans go at the moment, won't be out of her last port, Mawson, until 14 March. *Extremely* late, they say, with the winter closing in. So all our operations are now geared to that touch-and-go conclusion to the season's activities.

7

The high drama of our departure from Hobart didn't belong to us! Hundreds, perhaps thousands, of citizens lining the wharves, a launch full of jazzmen playing some splendid Dixieland as they cruised in and out of the docks, helicopters in the sky, and every small craft that could bear a sail, and a great many that couldn't, at sea in the Derwent on this fine afternoon, sunlight glancing off the boats' wakes and plumes of smoke—bushfires, beacons?—from the wooded hilltops of Hobart which suggest a land still under siege. A heroes' farewell?

No. As it happened, we cast off and slid quietly down the estuary as the first yacht home in the Sydney–Hobart race came belting up from the south, its great blue spinnaker clawing out ahead, a gallimaufry of welcoming boats playing around its path, hooters acclaiming its achievement—we added our own siren to them as we steamed past. *Apollo*, someone said she was. It was rather moving. She was sailing in to haven as we were leaving for visions and challenges unknown. She was finishing an adventure, we were starting one. They were home, and we were soon going to be far from home.

Already some of the unexpected or unremembered realities of shipboard life were apparent. I'd forgotten, for instance, how damn noisy a ship can be. Not the *Apollo*, perhaps with the swish of the water along her hull and the mere creak of the wind in its gear, but a complex floating machine like the *Icebird* creates an immense volume of noise: engines, air intakes and exhausts, whistles, announcements, falling crockery, slamming doors; even on the bridge there are clattering telex machines, shouts from people trying to make themselves heard on radiophones and the pinging of the satellite navigator as it gives us a new fix. Only up at the bow, as Peter Gormly later quietly pointed out to me, can you hear the real Antarctic sound of a ship's pushing her way through an icy sea.

There are rites of passage as we drive south, with some fellow-feeling—as featureless day succeeds to featureless day—for the ancient mariners who wondered if the day would come when they might fall off the edge. About half-way to the Antarctic coast, and only three days out, for our ship may seem to plod but it eats up the miles, we cross the great Pacific–Antarctic Ridge. The sea shoals from 12,000 feet, say some 4000 metres, to seven or eight thousand feet, 2500 metres, as we slip over the divide we cannot see. Now we are down to 56° South and well into the Antarctic Convergence, the point where the cold waters of the Antarctic sink beneath the warmer waters of the temperate seas, and where the mixing brings an explosion of food and predators. We have seen the albatross for some time, but now we see the brown petrels, the cape pigeons so fondly remembered from the Tristan da Cunha voyage of 1982, cheekily flashing their magpie colors in our wake, and—surprise—muttonbirds. In my provincial mind they're Bass Strait birds, but as love laughs at locksmiths so they laugh at geographical 'typing'. I've read somewhere, Dom Serventy's writings perhaps, that they're the most numerous of all bird species.

Yes, the pace of our involvement with Antarctica is now increasing. Odd items of news creep through the ship, the way news gets around even when newspapers have long been forgotten and no-one bothers to listen to the radio. The footsteps of Scott relief expedition on the *Southern Quest*, which left Australia before us against the warnings and rumblings of my *patron* Barry Jones, reports 400 somethings of pack-ice in McMurdo Sound. *Miles* of pack-ice? *Kilometres* of pack-ice? It doesn't make very much difference. It's a hell of a lot of pack-ice.

Later on we'll be more professional about this. We'll know to ask *What kind of pack-ice*? Four-tenths? Eight-tenths? Ten-tenths? Each demands a different response and a different kind of ship. And is it tight pack or loose pack? This can make the difference between success and defeat, medals or extinction. So, we're a bit apprehensive about that *Southern Quest* report. The old hands are unimpressed. The coast we're making for, the coasts of Adélie Land and Victoria Land, are traditionally relatively free of ice. That's how d'Urville got down there, and Douglas Mawson, though Queen Victoria never made it.

A flurry of snow reported from the bridge. Suddenly we seem a long way from the tar which is melting at the moment on Australian roads.

And then Thursday, the day on which so much happens and the pace of our lives suddenly quickens. For Brendan and me the day started on the bridge at 8 a.m., alone there with *unser Kapitän* Ewald, as we stood before the computer panel on the chart table and watched 59°59.99′ become 60°00.00′. We were formally in the Antarctic, and we shook hands. Not, mind you, within the Antarctic Circle—that is another matter. But we were within the area defined by the member nations of the Antarctic Treaty as being, for their purposes, the Antarctic. For instance, from this point on we could not throw any rubbish overboard, and it all had to be stored until our journey back homewards reached this point.

And then, an hour later, and very appropriately, our first iceberg, far away out there on the port beam, barely visible, a tiny triangular sail just peeping above the horizon. You might look a dozen times and not even see it: a mere "dash of white on a far horizon", I noted at the time, the kind of little flick of paint that a Fred Williams might, almost contemptuously, add as a highlight to one of his paintings. But, as the Australian poet has it, "reverberant of days to be". The ship's mournful siren—for some reason the German word is *Typhon*—blared out over the deck cargo piled high before us, and over those grey seas. Someone had won the ship's sweep. (He bought beer for his mates.)

Michael Madigan looked through the ship's binoculars at the distant iceberg, this skirmishing reminder of great battalions firmly sited on their own ground, a world that doesn't need to know us. "So we *are* invaders," he said. I think all who heard him felt a little shame.

At eleven, I caught sight of our second berg, a peaky berg on the port bow which we closed with fast. We all knew that later we should see plenty of ice, but the impulse to photograph our first bergs was as impossible to withstand as the impulse to photograph the first baby. It wasn't the berg that mattered; it was the accreditation. Water into ice changes its state. By witnessing this happening we were symbolising our own change of state.

From these first bergs the intimations of the South increased hourly. The sea became littered with 'growlers' and 'bergy bits': growlers the smaller pieces of decayed ice which (when driven together by wind into pack) moan and grumble as they ride against each other, the bergy bits larger pieces, more identifiably the remnants of bergs, often illuminated from within by splendid though chaste colors: greens and blues, a marvellous ethereal blue.

And then, at nine in the evening, and still perfectly light—we were moving away from the night—the most wonderful tabular berg: a great continent of an iceberg. We had seen the skirmishers, and passed them by. Now we saw power, and might. These glistening ice castles were so remote from us, so contemptuous, outliers of a world that didn't need to know us.

The seas are calm, almost humiliatingly so after the tales some of us have read of ships in danger of foundering and of dogs and horses washed overboard. Ewald tells me we are slipping down between two barometric 'lows', as a group of us drink schnapps and cold beer with him in his splendid day-cabin.

The Germans joke with us about the scale of manning on Australian ships, telling us—inaccurately as it turns out—that an Australian ship would need four times the crew of a German one, and that every Australian crewman requires a cabin like Ewald's. It's in good humor, but later on I realise it's part of a little propaganda war they run.

We talk of the pod of thirty pilot whales we saw during the afternoon, and around which the ship circled several times. This gives us hope that we will some time see the great sperm whales, their heads patterned with scars from battles with the giant squids, and the mighty Blues, at seventy tons and eighty feet the greatest of creatures, blowing twenty feet into the air before they roll and dive. Poor fools we! Our fellow men have cleansed these seas. Apart from the odd sighting of a small whale they are sterile of the great mammals. Later we learn that there are only about 1100 Blue whales left, spread over the vast Antarctic waters so that it is now doubtful whether they can find each other to breed.

A "Captain's dinner" that evening for the elect—my invitation comes round every few days, and sometimes one of the rough diamonds on board ignores the noticeboard injunction to appear in "neat casual" clobber and to the anger of Ewald turns up aggressively clad in stained working dress, to show his contempt for those who reach for the niceties of life in these latitudes. (Nor is the dinner all it seems: a sharp-eyed one discovers the steward decanting cask wine into impressively labelled German bottles, and Captain Ewald defends this economic action vigorously when he is rallied about it.) Indeed there is a constant submerged tension on board or, rather, a series of them: between the professionals, scientists and the like, with their toffy accents and degrees and eccentric senses of humor, and the diesos and tradesmen; between the 'round-trippers' and those going down for the rest of the summer; between those going down for the rest of the summer and those going down for the winter as well—who, of course, regard themselves as the *real* Dan McGrews.

And another small strain is also beginning to emerge: between the three journalists on board, Bob Beale and Paul Wright (photographer) from the *Sydney Morning Herald*, and me from the *Australian*, on the one hand, and the 'authorities' on the other. Graeme Manning, our conscientious and decent voyage director, and his mates back in the Antarctic Division in Hobart, remind me of Shakespeare's "poor cat in the adage"—"letting 'I dare not' wait upon 'I would'". They *want* reports about Australia's Antarctic activities to get back home. After all, the future of our activities in Antarctica depends on selling them to the Australian taxpayer. On the other hand, so much can go wrong in Antarctica. There might be 'wrong impressions'.

We, the scribblers, want to promote Antarctica, its Treaty and Australian activity; and we believe that stale news is no news. The issue arises because tomorrow we put our inspection party ashore at Dumont d'Urville. We think we should go with them, if the French will have us. Failing that, we believe that we should be able to send the news that the inspection is on as soon as it starts. And now they're telephoning and telexing Hobart and Canberra to get permission for us to say what is happening. I note in my diary: "Beale and I despair, not for ourselves and our desires, but at the pusillanimity, the lack of vision and initiative, the fear of openness, of the Australian and the Australian public servant."

At the Captain's dinner, and by chance, no Germans are sitting at our table. The conversation turns to German atrocities in the Second World War. We are told that the Germans on board say that "others committed atrocities too". This seems to satisfy the young Australians present. God help us all.

I suppose it might be said that few of the Germans on the

Icebird had been born at the conclusion of the war. And I remember young Germans like them I met in Berlin in 1971, anxious to forget rather than analyse the past: the 'fatherless generation'. But . . . I have been to Auschwitz.

8

Diary, 3 January 1986

4 a.m. "You should tell Barry Jones that this is where God is," says Brendan Doran, the only other passenger in the wheelhouse. The sun, just risen from its perfunctory dip below the horizon, is slanting horizontally into the bridge. Around us is the grand review of the Fleets of the South – a grandiloquent phrase for a scene nevertheless of the utmost majesty. Scores, hundreds of bergs of a variety defying description: small islands with cliffs brilliantly lit by the sun; rounded bergs, like lumps of sugar damply collapsing on themselves; aircraft-carrier tabular bergs; weird grotesqueries of bergs, rococo delights for an eighteenth-century gentleman; rabbit's-ear bergs from the children's nursery; neat little forts, turrets sharply defined, only a king's standard absent.

They lie across our path, they stream past us on either side as we pursue our steady 11.6 knots. Sprinkled over the steel-blue sea, now thrust aside by our bows, are the 'bergy bits', the decayed and worn-out stumps of bergs, cotton wool on a shaven face, Norm Gunston bergs.

And ahead, a few hundred yards, is the pack itself, the tough icing on God's cake, the franc-tireurs before the massed forces behind. We thrust the floes out of our way, but not too contemptuously. "Remember," says someone quietly, "they're floating lumps of concrete."

That man Doran was right about God. This is heaven. The beauty is transcendental. Nothing I have seen or read has led me to expect this. I hadn't realised that the South means, emotionally and aesthetically, a life lived on quite another plane.

Gateway to heaven and gateway to hell.

LATER

That was a wonder-hour, as we dodged and thumped and bashed our way through the mush, disturbing two lazy crabeater seals as we thrust their comfortable floe out of the way.

I went back to bed for two hours and then, when I got back to the bridge after ham and eggs, was surprised to see we were in clear water again, though still plenty of bergs about. And so on the bridge pretty well all day, with most of the ship's company, finding ever new ecstacies as we steamed south. And then—Antarctica itself. The black rock of the Ile des Petrels in sight on the port bow, the site of the French base, and behind it the great whiteness and the grey smudge of the polar icecap, rising to 3000 feet. By now we are over the narrow continental shelf, and the masses of great bergs around us are stranded.

Ewald is distrustful of all he surveys. We edge our way delicately towards the continent. Alistair, our only Australian officer, is out ahead in the *Chicken*, the *Icebird*'s stout little tender, taking soundings and radioing them back to the bridge. And I stand beside the bridge computer as we do this, determined not to miss the Antarctic Circle coming up—and there it is: 66° 33.5′. I remember how happy Shackleton's men in their tents on the ice in the Weddell Sea were when, on 21 January 1916, they crossed the Antarctic going *north*. For them it was an augury that they might live. For us, going south, it means that we were truly in Antarctica. The rite of passage came later.

Then we anchor, right up against the little archipelago. There is the station helicopter ferrying construction materials down to the airstrip the French are building across the penguin rookeries, against many furious environmental protests. There, higher up on the snow slopes, we see for the first time the characteristic fawn color of more penguin rookeries, snow and rock tinted by droppings. They are cheek-by-jowl with parked construction machinery and surveyors wandering around, our introduction to the insouciance of the Adélie penguins, named for the land named by Jules Sebastien-César Dumont d'Urville after his wife, with whom he was soon to be incinerated in a dreadful railway accident near Paris, fire on the snow indeed. The penguins, in their native dignity and disdain, echo for us the message of the icebergs. I say to someone: "There's something wrong in coming so far and finding people."

Which leads to a discussion with Anders Karlqvist, of the Swedish Polar Research Secretariat. Anders is a rangy type, given we find out later to wandering around the snow in knickerbockers and long socks, like a gentleman out for an afternoon's skiing in his homeland. He has a refreshingly sceptical turn of mind, as do other foreign observers on board, which serves as a contrast to Australian earnestness, our attempts to persuade ourselves of our mission. What is the best way of approaching Antarctica? He talks of the recent Beardmore Glacier conference put on by the Americans, partly to demonstrate to the Africans and other envious ones, looking at what may be in Antarctica for them, that commitment to Antarctica is no light undertaking. Who would want to travel to Antarctica, as they did, in a windowless aircraft: "sealed in a great container", as Anders said? We have done it the historic way. We had it easy, of course, compared to the old-timers, but we travelled the path they did, and we paid our respects at the gate. "You can only cross the Antarctic Circle for the first time once in your life," I said to Anders. He replied: "Exactly."

The constant daylight is disturbing us. So is the continual excitement and the flooding in of new impressions. The habit of sleep recedes. "In Eskimo villages," says Anders, "children come to your door at midnight and ask to borrow your skis. You don't need sleep, you know. You just think you do." But Peter Gormly said to me over a beer in his sick-bay this morning: "You'll be so glad of night-time when you get back."

And this very day Nita, Joanna and Ray, and other friends, are also steaming through seas, higher seas than these, to land on a deserted coast in Bass Strait and to live among penguins. As a family we do create some odd circumstances for ourselves!

9

For the first time in over twenty years Australia is exercising its rights under the Antarctic Treaty of 1959 to inspect another country's station in Antarctica.

Three Australian observers landed at 6 p.m. today [3 January 1986] at France's Dumont d'Urville base in Adélie Land to conduct an inspection designed to establish that no treaty obligations are being evaded.

Opportunity is being taken of a visit by the *Icebird* to Commonwealth Bay, the site of Sir Douglas Mawson's 1911–14 Australian Antarctic Expedition, to visit the nearby French base. Members of the private Project Blizzard expedition, who landed on 10 December from the *Southern Quest* to survey the Mawson site and hut for conservation purposes, are to be picked up at Commonwealth Bay.

The only previous inspection visit of other nations' Antarctic bases was in 1963, when American and Soviet bases were inspected. Australian bases have been inspected from time to time by United States observers.

The three Australian observers, appointed under Article 7 of the Antarctic Treaty, are Dr Patrick Quilty, Assistant Director (Science) of the Antarctic Division, Graeme Manning, operations manager of the Antarctic Division of the Department of Science, Brendan Doran, of the Antarctic Division of the Department of Foreign Affairs. They carry a gift of a dozen selected bottles of Australian wine, and a presentation plaque, for the French. The inspection will finish about 1 a.m. Saturday, by the light of the midnight sun. Dumont d'Urville lies just within the Antarctic Circle.

As is normal, the French base was given only twenty-four hours direct notice of the inspection, which was advised direct from the *Icebird*, a German polar vessel under charter to the Australian government and now on the sixth of the current series of Antarctic supply voyages. The *Icebird* is lying off the island on which the French base is situated in an ice-laden sea, surrounded by huge stranded icebergs, with the great mass of the Antarctic continent rising into white mists beyond.

Infringements of the Antarctic Treaty relate to such matters as disposal of nuclear wastes, environmental abuse and weapons testing and deployment. There has been some international criticism of the airstrip under construction at Dumont d'Urville which has been alleged to affect local penguin populations. Periodic use of the inspection provisions of the Antarctic Treaty is regarded by all parties as desirable and as emphasising the benign aspects of the Treaty, thus creating useful precedents. The Antarctic Treaty is claimed to be the world's most successful disarmament agreement.

It is understood that Australia, now adopting a more forward policy in Antarctic matters, will regularly conduct inspection visits of other nations' stations in future, and in turn expects and welcomes visits from them.

(*Australian*, 4–5 January 1986)

10

So near and yet so far! We wanted to get ashore at Dumont d'Urville, of course, but the 'observers' had to go first, to throw their hats in, as it were. By the time they were carted around, and then wined and dined as the French thawed out, and finally brought aboard again with an invitation from the French for all to visit the station, it was already early morning. By the time I was awake the weather had changed, we had pulled out and we were steaming through fog, rough seas and a forty-knot wind, eastward to Commonwealth Bay.

Our 'observers' were fairly close-lipped about what they had seen ashore. Our own observations were that there was probably plenty to comment on adversely, if anyone wanted to. The French were quite obviously going ahead with their airstrip, and be damned to outside opinion. *Pourquoi-pas*? Their ride-the-whirlwind attitude was no surprise; it was only a few months since their crazy terrorist sinking of the *Rainbow Warrior* in Auckland harbor, something that was in all our minds. I wondered if they had any inkling of the heavy cargo of Australian resentment the *Icebird* carried.

My guess is that our 'observers' behaved like gentlemen, in the Sir Humphrey Appleby tradition, content with making a modest point. But there was much they could have said. Newcomers to Antarctica as most of us were, we were horrified at the great conveyor-belt stream of rubbish of all kinds that was being poured down the snow-slopes and into the sea without ceasing. This cynical despoliation would have worried us less if it had come later, when we saw what Australians were also capable of doing.

But we did have a magical hour or so at Dumont d'Urville. Fifteen of us were taken inshore in the *Chicken*, to cruise in and around the islands and inlets and right under the great cliffs of the Astrolabe Glacier. Blue ice slashed its heavenly color into the white crags above us. "No-one is to talk," said Ewald as we passed under the overhangs. The resonance could have brought down a hundred tons of ice on us. D'Urville himself said here: "One could have believed oneself in the narrow streets of a city of giants." We passed within feet of great colonies of Adélies, hundreds of thousands of them perhaps, standing upright and flapping their wings at our intrusion. Alistair, our supercargo, jumped onto a stranded floe and hacked his way down to clean old ice with an ice-axe. We brought chunks back and had them in our whisky afterwards: "Between ten thousand and a hundred thousand years old," said Anders.

11

The next day I write myself a note:

Overnight steaming from Dumont d'Urville to Commonwealth Bay, though there is no night. Outside, driving snow, some of it drifting in through our part-open porthole. A temperature of 0°, Force 8 or 9 on our port bow, an angry sea. Visibility less than 500 yards—plenty of icebergs out there, and I hope they have the radars switched on. This is the first time we have seen seas breaking in anger on the weather side of the bergs: they seem unmoved.

Faint sounds of pop music from some other cabin. A couple of bridge schools going somewhere. The stickybeaks have deserted the bridge. Too bad for the philatelists that we didn't get ashore at Dumont d'Urville. French Antarctic stamps are available *only* at the station, and letters so stamped are highly prized.

Most of us are glad for a quiet day. The events of yesterday, when we stepped across the Antarctic threshold, have taken toll of us all. Tonight there'll be some down in the pub, some watching *Gone with the Wind* on video in the mess. (We had *A Night at the Opera* this afternoon—those who saw it found it the humor of another age.) Many are spine-bashing. Eating palls, though Uwe, who looks as a cook *should* look, a tribute to his own cooking, is never happier than when someone is complimenting him on his sauerkraut. Tonight there was soup, chops, fried rice, peas, boiled potatoes, strawberries and cream, German beer, Australian wine.

Our cabin floor shows the signs of the events of the last twenty-four hours: Antarctic-issue rucksacks, great leather boots and woollen socks, 'ventiles' (the windproof overlays the importance of which is everlastingly impressed on us by Geraldine, our deputy leader, and by the training films), cameras, Antarctic 1986 T-shirts cunningly organised and sold to us by the army larc drivers in aid of their (drinking?) funds, and an empty carton from a bottle of duty-free Black Label whisky. Private stocks of grog are discouraged on board, but most cabin cupboards have a few bottles nestling among the life-jackets.

12

5 January 1985. 7.30 a.m., on the bridge.

We are driving cautiously through fog at ten knots—but there are no icebergs around. We are an hour off Commonwealth Bay, said to be the windiest place in the world, with an *average* wind speed over the year of forty-four knots. Those ashore and waiting for us radio that it's just half that at the moment—in other words, a nice morning! We've decided, Graeme Manning tells me, to go straight in and start work. Graeme beams. It puts him on schedule.

Snow is falling but not much is lying on the ship. It's just above zero, 1°C. The sea is down to a 'slight'. The ship is not stirring yet. Up here we have only the officer of the watch, Bill Ware, the ever-cheerful meteorologist, Graeme Manning and me. Bill fusses with his met log. (We transmit eight observations a day to the Bureau of Meteorology in Melbourne, where it goes into the data-bank for southern hemisphere analysis. Bill says these high latitude reports are of real value because they are so uncommon and so widely scattered.)

Ewald our skipper—jutting Captain Cuttle beard, red windcheater, blue jeans, tan moccasins—has just irrupted into the wheelhouse in his no-nonsense way, bowing his head not to his God but to the radar console. He's just rung up Uwe to order orange juice and a fresh roll with cheese for breakfast, to be brought to the bridge.

Off goes Bill with his sea-temperature thermometer and a coil of yellow nylon rope. The bridge sea-temperature gauge doesn't operate below zero, presumably on the grounds that at that temperature we should be stuck in a block of ice. But salt water, as we've found out, doesn't freeze at zero, fortunately for us. Here comes Bill back in now, shrugging the snow off his shoulders. He's got his water sample and is 'acclimatising' his thermometer in it. The water temperature turns out to be minus 0.6°.

And now the snow is coming down hard and the sea has a lot of ice trash in it. Visibility two miles, says Ewald, pointing out an iceberg ahead. I argue with him and say I can't see more than 200 metres.

Ten hours' sleep last night, the dark blind pulled down against the light, and sleep badly needed. I felt so fresh this morning that, to the amazement of my cabin-mate Brendan, I vacuumed the cabin floor.

"We're going in!" The phrase, even forty-five years on from the jungle war, still brings a sinking feeling in the stomach.

Graeme says he has five or six campaign and service medals, from Malaysia and Vietnam, but the only medal he really wants is a Polar Medal. Many of us would agree.

At breakfast now. Someone looks out the window. "Either that's a bloody big iceberg or it's the coast." In fact it's the coast: the first of Australian Antarctica that we have seen.

13

Douglas Mawson was born in Yorkshire and arrived in Australia in 1884, at the age of two, with his father and mother. He studied engineering and science at the University of Sydney after passing through the famous Fort Street Model School. He was strongly influenced by the remarkable Professor Edgeworth David, one of the pioneers of scientific geology in Australia, and he became increasingly interested in that subject. Following some original research in the New Hebrides, now Vanuatu, in 1905 Mawson joined the staff of the University of Adelaide, immediately making energetic investigations into the geology of South Australia. When Mawson was sixteen, and before he had left school, his headmaster had said that "if there be a corner of this planet of ours still unexplored, Douglas Mawson will be the organizer and leader of an expedition to unveil its secrets."

In 1907 Ernest Shackleton was passing through Adelaide on the first of the three expeditions south which he led. Shackleton had already been to the Antarctic, on Robert Falcon Scott's *Discovery* expedition of 1901–04. With Scott and Edward Wilson he reached a record 82°16′ South, though this did not even take them off the Ross Içe Shelf. The party, though, was in poor shape, and Shackleton was compulsorily repatriated by Scott in 1903, amidst ill-feeling. Mawson asked Shackleton if he could have a place on the *Nimrod* for the round trip south, in pursuit of his geological interests. Shortly after, both Edgeworth David and Mawson were appointed members of Shackleton's party.

Mawson was in Antarctica in 1908 and 1909. With David and the surgeon Alistair Mackay he reached, for the first time, the position of the oscillating South Magnetic Pole, manhauling sledges 1260 miles. It was a magnificent exploit, and David later called Mawson "an Australian Nansen". On his return home Mawson argued the importance of further scientific work in the region west of Cape Adare, was unsuccessful in approaches to Shackleton and Scott for support for this project, and in 1910 launched his own appeal for an Australian Antarctic expedition.

Mawson's expedition sailed in December 1911, dropped off a party on Macquarie Island, and on 8 January 1912 discovered a wide, ice-free bay, some 700 miles west of Cape Adare, on an unknown coastline, which they named Commonwealth Bay. Within this bay was a rocky promontory, Cape Denison, and beside it a convenient, if shallow, boat harbor. The site had much to offer: not only access from the sea, but access to the icecap; rocky footings for buildings; penguins and seals for food and fuel, when necessary.

But they did not yet know of the appalling climatic conditions at Cape Denison. Later Mawson was to write: "We had found an accursed country." In May the monthly wind-speed *average* was sixty miles an hour.

With stores landed, and the *Aurora* left to establish a western party, the eighteen at the Cape Denison base set to and within ten days erected their twenty-four-foot square main hut, onto which they later added an eighteen-foot extension as a workroom. Scientific programs were established, which culminated in what was known as the Far Eastern expedition, when Mawson, with the Royal Fusilier B.E.S. Ninnis, and the Swiss mountain expert Xavier Mertz, marched 310 miles out over the icecap.

Apsley Cherry-Garrard, of Scott's second and fatal expedition, called the journey to Cape Crozier and back, to observe emperor penguins, *The Worst Journey in the World*. It was bad enough, but there is not, in the annals of Antarctic exploration, any survivor's story to equal that of Mawson on this expedition. Mawson and Mertz turned back when Ninnis plunged into the fathomless Black Crevasse, with the sledge carrying most of their food, and with their best dogs. Twenty-five days later Mertz died, probably of vitamin A poisoning from the dogs' livers they were eating. Mawson still had a hundred miles to go. It took him thirty days. Three days after leaving Mertz's body Mawson removed his socks, and the soles of his feet came away with them. A few days later Mawson fell through a crevasse himself and, spinning on his harness rope, he gave up: "I well remember how I looked forward to the peace of the great release." Then he remembered Robert Service's lines, "It's the keeping-on-living that's hard." Mawson got himself out and, finally dragging himself to within a mile and a half of the base camp at Cape Denison, saw on the horizon the relief ship leaving. He, and a small party that had been left behind in the hope that he would arrive, had to stay another year. His expedition of 1911–14 was termed, in 1928, "the greatest and most consummate expedition that ever sailed for Antarctica."

Mawson returned to Cape Denison once more, in January 1931, as leader of the second BANZARE (British, Australian, New Zealand Antarctic Research Expedition), which had been set in motion partly because of the French claiming Adélie Land in 1924.

He landed from the *Discovery* on 5 January, and was greatly intrigued to see that his old headquarters of 1911–14 was still standing in good order, apart from the wind erosion of some timbers. Inside his hut, "great numbers of delicate ice crystals hung in festoons." Later he and his companions climbed what came to be known as Proclamation Hill, the peak of a rocky ridge lying to the east of the hut. From this point, overlooking the little valley he knew so well, Mawson claimed for the British Crown King George V Land, defined as that section of Antarctica between the 42nd and 160th degrees of east longitude.

And that is where the trouble started.

It was an astounding claim. It covered 2.5 million square miles (6 million square kilometres). Even when the 42nd degree was later slightly abridged to 45°E it meant that, added to the Ross Sea sector claimed by Britain, amid much controversy, in 1923, and to the so-called Falklands Islands Dependency (now British Antarctic Territory), the Crown claimed some three-quarters of Antarctica measured in degrees, and about the same in land mass.

The British later passed the Ross Sea sector to New Zealand, and in 1936 the sector claimed by Mawson to Australia. Lesser breeds were not impressed. While the Queen of England remains Queen also of Australia and New Zealand, her claims remain just as they were in 1931. Even if we regard the sector of Antarctica claimed by Australia as quite separate and distinct from other claims, it means that Australia regards some 42 per cent of the continent, an area twice the size of Western Australia, as its national territory. To put it another way, 0.35 per cent of the world's population claims 10 per cent of the world's land area.

As one of the foreigners on the *Icebird* said: "We might let you get away with 5 per cent. But 42 per cent? You must be joking!"

14

Let us now try to sort out who owns Antarctica, or who thinks they own Antarctica.

First, there is a long-standing argument as to whether Antarctica in international law was *terra nullius*, that is, territory open to claim by interested parties, or *res communis*, which means that, like the high seas and outer space, Antarctica belongs to the international community.

The first view is obviously supported by all those countries which claim sectors of Antarctica—countries which, for the most part, recognise each other's claims.

The second view may not be positively supported by, but at least has considerable relevance to, the view of diverse countries and interest groups. These could include the Soviet Union, the United States of America and other 'non-claimants', who have refrained from asserting *any* territorial claims in Antarctica; some third world nations, led by Malaysia, who oppose the Antarctic Treaty system as a form of gentleman's club and wish Antarctica to come under the control of the United Nations; and, of course, the environmental groups which in the main wish to see Antarctica as some form of world wilderness, with minimal human intervention.

Second, we have the nations who actually have staked territorial claims in Antarctica. They are Britain, Australia, New Zealand, Norway, France, Chile and Argentina. Three of these claimants, Britain, Argentina and Chile, dispute the same territory. (To put that another way, five of these seven nations recognise each other's claims. Chile and Argentina recognise none except their own.) On the Antarctic Peninsula, that long fore-finger of Antarctica that pokes up towards South America, there are—or have been—British and Argentinian bases within a few yards of each other, pretending that the other is not there.

After the Second World War the position of these seven nations became increasingly embarrassing. A resources-hungry world, and furthermore a world in large measure liberated from colonial rule, became increasingly aware that there were a few fat boys sitting around the tart and pretending it all belonged to them. The fat boys may have been able to ignore most of the puny fellows who were protesting, except for the fact that among them there were two grown-ups who, if they wished, could send the fat boys packing: the Soviet Union and the United States. Both had long-term interests in and involvement with the area. The Russian Fabian Gottlieb von Bellingshausen had been among the first to sight the Antarctic continent, in 1820, and the Soviet Union claimed whaling and scientific interests there. American exploration and research in the interwar period, and since the end of the Second World War, had been exemplary. They could not be ignored.

Thirdly, the Antarctic Treaty of 1959. This presented Australia and other claimant nations with an opportunity to get off the hook. The Treaty, as originally signed, encompassed the claimant nations, and in addition the Soviet Union, the United States, Belgium, Japan and South Africa. (Poland, Brazil, West Germany, the German Democratic Republic, Italy, China, Uruguay and India have since joined the Treaty as full, 'consultative', members. There are also eighteen countries which have 'non-consultative' or, more correctly, 'acceding' status within the Antarctic Treaty: Bulgaria, Czechoslovakia, Denmark, Finland, Canada, Hungary, the Netherlands, Papua New Guinea, Peru, Romania, Spain, Sweden, Cuba, South Korea, North Korea, Greece, Austria and Ecuador. Promotion to full consultative status depends on some record of significant scientific work in Antarctica.) Behind the Treaty, which was ratified in 1961, lay the success of the International Geophysical Year of 1957–58, and the fear of the United States that, unless international bickering over Antarctica was laid to rest, the Soviet Union might step into the continent on its own account. Australia, at first, opposed the extension of the scientific cooperation of the International Geophysical Year in Antarctica.

The Treaty lays down the following:

- Antarctica shall be used for peaceful purposes only.
- There shall be freedom of scientific research in Antarctica.
- All claims to territory in Antarctica shall be held in abeyance; disputes shall be set aside while the Treaty is in force.
- There shall be no testing of nuclear devices, or disposal of nuclear waste, in Antarctica.

A subsequent and separate Convention on the Conservation of Antarctic Marine Living Resources (1980) extended the agreement of Treaty members and others into the area of the conservation of marine life in Antarctica and Antarctic waters. (The world headquarters of this CCAMLR—pronounced 'camelar'—organisation are now in Hobart.) Whales and seals are the subjects of other agreements, but are partly covered in this one, which takes a unique ecosystem, as opposed to a specific management, approach. A principal concern of the Convention is with the exploitation of krill resources, krill being the small shrimp-like creatures which play a vital part in the Antarctic marine food-chain. CCAMLR unfortunately is not above suspicion. Scientists in particular are increasingly coming to see it as a front for those nations whose main interests in the Antarctic are mercenary.

What is not stated in the Antarctic Treaty is of as much interest as what is. For a start, the Treaty means that any nation signing it can establish a base or undertake scientific research anywhere on the continent. Thus Australia, from its point of view, has found itself the somewhat reluctant host to no fewer than four major Soviet bases: Leningradskaya at the eastern limit of 'our' territory, Molodezhnaya at the western extremity, Mirny in the middle and, well inland at a height of 11,500 feet, Vostok. Some see something a little sinister in the accurate 'bracketing' of Australian Antarctic Territory by the Russians, but it may be no more than coincidence dictated by topographical considerations.

It is true that, even before the Antarctic Treaty, other powers—if they had the clout and the resources—could go anywhere they wished in Antarctica, and often did. It is also true that, even with the Antarctic Treaty, there is no way of stopping nations outside it from doing the same. (India did, in fact, take this bugger-you step shortly before she joined the Antarctic Treaty organisation, and it caused quite a diplomatic flutter; and Malaysia today (1988) is talking about it.) But at least the Treaty requires those subscribing to it to *tell* each other about what they intend to do or what they are doing, and inspections, as we have seen, are allowed and even encouraged. So—some countries would like to see South Africa expelled from the Treaty, as she has been from many international bodies. But, if she were, she could test nuclear weapons, which it is suspected South Africa possesses, in the Antarctic. So—South Africa stays.

Again, we may note that, while the Treaty goes a long way towards implying that the only reason for any nation being in Antarctica is scientific, it doesn't actually say so. When nations, as well as individuals, start talking about ideals, it is time to look to one's wallet. Science in Antarctica is a cover-up for power and resource and even, perhaps, military politics. Of course a lot of scientific work has been done in Antarctica. In applied biology, in atmospheric physics, in glaciology and in many other areas much of this science is of very considerable long-range importance to the management of the affairs of the human community. Here, at least, scientists feel they are at the helm, working at the frontiers in two senses. They sniff the cold, dry Antarctic air with delight, dreaming of the conferences they will attend, the papers they will see published, the degrees they will earn. The invariable belief of scientists, that all they do is Good, in Antarctica advances to an even more transcendental plane.

But nations are in Antarctica, alas, not because Presidiums and Senate committees believe that the objective pursuit of science will nurture the questing mind of the species and will lead, through progress, to a happy condominium of the future. They are in Antarctica because of greed, because of fear and for national aggrandisement. (To be fair, one should add also that they are there because of prudence.) If yumpies are young upwardly mobile professionals, then the flags one sees in Antarctica are those of numpies. The hidden motto of the Antarctic Treaty is "What's in it for us?"

"See how these Christians love one another!" an ancient Roman is said to have remarked ironically. It is not pointed out often enough that, behind the clap-trap about international cooperation under the Antarctic Treaty, lies all too often a lamentable *lack* of international concern for the welfare of Antarctica. In the King George Islands group in the South Shetlands no fewer than *eight* Antarctic Treaty nations have research stations; thus in a restricted area duplicating numerous facilities, sending identical meteorological reports homewards, conducting overlapping research, destroying precious areas set aside for scientific conservation—including the only beach in Antarctica where three separate species of penguin bred—and even, on one occasion, in 1977, witnessing the bulldozing into the sea by one Treaty power (Argentina) the research station of a country, Italy, which has since become another Treaty power.

And in the summer of 1985–86, the period covered by this

book, both the Russians and we Australians had bases in the Larsemann Hills area, about 70 miles to the west of Davis. These two bases were 1600 metres apart—and no efforts were made by either party to share facilities or research. Under such circumstances as these one can only feel sympathy for the unfortunate sea-birds and penguins around Antarctica which could end up carrying the identification tabs of several nations.

Indeed the issue of how long we can go on in Antarctica pretending that the other nations there do not exist—except when we want their help in an emergency—is (in 1988) about to become a critical one for Australia. The Russians have announced that they are about to establish the 60-bed "Progress" station in the Larsemann Hills, one of the rare ice-free coastal environments of Antarctica, with excellent access from sea to land and from coast to the continental dome. It will be the most favorably sited of any Soviet station except Molodezhnaya, their largest, and will probably have associated with it an intercontinental-flight standard runway, which could well have great significance for our own air operations in Antarctica. There has been no consultation about the establishment of this new station, and no international environmental planning.

It may be the Russians' fault more than ours, but here is an example of a lost opportunity for international cooperation, the pooling of resources and the sharing of at least some facilities. The difficult question the new Soviet base raises for Australia is how we can justify the maintenance of a seasonal research base on the doorstep of another country's wintering station. Nor is this likely to be the last matter of its kind to affect us. Many believe we are on the eve of a Chinese presence in Australian Antarctica. Given the fact that most of the coastline is one of ice-cliffs, with strictly limited areas suitable for sea access and the establishment of stations, future inroads by other nations are likely to place us again in the position of having unwelcome neighbors. All this reminds us that the Antarctic Treaty as it stands at present is an anarchist's charter, allowing freedom without responsibility, and that if the Antarctic Treaty nations were really serious about the welfare of Antarctica as part of the welfare of mankind they would have a secretariat of some kind which would actually *manage* intrusions into Antarctica so that selfish national interests were not paramount, as they are now.

How sturdy is the Antarctic Treaty? Could it fall apart? This is one of the nightmares of those countries which, like Australia, see no other protection for their tenuous claims. The simplest way for the Antarctic Treaty to disintegrate overnight would be for either the Soviet Union or the United States to withdraw from it. That is why those countries are handled by countries like Australia with kid gloves. It is true that we regard the Soviet Antarctic bases in 'our' sector of the continent as, in theory, subject to Australian law, but do not press the matter too far. We have issued the Russians every year, free of charge, their Australian radio licences, and by this we think we are making a point, even if they do use the licences as lavatory paper. But we stop there. We do not insist on their paying for those licences. We do not demand that they register their vehicles in the Australian Capital Territory. We do not point out to them that they are subject to Australian law, that offences against the law should be reported to the Australian authorities, and that a murder, for instance, committed on a Soviet Antarctic base should result in a trial in an Australian court. We have enough sense to realise that to be consistent in these matters is to make ourselves look ridiculous. Our only hope of getting something from other nations, in terms of say mineral royalties, is by playing the game of "constructive ambiguity", as they call it in our Department of Foreign Affairs.

There is of course no doubt that, if the Soviet Union or the United States were to see their national interests best served by withdrawing from the Antarctic Treaty, thus destroying it, they would do so with no compunction whatsoever. A major change in the political climate in either country could result in this. So could exasperation at excessive demands of the 'claimant' countries for royalties on minerals extracted, for instance. (As things stand at the moment it is most unlikely, but it is the way things could go. Australia has been angling for at least token royalties to be paid on any minerals extracted in 'its' territory.) Significant unregulated activity in Antarctica by non-parties to the Treaty could also result in withdrawals.

As a matter of last resort, and if there were indeed any danger of an imminent collapse of the Antarctic Treaty, the 'claimant' states could abandon their claims, thus turning the Antarctic Treaty powers into a genuine consortium, and Antarctica into a condominium of the Treaty powers. This, of course, would strengthen the opposition of those who regard the Antarctic Treaty as a club of the privileged, for the Treaty powers would not only exploit Antarctica's minerals in their own interests but would be in a position to say yea or nay to 'outsiders' applying for exploration and exploitation rights. The Treaty powers might then have to institute some kind of police or military power to safeguard their position as the guardians of Antarctica, thus abrogating, at least in spirit, the Treaty's opposition to a military presence on the continent! Although New Zealand has wavered, more than once, on the matter of maintaining its claim, the wholesale abandonment of claims is, however, most unlikely; for it would strengthen the legal case of those who argue that Antarctica is part of the 'common heritage' of mankind.

Piquancy is added to the whole situation by the fact that, in 1991, any full member can ask for a review of the Antarctic Treaty. It is possible that nothing may happen. On the other hand some matters which are now high on the Antarctic political agenda were not regarded as significant when the Treaty first came into force in 1961, above all the matter of mineral exploitation, which carries in its train the problem of national claims to Antarctic territory, especially perhaps where they overlap, as in the case of Argentina, Chile and Britain. Diplomats reach for the whisky bottle when 1991 is mentioned. If the apple-cart is upset, it may take a long time to retrieve the apples.

So we live in interesting times! Little wonder that the field of Antarctic law is a growth industry.

Fourthly, there is the proposal, already referred to, that Antarctica should be managed for the benefit of all nations through the United Nations Organisation. The argument for this, of course, is that the continent is a resource from which all people should benefit and to which they should have access on equal terms. The model that is sometimes used to support this argument is the Law of the Sea, by which in 1970 the United Nations agreed that the mineral resources of the sea-bed of all oceans were the "common heritage of mankind." The main arguments against the "common heritage" position are that the Antarctic Treaty exists; that it runs Antarctica reasonably efficiently; that legal claims to Antarctic territory already exist; that Antarctica is 'occupied', whereas the deep sea and space are not; that the Antarctic Treaty does not exclude those prepared to put their efforts where their mouths are; that the consultative members alone represent 80 per cent of the world's population; and that the Law of the Sea is concerned with exploitation, not conservation. (Of course the cynics will argue that that is what the Antarctic Treaty powers have in mind also.)

Fifthly, there is the 'world park' option for Antarctica. (Interestingly, this *could* be compatible with the 'common heritage' argument.) Given the selfishness of man, especially when organised into national states, such proposals seem idealistic and delusionary. Or rather, they would, but for the fact that the world-wide campaign for the exclusion of 'exploitation' from Antarctica is a formidable one, that it has a great deal of logic as well as simple idealism on its side, and that it is certainly going to influence future decisions about Antarctica, whether it wins all its points or not.

The environmentalists hold that the nature of the Antarctic Treaty is changing, that from being a 'conservation' regime it is being twisted into an 'exploitation' regime. Geoff Mosley, the former Director of the Australian Conservation Foundation, has written that "if mining activities were to be permitted that would be the end of Antarctica's status as a wilderness. Antarctica would no longer be a marvellous example of environmental restraint to inspire the world." It is argued that, once the step of allowing prospecting in Antarctica is taken, this will inevitably lead to mining, and mining will lead to arguments for other industrial activities, including processing.

This is a powerful argument for those of us who have seen how frangible the Antarctic environment is even today, when relatively puny forces are deployed there. When we think of the limited areas of ice-free coastline suitable for deepwater ports and the associated towns and installations; when we consider that these same small areas support most Antarctic wildlife; when we remember the difficulties of disposing of waste in Antarctica, and the reluctance of those running Antarctica to waste manpower and shipping time, in the precious few months in which Antarctica is 'open', on removing the mess we make; when we read of the vandalism which has destroyed the historic environments of the huts still standing of expeditions of the 'golden age'; when we are told that vehicle tracks across stony ground on Ross Island are still plainly visible ten years after they were made; when we learn that cement dust from building operations at Casey base has destroyed the rare lichens we are supposed to be protecting; when we remember that conveyor belt pouring a ceaseless flow of muck and rubbish down the slopes and into the sea at Dumont d'Urville—when we reflect on all this and much more it is impossible to imagine that to take minerals out of Antarctica is not to rape it.

Just to take one example of 'what may be'. We already know that there are prospective oil sites around something like a third of the Antarctic coastline, including the Weddell Sea, the Ross Sea and the 'Australian' Prydz Bay area. Almost all life in Antarctica is marine-based; the whole great chain from the little krill to the great whale, from the stolid penguins to the elusive snow petrel, is interlocked. Now, the extraction of the oil which we know is there presents hair-raising difficulties. Just think of the fate of a conventional oil rig with an iceberg the size of a football ground bearing down on it. The rig would be brushed away as we brush away bush flies at a picnic.

Oil, however, will be taken out of Antarctica just as soon as someone wants it badly enough and is prepared to pay for it. New technologies will be developed. Indeed, they are in place already in the Arctic, where icebergs are shoved out of the way of the oil-rigs by ice-breakers, and where the drill-holes may be capped well below the level of the sea bed, and the rigs moved away to safety, where this is not possible. These techniques will be exploited in Antarctica if a 'minerals regime' is launched there. Then, sooner or later, something will go wrong, and there will be a major oil spill. This will have dramatically sad effects. It is likely to anywhere, as we have seen to our cost in the past, but the Antarctic cold dramatically slows down all biological degradation. The bodies of Scott, Wilson and Birdie Bowers, left beneath an icy cairn on the Ross Ice Shelf in 1912, are still there somewhere, on their long voyage to the sea, in 'perfect' condition. The slicks will spread across the cold seas, they will coat the floes, they will wipe out the krill, they will entrap the penguins, starve the seals, even climb the rocks and kill the delicate Antarctic lichens. It could be a desecration on the grandest scale that even the human species has devised.

And is it worth it? ask the 'world park' people. The history of the twentieth century has not left the world's people with much to be proud of. The eighteenth century left us with a view of reason in human affairs, the nineteenth with a vision of scientific and industrial progress. The twentieth will be viewed as a century of barbarism and retreat, on its gravestones engraved AUSCHWITZ, HIROSHIMA, ENVIRONMENTAL DESTRUCTION. If we can keep our grimy fingers off Antarctica, if we can keep it free of our droppings, we not only hand on to the future the world's last great unspoiled wonderland, we not only allow that future the privilege of deciding for itself what Antarctica should mean to it, but we have a chance of redeeming something of our own reputation, of showing that we can rise above our viciousness.

This vision, then, is both moral and practical. The morality we have discussed. It is practical because it treats Antarctica as one huge, permanent spiritual and scientific resource for mankind, these values even in money terms transcending by a million times the value of mineral wealth to be dragged out of the area.

Australian conservationists see Australia as in a specially favorable position to advance this concept. Australia claims a vast section of Antarctica, which it could nominate for World Heritage status with the United Nations, though this would be regarded as provocative by non-claimants, who would question our right to make such a nomination. We are a founder member of the Antarctic Treaty. Few if any nations are more closely related strategically to Antarctica. We stand somewhat apart from the great empires, and have a modest reputation as an independent, non-colonialist nation. One way and another we have been involved in Antarctic exploration from the very beginning. Indeed it can be claimed that the first person ever to step ashore on the Antarctic mainland was the Norwegian–Australian Carsten Borchgrevink on 24 January 1895. (Though personally I believe the honor lies with the men of Dumont d'Urville's expedition who landed on the offshore islands of Adélie Land on 21 January 1840.)

The 'world park' view, then, holds that the Antarctic Treaty powers should nominate the entire Antarctic continent as part of the world's natural heritage, and that the Treaty powers should negotiate an overall Conservation Convention for Antarctica, with provision within the Convention for the establishment of Antarctica as a world park, that is a 'wilderness area'. This is in effect a plea to maintain the *status quo* of Antarctica, to reinforce the original intent of the Antarctic Treaty as a scientific and conservation treaty. Scientific exploration and research would continue. Existing bases would remain, if required, and new ones could be established by agreement. The present 'zoning' system, whereby certain key locations are designed as Specially Protected Areas to which access is only available under permit, would remain, and no doubt be extended. Tourism, as with any park, might well be encouraged, under controlled conditions. Mining would be banned. So would fishing, disgracefully permitted at the moment.

The more you think about it, the more sensible it seems. But the 'world park' option requires educated, courageous and imaginative minds. These are in short supply, particularly among Antarctic bureaucrats, the inhabitants of government ministries and politicians—Australian or otherwise. On the *Icebird*, if there were those—apart from the Project Blizzard people—who thought this way, they kept quiet about it. It was a long way to swim home.

15

You could be forgiven for thinking that life had not established here. But look, and tread, carefully and a variety of delicate plants and animals are revealed.

Small carpets of moss are green oases where water drips down from melting snowdrifts. Splashes of colour on the rocks are crusty lichens, spreading imperceptibly over the surface as the centuries pass by. During the brief summer, bubbling streams of melt from glaciers contain rich green, orange and even purple growths of slimy algae. Numerous small ponds form and there are also many large, permanent lakes in which these simple plants abound.

Amongst the vegetation the animals lead their hidden lives. Pin-head-sized mites crawl around on their eight legs and nematode worms thrash about in the thin water films covering the mosses. In the lakes microscopic rotifers and minute 'water fleas' browse on the floating algae.

This life is incredibly hardy whilst paradoxically being extremely fragile. Hardy because it survives deep-freezing, a long winter darkness and possibly intense drying year after year. Fragile because it is so slow in growth that a single careless boot could wipe out centuries of existence. The inconspicuous plant life of Antarctica is for that continent the equivalent of the rainforest in the tropics and it needs equal protection.

Paul Broady: "Antarctica – The Threatened Continent", in *Habitat*, vol. 11, no. 5, 1983.

16

Diary, 5 January 1986

Up early to catch the first sight of Commonwealth Bay and the Cape Denison area through the murk. As we edge inshore we look with awe at the great cliffs of the icecap edge as it slides into the sea. Later I learn that Mawson's photographs show that the shape of the coastline and the nature of the ice edge, hundreds of feet high, are much the same today as in his time – one piece of evidence, perhaps, in the debate on 'is the ice retreating?'. Above all I want to have the past foreclose on me. I want to be precipitated back those seventy-five years and come into physical contact with Mawson and his men.

And there the ice-cliffs end and a couple of rocky promontories thrust out into the sea. Offshore, what Mawson called "an archipelago of islets". On the rocky point nearest to us a single pole can be seen. Later I find out that it is all that remains of the cross to Mertz and Ninnis, but there was no time to ask, for someone was pointing and saying to me, "There, look, just appearing over the ridge, it's brown, it's the roof of Mawson's hut." I don't know if it was a great moment for the others, but it was for me. I felt a rather embarrassing rush of patriotism. This is where we Australians put our roots down in the south – or, rather, blew holes in the rock to hold the stumps of our first building. Let our foreign friends on the *Icebird* have their little jokes. They are Johnny-come-latelies.

I got ashore in the first larc. That's a quick way of covering quite a feat. By the time I had climbed into full Antarctic gear, boots, cords, woollen shirt, sweaters, ventiles, fur hat, and then slung round me camera, video-camera, heavy battery, pack, and then struggled into a too-small lifejacket, the climb down the Jacob's ladder to the heaving larc, unable to see where I was going, was quite a feat. Cries from below of "When we say LET GO let go—we'll catch you" required rather more faith in the common soldier than I could summon up. Especially with the previous day's lecture, describing what happens to someone who falls into the sea between the larc and the ship—it is nasty—still firmly in mind.

The larc revs up and we are off towards those islands, with some agonised cries from the helmsman of "Which side of the bastards do we go?". We'd be thrown about if we weren't packed so tightly—the affectionate embraces in which we clasp our neighbors would cause some asides about incipient homosexuality if this were a seminar on Australian literature. Bloody cold, grateful for the fur flaps fastened across our faces. We head for an island, a mushroom island, a stalk of rock and a great cap of ice and snow. The ship sinks behind in the sea-mist and it feels very lonely.

Then round the islets and into Boat Harbor, calm and compact. Mawson was right: "a beautiful, miniature harbour completely land-locked". Up to the cod of the little bay through friendly, smooth waters. The larc lumbers up on its great wheels to sit snugly under the overhanging ice, conveniently at a level at which we can just step ashore.

Strange people carrying boxes down to the larc, putting them down to shake hands with us. These are the Project Blizzard people, the reason we are here. We greet them with some respect. They had come down in the North Sea trawler *Southern Quest* as a private expedition, and had spent nearly four weeks ashore working hard at maintenance work on Mawson's hut and making a detailed topographic survey. They are enthusiasts, but skilled and sensible ones, and it's good seeing something down here being done outside the shelter of an official umbrella. Full marks to Barry Jones and the Antarctic Division for co-operating with them and agreeing to pick them up. Low marks to the Heritage and Environment people in Canberra who don't themselves know what to do with the problems of Mawson's hut, but resent others getting worked up about it. [For the Project Blizzard story see

Jonathan Chester's splendid book *Going to Extremes* (Doubleday, Sydney 1986).]

What with the introductions and the Adélie penguins standing alongside us and giving us the old sideways look, and veterans saying, "Careful where you're standing—that's an ice crust and there's a melt stream underneath", it took an effort to remind myself that I had just taken my first step onto Antarctica. We were lucky. For once the notorious Cape Denison wind was absent. For much of the time they had been here the Project Blizzard people had found it not worth while emerging from their shelters until the afternoon, when the katabatic wind died down. But today was quite calm, with the temperature disconcertingly just a fraction above zero, the constant light snow tending to turn into rain. This, they tell me, is not good news in Antarctica. Ice and snow are much preferable to slush, and in any case our clothes are designed to protect against cold and wind, but not against water.

Next to the landing, and the first thing we see is a desiccated seal carcase, a rope round its flippers, a ghastly sight. Mawson's, they say. No doubt killed for the dogs in the last days of his stay, but never cut up. Here the great body is, to remind us that, with few bacteria about in this cold-cabinet, nothing decays. Anders tells me later of seventeenth-century corpses emerging from the permafrost in Spitzbergen, their clothing wonderfully preserved.

The Project Blizzard people have been marvellous. Jonathan Chester, the photographer, and Angela McGowan, the archaeologist, took charge of those of us in the advance party in a long tour of the whole base. Not, at first, to Mawson's hut, but across the floor of the valley and first to the Magnetograph House, up on the edge of the valley's eastern ridge. This is the only one of Mawson's buildings that is still sealed from the weather—the laboratory where Eric Webb made his continuous records of magnetic variation, working in darkness with photographic paper. I'm amazed that the building, of pine boards, seems so little affected by the attrition of the mighty winds and the snow-blown particles. Not much bigger than a car case, and reminding me of the cubby I built for our kids in the garden at Mount Eliza, there are still visible shreds of the sheepskins with which the exterior had been lined to maintain an equable temperature inside.

Some of the party climbed through the top of the stable-door entrance to the Magnetograph House and penetrated the labyrinthine interior, but didn't see much, so we moved on to the few sticks that are left of the Magnetic Absolute Hut nearby, laughing at the 'changing the guard at Buckingham Palace' antics of the file of Adélies down below us on the flat. Then along the stony, broken ridge and up to Proclamation Hill. I was astonished at the diversity of geological specimens, quartzes and slates and basalts and heaven knows what other varieties of flakes and gneisses brought down by the ice sheet over unimaginable periods of time from some antediluvian deposit inland, but I was too out of breath at the climb to linger until we got to the high point.

And turned around to gasp. Down below, on the eastern side, the frozen waters of the Round Lake, where Mawson's mob drew their water and where they once skated. But on the other side, looking back across the little valley to the high ridge on the western side, with its penguin rookeries and the pole of the Mertz–Ninnis cross, a superb symphonic composition in Whistlerian grey and white—from our feet the black rocky decline to the valley floor, perhaps 200 feet below; then ice and snow, the brown roof of the main hut poking out above the drifts; further across to the next rise, the ANARE emergency Granholm hut and the little red portable 'apple' huts intrusive on the lower slopes. To our left the great slope of the icecap descent into the valley, studded with black moraines, the pathway for Mawson to the inland. To the right the two capes, Boat Harbor busy with traffic today, the seal and penguin rookeries; the snowy Mackellar islets offshore, and far away in the mist a ghostly ship, looking more like the *Flying Dutchman* than the *Icebird*. Suddenly the bits started falling into place—it seemed almost homely, and I could only wonder that beauty could be constructed out of such unpromising materials.

The snow was now driving around us, melting on our ventiles and dampening our camera lenses. I know of old how taking pictures stops you looking at things, and I told myself to *look* and *think* as well as just record. It was a moving moment. Just by us, at the site of the anemometer their father C.T. Madigan tended for so many months, Russel and Michael Madigan were paying filial homage, the snow coating Russel's spectacles. And now Jonathan Chester was reaching into the canister attached to the pole on the peak of Proclamation Hill, drawing out the message that Mawson left here fifty-five years ago to the day (a facsimile, actually; the original is in Canberra) and reading it to us:

I, Sir Douglas Mawson, do hereby proclaim and declare to all men that, from and after the date of these presents, the full sovereignty of the Territory of King George V Land and its extension under the name of Oates Land situated between Longitudes 142 and 160 degrees east of Greenwich and between Latitude 66 degrees south and the South Pole.

There's a verb missing somewhere there. Mawson, not me.

A scramble now down the hill, over the curious crescent line of gneissic rocks behind Mawson's hut: I would have called it a moraine, as Mawson did, but the revisionists these days call it a raised beach. Over a jumble of fallen wires, the stays for the great oregon mast, now lying splintered nearby, over which the first radio transmissions from Antarctica went out. And now to the back of the hut and the side, where the hangar was for the Vickers monoplane that never flew, a mess of four-gallon petrol tins, heavily rusted, sliced into with an axe, perhaps by the Mawson party before they left.

And now there's the start of the ice tunnel that leads into the bowels of the hut, just big enough to enter, a rabbit-run, twisting its way for ten yards or more, slippery, cold and claustrophobic. Outside there's a Honda banging away, sending power into the hut for a fluorescent light, but the tunnel is dark. Bloody cold on the hands, too, that icy floor—I stopped crawling to don gloves. And then into the cave of the Ice Queen. Angela is there, holding up the light: rows of bunks, shelves with old tins and jars, a line of open boxes with flour and other foods, all looking perfectly edible, a shelf of the paperbacks of Mawson's day—*Memoirs of Sherlock Holmes, The Greatest Gift, On Tour with Troodles, To Pleasure Madame*, William Le Queux's *The Mysterious Mr Miller.* Old newspapers, too. A row of pharmaceuticals, labelled POISON, and with them a bottle of Heinz India Relish.

Almost impossible to take pictures—lenses cloud in a second. This is a museum, perhaps, but it's a very odd sort of museum. Above my head the loft is collapsing with the weight of the ice it holds. A Project Blizzard fellow is attempting to support the split timbers with tubular props we have landed from the *Icebird* that morning—that much at least Canberra have permitted to be done, but there's a great deal of ill-feeling towards Canberra, and not just among the Project Blizzard people, that they won't allow the holes in the roof to be sealed, the holes through which the snow is being blown to turn into ice. The Madigans, who were in the hut just before me, and who had nourished a wish to lie in their father's bunk, found it a great block of ice. The floor is ice. The stove is just visible through more ice. This is a morgue rather than a museum.

Unless it be a museum to bureaucratic mindlessness.

Still, what a moment! When I discuss it with Anders Karlqvist later he smiles a European smile as I declare that, not having Great Pyramids in Australia, we have to make Great Pyramids out of what is to hand. "Seventy-five years old!" says Anders. "Seventy-five years old and a national monument! I have eaten in restaurants in England that are a thousand years old."

Bugger Anders. Look, I turn the corner, under the fingers of ice that hang from above. There is Mawson's bunk, with its ticking pillow. There, on the shelf by his head, are his peppermints. And there is the collapsible chair in which he sat and thought by himself, though now it has a cushion of ice on it and he would find his ruminations chilly. A spare refuge for a spare man. In the main room, so far as I can see behind the ice falls, are the bunks, each with initials burnt into them with a hot poker. There's Eric Webb's—with the metal badge of his Christchurch school still fastened to the wall above it. And there's FJH, bringing Frank Hurley back for a moment even more movingly than his photos do. Look, it's all a great story. "To strive, to seek, to find and not to yield"—Tennyson's words are on one of the memorials of the Scott expeditions. High-sounding Victorian emotions if you like. Very old-fashioned to be moved by that kind of thing today; we like antiheroes, not heroes. Indeed in these deconstructional days we are inclined not to believe in heroic motives at all. Perhaps the explorers by our standards were a rather simple-minded lot, with their schoolboy jokes, their transvestite entertainments, their pictures of the King and Queen on the wall. But perhaps we shall discover one day that they weren't that simple-minded at all. Single-minded, perhaps, but not simple-minded. Their stories are stories of compassion, humor, courage, love. And of vision. Instead of listening to dreadful songs about impossible dreams they went out and lived them. Most of them were humble men from humble origins to which they returned. The few explorers of this era whom I have known—Raymond Priestley and Herbert Dyce Murphy among them—were self-evidently *good* men. Yes, bugger you, Anders.

Anyway, by now I was rather drained of emotion, and slithered out of the hut to today's world. The thaw had at least revealed that Mawson's men cared as little about their environment as we do today. Poking through the snow were dog chains, old insulators, pieces of coal, discarded clothing, an old boot, blubber, penguin skins, bolts and a stove plate. "That," said Jonathan, "is a relic of the first Antarctic barbecue—Mawson had one here when he came back in 1931." All trivial, all discarded, and all reminding us of the way dead men once lived.

I linger for a moment by the Transit Hut, the remains of the little astronomical observatory just to the east of the main hut. It was built of scrap timber covered with canvas; today, its dilapidated walls are chiefly interesting as a show-piece of wind erosion. The pine planks have been deeply engraved by the wind and the ice particles it carries; nails sticking out an inch or so from the present surface indicate where the original surface once was. It's another of the many lessons we are starting to accumulate: not to take the South for granted, not to imagine that, because it's quite a calm day today, it's always like this.

I make for the Granholm hut, an ugly thing put up about ten years ago by the Antarctic Division. Later I hear that there are plans to move all evidence of later intrusions from this little valley, and I'm grateful. The Project Blizzard people may be environmentally conscious, and I'm grateful for the cup of hot soup they gave me at the Granholm hut, and the water and tea, for Antarctica's a thirsty place, but I don't like the row of plates on posts that they have erected just by the landing place at Boat Harbor, commemorating donors to their work. Typical Australian inability to see ugliness when one creates it oneself. Graeme Manning has been prospecting over the ridge to the east, in the Cape Gray direction, for a future ANARE summer station. I'm delighted when he tells me that, not only will there be no sign of the new station from Mawson's valley, but also that it is hoped that not even Boat Harbor will be used. And that the summer station people will keep an eye on the integrity of the Mawson site. Well, we'll see.

And now a solitary trudge up the ridge to the Mertz–Ninnis cross. We've been told to stay in sight of each other, and there's a minor panic later on when the Madigan boys are seen disappearing in the distance up towards the polar icecap, presumably on the first leg of their sortie to Amundsen-Scott Base at the South Pole. But I find myself, for the first time on this trip, a lone ranger plodding carefully around the homes of thousands of penguins. The rocks are brown with countless generations of penguin pooping, the smell is overpowering and like very bad fish-paste, and my intrusion is marked by a few protesting squawks and the odd bill half-heartedly thrust my way. Indeed, it's a miserable day on the rookery. Instead of bracing sub-zero temperatures we have wet snow turning to water as it settles on the birds. The adults can cope with it, but the downy black chicks, now beer-bellied and standing about a foot high, have not of course got their adult plumage, are *not* waterproof, are looking—as grandma would have said—like drowned rats, are going to die before they ever see the sea. Or at any rate thousands of them are, of pneumonia or whatever miseries afflict penguin chicks. It's a nasty reminder of the pitilessness of nature, and one I could have done without on this auspicious day.

At last at the top, and under the cross, I sat and for the first time lit my pipe, relaxed and marvelled that I was here. Below me to the west Land's End and the start of the ice-cliffs of Commonwealth Bay. Below me to the east the whole panorama of Mawson's valley again, but this time from the side opposite to Proclamation Hill. It's all serene from this height, black rock, white snow, grey sea, ice pools—the color pattern is taken up and repeated by the penguins. The Project Blizzard people packing and loading, the 'tourists' who have come ashore from the *Icebird* in successive larc trips, from this distance seem little more than busy penguins themselves.

Inland there's first a gradual snow slope up to a white ridge. A penguin file, mere dots at this distance, are traversing up it. Above this first long ridge and far back, blending into the snowy sky, there's a higher and further ridge—two or three kilometres inland, they say, but for all I could tell it could be ten times that distance. Beyond that—well, beyond that there is nothing, or everything. To look at that vast, endless, featureless, terrifying nothingness, and then to glance back to this tiny, impertinent bridgehead on the confused shore just below me, is a quick course in humility. Yet in the old days men did struggle up such courses and worse to the Antarctic plateau not knowing what lay ahead. Albert Armitage and his party were the first. They reached 9000 feet early in 1903. I think of them.

But enough. It's been a big day, emotionally as well as physically. Back down the hill, always harder than climbing up, and a few minutes' rest in one of those ingenious 'apple' huts, red fibreglass igloos which they bolt together and stay down to the rocks with cables. Down to the shoreline and a wait until a small party, thinking no doubt of hot showers back on board the ship, is assembled. 'Doc', our army captain in charge of the larcs, says the seas are getting up. The Adélies saunter backwards and forwards through us, so that I almost expect one to select a lifejacket from the snow-covered pile and don it. A climb into the larc, and off out to sea—the ship is remote now, in deeper mist. Pat Quilty points to the water: "That's grease ice. It looks like oil on the water. It means the water is making up its mind to freeze." A nasty sight as we come alongside *Icebird*: there's a five-foot angry swell, and the larc is not only plunging in a crazy, erratic manner, but every now and then smashing with a great bang into the side of the ship. Doc is spreadeagled on our stern desperately trying to snare the springer cable laid along the ship's side with his boat-hook. Those on board, ten or twelve feet above our heads, fling us fore and aft ropes, which help. The army men push my comrades up onto the wire along the top of the side-screen, and from that, at the right moment, on to the ladder: NOW GO! Some clutch it, their legs dangling until they get a foothold. It's all pretty hairy. Graeme Manning, in his Soviet fur hat, leans out and calls to me from the deck above: "Would you like to stay in the cabin, Stephen, until later, when we lift the larc aboard?" I spurn his thoughtfulness—I may be fat and sixty-three but if the other buggers can do it so can I. I stand at the plunging edge. Two soldiers support me, a reserve behind. We have a few bad moments and some aborted attempts to swing onto the ladder. Then a moment of stillness, the larc and the ship steady for a second against each other, and I step over and climb up easily. The spectators lose interest when they see me safe.

And so to that shower, and Pat Quilty into the cabin for a whisky, and we talk for an hour or more with the affection and warmth of comrades who feel they have done something dramatic together—about the day, and the place, and Patrick's ancestors, and much more.

17

On Sunday, fifty-five years to the day since Sir Douglas Mawson claimed British possession of King George V Land from Proclamation Hill above Cape Denison, the Australian Antarctic charter vessel *Icebird* called at Mawson's Australian Antarctic expedition base of 1911–14 to load the seven members of Project Blizzard's second expedition.

They had spent the past four weeks in survey and assessment work connected with preservation of the original expedition hut, Australia's only significant historical site in Antarctica.

Loading was successfully completed with the aid of a crack army team handling amphibious vehicles in difficult conditions. Despite above-normal temperatures and constant wet snowfall, fifty members of the Australian National Antarctic Research Expedition's party were able to examine Mawson's base site in detail and crawl through a ten-metre ice tunnel into the heart of the hut to inspect the bunks, food, supplies and other memorabilia left behind seventy years ago.

In Mawson's small room, his pillow was on his bunk and his super-strength peppermints were on a nearby shelf.

All members of the visiting party were concerned about threats to the continued existence of Mawson's hut, now largely filled with hard snow and ice that has entered in recent years through gaps in the roof.

The weight of the packed snow and ice is splintering essential timbers, although emergency strutting was done with material landed yesterday.

The Department of the Environment in Canberra has barred Project Blizzard staff from doing immediate and essential conservation work, including sealing gaps and clearing the hut's interior as recommended after the first expedition a year ago.

The Project Blizzard leader, Sydney architect William Blunt, 32, now on board the *Icebird*, said: "There has been no maintenance on Mawson's hut for seventy-four years and present conditions makes implementation of our recommendations imperative.

"We have accumulated massive documentation but the vast input of community donations and voluntary work in the past two years has been in part negated by governmental obstruction and opposition to our carrying out emergency conservation work.

"A great opportunity has thereby been lost. Project Blizzard, with its thousands of supporters will not accept further involvement until and unless more satisfactory support from the Department of the Environment is forthcoming."

Mr Blunt's views were supported by all who made Sunday's site inspection.

The voyage leader, Mr Graeme Manning, and other officials of the Antarctic Division yesterday investigated the site for a future Australian summer station one kilometre east of Mawson's base and consider its potential satisfactory.

An alternative site for a summer station at Cape Gray, thirty kilometres east of Cape Denison, was investigated from the sea but rejected because of offshore reefs and landing problems.

(*Australian*, 7 January 1986)

18

AN AFTERWORD

There were nine huts built in Antarctica by expeditions which visited the continent before the First World War, of which six remain in reasonable condition. The earliest is that of Borchgrevink (1898–1900), at Cape Adare, in New Zealand Antarctic Territory. On Snow Hill Island on the Antarctic Peninsula (which we used to call Graham Land) there is Baron Nordenskjöld's hut from the Swedish expedition of 1901–04. Next in age comes Scott's *Discovery* expedition hut of 1901–04, on Ross Island, then

Shackleton's 1907–09 hut at Cape Royds, also on Ross Island, and then there is Scott's hut of 1910–13, at Cape Evans on Ross Island. Lastly there is Mawson's hut at Commonwealth Bay.

Two huts, Amundsen's of 1910–12 at the Bay of Whales, and Frank Wild's on the Shackleton Ice Shelf, have disappeared into the sea. Both were built on sea ice. Wild's base was an offshoot of the Mawson expedition. One further hut, Campbell's Scott expedition hut of 1910–13 at Cape Adare, is in ruins.

It is a good record of survival; in a way it's a bit like finding Ulysses's camp sites intact. It's a tribute to the construction of the huts themselves, of course, but they were never intended to serve as pilgrimage places for posterity, and probably the main credit for their continued existence must go to the snowdrifts which build up around them.

Although these huts survive, most of them have been quite frequently visited, tinkered with and even to some extent looted. Even Mawson's hut, the only surviving shelter on Australian Antarctic Territory, and with its surrounds probably the least disturbed of all these bases, has suffered in its time. Until the mid-1950s the hut was in excellent condition, inside and out. Then a party of US helicopter pilots left it inadequately sealed, and our troubles began. About the same time some of the hut's contents were looted/souvenired (choose the word you prefer) and taken to Paris. Recently this material has been returned to Melbourne, but not—and there are hard feelings about this—to the Antarctic Division.

Mawson's hut has been called by Michael Pearson, of the Australian Heritage Commission, "a uniquely Australian contribution to Antarctic hut design" *Heritage Newsletter*, June 1987). It appears to have been based on a standard prefabricated Australian homestead design, with a pyramidal roof and verandahs which could be, and were, enclosed. The stumps, set in holes blasted into the rock, provided strong foundations. (Mawson's decaying gelignite caused some concern to the first Project Blizzard party, who found it near the hut in 1985.)

Dr Pearson visited the Commonwealth Bay site in the summer of 1986–87. An assistant director of the Australian Heritage Commission, he is also a member of the Antarctic Historic Sites and

Monuments Advisory Committee, set up by Barry Jones, the then Minister responsible for Antarctica, in 1986. (Astonishingly, considering Barry Jones's lifelong interest in, and practice of, historical research, the committee does not include one historian.) Dr Pearson, who was unable actually to enter Mawson's hut, claims that it would be impossible to preserve it on the 'let's walk in and have a look' basis applying to the huts on Ross Island. The tongue-and-groove cladding is no longer weatherproof, if it ever was completely so; the whole hut would have to be covered in "some form of impervious cladding" and regularly cleared of intrusive snow; and to remove the ice within the hut would have a detrimental effect on the hut's fabric. Dr Pearson appears to believe that the hut is best left full of ice, with some maintenance of "falling structural elements".

I believe that Michael Pearson is far too pessimistic. I also believe that, while the Heritage Commission shelters behind the timeless bureaucratic defences of 'hastening slowly' and 'considering the options', it has shown such a lack of enthusiasm for Australia's Antarctic heritage that it would appear to regard the whole issue as a nuisance. Perhaps one of the problems is that Mawson's hut doesn't lie within a Commonwealth electorate. Support from the Heritage Commission and the Department of the Environment for the inspired and courageous efforts of the Project Blizzard teams has been scandalously lacklustre, as I have said. I believe that Mawson's hut can be repaired and placed in a reasonably sound and weatherproof condition. And I believe that it is important for our national self-respect that this should be done.

I am not alone in this. William Blunt, who was the leader of the two Project Blizzard teams to Commonwealth Bay, who is a Sydney architect, and who probably knows as much as anyone living about the problems of Mawson's hut, inside and out, believes that it is quite practicable to preserve the hut in reasonable condition. The chief problem of snow entry is with one section of the roof. This could be removed, sarking inserted and be replaced. The wall cladding, he believes, is in reasonable condition, and in any case is protected, during the worst weather and at its most exposed points, by snowdrifts. Certainly there would need to be regular maintenance. Unfortunately the new ANARE summer base in the Commonwealth Bay area seems unlikely to be occupied long enough each season to make this possible, but when the French complete their airstrip at Dumont d'Urville, only 200 miles away, it should be possible to fly a small party down from Hobart and helicopter them in to Commonwealth Bay for this purpose. It will be interesting to see if the inclusion of Antarctica in the same Canberra portfolio as Environment and Heritage, from 1987, brings any improvement in this scandalous situation.

As regards the ice which fills two-thirds of the hut or more, Blunt believes that it need not all be removed. The only objection that I can see to some ice remaining within the hut is that it is that ice which, during the warmer summer months, creates an internal humidity which certainly affects the artefacts within the hut, and perhaps some of the timbers themselves. I cannot see why, with the removal of the ice and the repair of the standing timbers, the hut cannot stand until wiser heads, in times to come, make further decisions about it.

Old Antarctic hands, such as John Béchervaise, have pointed out to me that under suitable conditions enclosed ice can be made to evaporate, to pass from the solid to the gaseous stage without in the process becoming water. This 'sublimation' takes place when the container is effectively sealed for some time. I am told that there is no reason why this process should not work at Mawson's hut. What it requires is for a few people to get off their arses, just as Mawson and his men did.

And, by the way, measures adopted under the Antarctic Treaty *require* Australia, as other nations, to "adopt all adequate measures to preserve and protect from damage the historic monuments situated in the Antarctic Treaty area."

19

7 January 1986, 7 p.m.

A featureless sea. The *Icebird* nods placidly as it drives forward at 13.1 knots. The satellite has just pinged the bridge computer to give us a new fix: Latitude 63°35′S., Longitude 129°11′E. In other words, 150 nautical miles (you rarely hear of kilometres down here) off Wilkes Land, standing well out to sea to avoid the pack. Not that the pack would worry us, but it would slow us up.

I think of Charles Wilkes, the American naval officer, and of how startled he and Dumont d'Urville must have been to sight each others' ships in just these waters, back there in 1840. We would be startled to sight another ship here in 1986 – though I am told that, further west, it is possible to run into big Japanese or Soviet fishing fleets, harvesting the krill. Wilkes and d'Urville each started to do the decent thing and to make contact with each other. In one of the most bizarre of Antarctic incidents Wilkes mistook d'Urville's intentions, thought he was being snubbed, got huffy and made off! It seems hard to believe that gentlemen were that sensitive, even in 1840. They never met again.

The bridge is deserted except for Jörg, the pleasantly-mannered young officer of the watch – second mate of the *Icebird*, in fact – and myself. My fellow voyagers' overheated cameras (and mine) are having a day off. Flurries of snow occasionally invest us, but that's as far as drama goes.

No whales. I think with sadness of how Mawson and other forerunners spoke of the leviathans as familiars, and of humanity's murderous instincts. At the moment there are not even any birds. The radar tells us that seven miles off to the west there's a mighty berg. We can't see it.

For most on board the evening is chicken Kiev for dinner (the 'Mombasa', that is 'slushy', in the servery tonight is my cabin-mate Brendan) and a film, "Mephisto". If it's the film about the German actor who compromised with the Nazis [it wasn't] it raises a lot of questions it would be interesting, but embarrassing, to discuss on this German ship. And this reminds me that they tell me that the Antarctic Treaty is the most successful example of an international disarmament agreement in history. Which in turn leads me to reflect on the obscenity that forty years ago young Australians like those on this ship would have been flying over Germany trying to kill these pleasant and talented young Germans who have us in their care, *and* their families.

If Antarctica meant no more than the opportunity for young people of many nations to display some idealism and enthusiasm

The wind-eroded cladding of Mawson's hut at Commonwealth Bay. The battens which reinforced a tarpaulin overlay are still in evidence.

Stephen Murray-Smith about to enter the ice-choked Mawson Hut at Commonwealth Bay, crawling along a laboriously-excavated ice-tunnel to his right.

Whodunnits mingled with nautical almanacs on the library shelf in Mawson's Hut of 1911–13 at Commonwealth Bay.

Condiment bottles and open boxes of foodstuffs, three-quarters of a century after they fed the members of Douglas Mawson's 1911–13 Antarctic expedition in the hut at Commonwealth Bay.

in an unusual setting, it would be worth it. And if it meant no more than to give those who are not young, and who will never see the great barriers, the spiritual delight of knowing that they are there, it would be worth it. These mean more than all the ingenious scientific experiments and gallant icecap traverses, though without the sense of purpose and achievement that such exploits give us, some of the wider inspiration might be weakened.

What is the point of something you can't see for yourself? Russel Madigan wants the Mawson hut at Cape Denison moved to Melbourne, and a replica erected in its place. He has his points—how *do* we preserve that jerrybuilt edifice, only designed for a season's shelter in the Antarctic? How, he argues, short of imbedding the lot in a cube of clear plastic, do we ensure that it will still be there in another seventy-five years' time? But the argument that to shift it back to Australia would enable hundreds of thousands to see it, where only tens see it now, misses the point.

You don't have to *see* Everest or *climb* it to be inspired by its presence in your mind. You don't have to worship at Chartres, or even to see it, to feel it belongs to you. Venice is more than a trip across the Grand Canal in a gondola. Mawson's hut, where it stands at Cape Denison, has a real life in the minds of many Australians which it could never have in an air-conditioned hangar on the banks of the Yarra.

20

From now the path was west, west, west, the clocks back an hour every couple of nights. We crossed the Antarctic Circle again, this time travelling north, for we went 150 miles out to sea before turning west for Casey base, thus clearing the pack-ice and leaving us only icebergs to worry about. As day succeeded to day, running our westing down, we began to realise the extent of this section of the sixth continent that we claim for ourselves. A thousand miles from Commonwealth Bay to Casey. Another thousand miles from Casey to Davis. Five hundred miles on across Prydz Bay to Mawson, and yet another 500 miles before we reach the edge of 'our' territory. (Actual 'as the skua flies' distances, in nautical miles, are Leningradksaya (near our eastern border) to Dumont d'Urville, 470; Dumont d'Urville to Casey, 700; Casey to Davis, 753; Davis to Mawson, 342; Mawson to Molodezhnaya, on our eastern boundary, 357.) And that doesn't take into account another 500 miles or so of Australian coastline *east* of Commonwealth Bay. Altogether some 3000 nautical miles of coastline, say 3500 miles, say 5700 kilometres. Of course the curvature of the earth has a constricting effect on the parallels of longitude, but it still came as a shock to realise, later on, when we got to Davis, that we were pretty well directly south of Bombay; and that Mawson, to which at one stage we were also bound, is south of the Persian Gulf! If Australians think about Antarctica at all, which of course they don't, their mental vision will be that our bases lie south of us. They don't. They lie a long way west. And that has both logistic and political implications.

We were settling down into a little community, and those of us of like minds were getting to know each other. Shipboard life was becoming a routine: meals, reading on the bridge, writing, yarning. It was interesting, for instance, in talking to the two Italian observers on board to learn of their backgrounds. Roberto Cervellati is an electronic physicist and scientific adviser to Enea, Italy's

nuclear and alternative energy authority. It's a big enterprise, employing 4000 people, formerly a nuclear energy authority only, like the British and French ones. When the Italian government decided to launch an Antarctic project—they were already ashore and working at Terra Nova Bay, on the Ross Sea—they decided to place the organisation into Enea's hands, and Enea invited Gabriel Riccardi, who works for an enormous state-owned engineering company, to join the team. These charming men, it occurred to me, were not chosen because they were starry-eyed visionaries, but because they were 'hands on' men able to see that Italy got value for money in Antarctica.

Roberto, who has the better English, has grey hair and, like so many on board, was trying to grow an Antarctic beard. I liked him and Gabriel because they viewed Australians quizzically, and they seemed to like my company, perhaps because I spoke clearly to them and explained unusual words and ideas. I'd already told them that I wanted their *pensieri segreti*, their secret thoughts, when we again sighted the Tasmanian coast.

And then to Ewald Brune's cabin for some of his Fürst von Metternich Rhineland champagne. I sat round his big table with Lee Ranford, Phil Gard the cargo-master, Graeme Manning, Geraldine Nash and Anders Karlqvist. The talk turned to Antarctic vessels, and in particular the ideal supply ship. Ewald thought the *Icebird* close to the ideal, though he'd have a stern better able to cope with following seas, and wouldn't have the superstructure and module on rubber mounts. This, he said, reduced the noise from below, but increased internal noise and caused jolting and movement.

Then we talked about the Greenpeace ship *Southern Quest*, now beset in the Ross Sea, somewhere near Scott Island so far as we knew. Ewald said the ship was hopeless for its job; the plates forward were strengthened but the frames were not, and ships of what he called the "tugboat type" sink when beset, as the ice mounts on deck and just pushes them down.

Ewald should know, for he has a tale to tell, and told it. In December 1982 he was in command of the MS *Gotland II*, 2186 gross tons, landing the German Antarctic North Victoria Land (GANOVEX) expedition near Cape Adare, at the entrance to the

Ross Sea. The expedition insisted, against Ewald's advice, on sailing south from Wellington too early in the season, in order to qualify for an income-tax exemption! The ship got caught in Yule Bay, and Ewald saw what was coming. Since the German base camp was many miles inland he got the helicopters off, and the helicopter fuel on to the beach, before the *Gotland* sank in 400 metres of water, taking a great deal of valuable scientific equipment with her. A nasty experience for a young skipper, but Ewald was quite debonair about it, fortified no doubt by the fact that the subsequent enquiry in Germany cleared him of responsibility.

A few days later, for his birthday, I wrote him a poor poem in dog German which made reference to the event:

Lieb' Kapitän

Mit besten Wunschen dieser Brief
In schrecklich Deutsch geschrieben,
Von allen die mit Ihnen fahren,
Um Ihren Geburstag zu feiern.

I switch to English, mit relief,
To celebrate Ihr Leben,
We'll sail with you to Hell and back,
And kein mehr *Schiff aufgeben*!

If gentle manners, kindly thoughts
And humor makes a skipper,
The *Icebird* is a lucky ship,
Who'll never find a fitter.

(*Schiff aufgeben* means "Abandon ship!")

One of the pleasures of shipboard gossip is the trivial information you pick up. Ewald told us that Gould Bay in the Weddell Sea is, at 78°50′ South, the furthest south you can get in ice-free water. He added that, to create a record that will presumably stand for some time, he once wind-surfed there.

21

Ewald has a pet charity, the restoration of a historic German Arctic exploration ship. From the noticeboard:

WHISTLING

The current bad weather conditions have caused the Captain to indulge in a close study of maritime history, maritime law, recent Antarctic incidents and old wives' tales. He has come to the firm conclusion that the cause of the current Force Ten gale is due to whistling. Offenders in future will be fined $5 for the SS *Stettin* Restoration Appeal. The amount will be debited to the Offender's ship account.

22

Verb sap.?

. . . the strategic interest of Australia in Antarctica is to have no reason to take a strategic interest in the region.

Cisca Spencer, in Stuart Harris (ed.): *Australia's Antarctic Policy Options* (Canberra, 1984), p. 120.

23

I have a delightful set of 1794 prints which depict "The Delights of Bacchus", in fact a set of toasts. In one of them a dilapidated-looking fellow in a tricorne hat is sitting at a table clutching his wine glass. The toast he is moving is "May the Eye of Science pierce through the mists of Obscurity". Unfortunately the poor fellow is one-eyed, and wears a black patch.

On the *Icebird* we now have a chance to see science at work, piercing those mists of Obscurity.

We are going to try to find the South Magnetic Pole.

For some time we have been wondering about the odd, gantry-like structure, a huge beam to which some devilish machine is attached, which has been poked out over the stern of the ship from several decks up on the afterthought sterncastle built right on the blunt end of the *Icebird.*

Then the word got around that we were going to make some kind of scientific history.

The Earth, of course, is a magnet. Were that not so compasses would not work. At first it was thought that the explanation of the magnetism of the Earth was that, since a compass needle mounted vertically behaves very much as does a similar needle above a ball of magnetised iron, the whole Earth must be a magnet. Then it was realised that, below a depth of thirty miles, the Earth's core is too hot to have magnetic qualities. There had to be some other explanation.

It is only in quite recent decades that agreement has been reached that in the main the Earth's magnetic field is produced by electric currents generated in the fluid core of the Earth as a result of the Earth's rotation.

A compass, unfortunately, points not to the North Geographical Pole—if it did, navigation by land and sea would be a great deal simpler—but to the North Magnetic Pole. At this point, as at the South Magnetic Pole, a vertically mounted compass needle (known as a 'dip needle') will stand at a right angle to the Earth's surface. The angular difference between True North, the point around which the Earth spins, and Magnetic North is known as the magnetic variation.

If this variation were fixed and permanent, again matters would be more simple. If a navigator wishing to travel north knew that at all times he must actually travel 8° west of the direction in which the compass points, his life would be rather easier than it is at the moment. But in fact the Magnetic Poles are in constant motion. The South Magnetic Pole has moved more than 1200 km in a north/north-westerly direction in the last 140 years, and the North Magnetic Pole has moved similarly though not, as it happens, in phase with the South Magnetic Pole. The issue is further complicated by the fact that at any one time there is no *one* magnetic variation, but a variation which itself varies according to where you are on the Earth's surface.

When James Clark Ross first established the position of the South Magnetic Pole in 1841 it was in South Victoria Land, not far from the famous Ross Island. By the time Mawson, Edgeworth David and Alistair Mackay actually reached it in 1909 the pole was 230 miles north of Ross's site, but still very much on dry land, so to speak. Three years later, when Eric Webb visited the position, the pole had moved some distance west. In 1952, when Mayaud stood above it, it was quite close to the French station of Dumont d'Urville. Its position was now computed mathematically to be out to sea from Dumont d'Urville.

And the project was that we should find the South Magnetic Pole by direct observation 'on the ground' and that we should lie above it. Quite romantic, really. We would be only fourth from Mawson.

Great doings on the bridge. The scientists had lashed their computers and recorders to the outside wall of the radio cabin. They darted around with grins on their faces and spent a lot of time going through the 'it's not working properly yet' routine. I felt tempted to offer them one of our catchphrases from Erith Island: "If all else fails read the instructions."

24

After a week of vectoring experiments using specially designed equipment on the bridge of the *Icebird*, and also hung over the stern on beams, Australian scientists aboard this Antarctic research vessel today [6 January 1986] established the position of the South Magnetic Pole by direct observation. It is believed this is the first time this has been achieved, other than by mathematical models, since 1952, and only the fourth time since Mawson, Edgeworth David and Mackay stood above the Pole in 1909.

At twenty minutes past two this afternoon the pole was at Latitude 65°13′ South and at Longitude 139° 55′ East, approximately 160 kilometres north of the French Antarctic research station of Dumont d'Urville. Several spot locations were observed of the wander-path of the pole. It is oscillating rapidly and moved fifty kilometres in a west/north-west direction in one hour. This is believed to be the first time this movement of the pole has been traced over a short period. The observations agree with the long-term observed movement of the pole in a north/north-westerly direction.

The project leaders for the South Dipole Project are Dr Patrick Quilty of the Antarctic Division and Dr Charles Barton, of the Bureau of Mineral Resources in Canberra. The group leader on board the *Icebird* is Rodney Hutchinson of the same bureau, assisted by Dr Patrick Quilty, Dr Gary Burns, Peter Yates and Matthew Sherlock of the Antarctic Division of the Department of Science.

(*Australian*, 7 January 1986)

25

Diary, 8 January 1986

Early breakfast with a couple of mates. A sign of our acclimatisation to the Antarctic scene is that the talk on such occasions is getting round increasingly to domestic topics. One of my companions, angry that the ship's bar does not open before dinner at night, a time at which at least the middle classes on board feel they want a drink, says of Captain Ewald—and referring to the recent *Nella Dan* besetment and the problems the *Icebird* met with in attempting to go to its rescue—"If he can stick a ship in the ice surely he can extend the bar times by half an hour." Unfair but funny.

The comments arose from a hectic hour I had with the larcies in the pub down below last night. They're in a high state of resentment at the way the army treats them. When they tell army public relations that half the time Australian Antarctic operations get publicity in the press, army personnel are involved, but never get identified, the army people say, "So what?" This then led to the next most important grievance, the price of grog on board—at $15 a dozen small cans of beer, more than a hundred per cent up on last year. They say this is obviously an attempt to keep them off the hops, and that therefore they are all the more determined to get on them. They're a good, tough, spirited mob, the only dissidents on board, and proud of their courage and skill. And they're right, I suppose: the only Australian soldiers on active service.

(A fellow at Casey later told me that he'd gone to a lot of trouble to order 200 dozen beer, a pallet of beer in fact, to be loaded at Hobart and sent down, to be shared among twenty. Of these 140 dozen were to stay on the base, the other sixty dozen to be drunk on board the ship, after first meeting the duty-free regulations by being landed at Casey. The Antarctic Division moved in and said there was no room on the ship. In my heart I found I could blame neither the Antarctic Division for its prudence nor the expeditioner for his wrath at the naked paternalism and lying. The Antarctic Division defends itself, in cases like this, by pointing out that there are frequently *time* limits in loading rather than *space* limits on board.)

Then an unexpected outburst at this same breakfast from one of my companions about the Antarctic Division in which he works, its cabals and dishonesties, a talk continued on the bridge. Later we watched a video on the Fuchs–Hillary crossing of Antarctica in 1957–58. Hillary emerged from the suave British commentary as a cheeky colonial upstart, which of course he was.

And so, in this episodic way, my day continued. A beer in the pub, with Ernst, chief cook and barman, trying to teach me the German bar-top game called Max, played with dice: "*Sehr kompliziert, Ernst.*" "*Nein, nein.*" Then a gin-and-tonic in Graeme Manning's fine leader's cabin, with him, Geraldine, Ewald and the Italians, and talk of classical education and Latin and Greek. Frankfurts for lunch, and talk there to Roberto and Gabriel of Scott and Oates and the Amundsen controversy.

Later. I casually count from the cabin window fourteen bergs around us, even from this restricted viewpoint. I am sad that I am already a little *blasé*. In fact I'm generally a little melancholy. I miss my family and wonder what they're doing. And I reflect on the people on board—good people, I'm sure, but hardly any share interests with me; so I can't be a good mixer. The deflation is good for my soul, but it is also demoralising. I'm pleased to be here and to see what is going on, but these pleasant, decent, ebullient, uncomplicated, timid Australians are no latterday Mawsons or Shackletons, Frank Wilds or Herbert Murphys. To be fair, they are as responsive to the delights of ice and bestiary as I am, for all I know more sensitive and moved, though perhaps in a less affected way. In all of them, I suppose, there is some response to the lines Mawson quoted from Robert Service: "Let us probe the silent places, let us seek what luck betide us." All are interested and prepared to do their best. A few will even have a difficult time in the field, but I'm not picking up any resonances from the 'heroic' age. Bureaucracies, professional (and justified) fusspots and knowledge capitalists abound now in Antarctica. I'm beginning to feel that the sooner all the 'frontier' guff is dropped and we set up permanent Australian townships in Antarctica—if that is the way we are going—the better. Heroics are out. Adélie Land is closer to Hobart than is Perth. A quarter of Sweden is above the Arctic Circle. Eskimos in Greenland live up to 74° North, and even further, on a permanent basis. At Roros, in central Norway, 5000 people live in a community where the temperature drops to −50°C, and school is declared 'out' when the classroom temperature drops below −12°C. Who are we kidding?

Yet myths can be sustaining. There is a selflessness, or at least a sense of service, on board *Icebird.* The young diplomat Brendan is *very* serious about the virtues of the Antarctic Treaty and works very hard for Australia; Bill Ware gets stuck into his met reports with a proselytising enthusiasm; the 'Mombasas' cheerfully do their dirty work; Gary Burns, one-time stamp-collecting schoolmate of my son David, is clearly a dedicated Antarctic physicist. All of this is impressive, and I should not forget it.

Reading Phil Law's *Antarctic Odyssey.* It's a good book. Very Phil—he wants to make sure you appreciate his role. But then, as Patrick Quilty says, his role was a great one, and he has never received his deserts.

26

I, KING NEPTUNE, am pleased to again welcome ye mighty vessel *Icebird* to my southern-most realm. I am also pleased to accept my friend of old, Captain Ewald Brune's, invitation to become acquainted with his latest load of dubious human specimens.

HOWEVER, my winged emissaries have advised me that this collection of said specimens is so smelly, putrid, filthy and, not to put too fine a point on it, totally repulsive, that I find myself required to prepared a suitably thorough ceremony to ensure that my southern-most realm remains unpolluted.

As such, I request your presence on the forecastle (the sharp end) on Thursday morning at 1000 hours local where I will preside over my Court of Cleansing. Please be advised that you are to present yourself punctually (late arrivals will attract my special attention) attired in ventiles and lifejackets.

P.S. As I am a warm-hearted ruler I offer you a way of appeasing my dislike for yourselves. A vessel which was commissioned when you were uncontemplated, the mighty steam ice-breaker S.S. *Stettin*, is being renovated in

Lübeck by public funds and will become a relic of a maritime era. For a small donation I shall look upon your cleansing with a new light.

P.P.S. I look forward to our mutual pleasure.

KING NEPTUNE

27

The ceremony, somewhat delayed, is to mark our crossing of the Antarctic Circle. I find out later that the ceremony is in fact an old one. On 19 January 1840 Dumont d'Urville, sailing south, was "officially warned" that the ship was about to receive the visit of Father Antarctic:

> After a shower of rice and beans thrown from the topmasts, I received a messenger on a seal, who brought me a message from his fantastic sovereign. I will spare the reader a description of the costume of the strange ambassador and the content of his epistle. [It sounds as though it was rather like the message we received.] I was pleased to see that our sailors had changed the traditional baptismal ceremony into a communion of another kind, that of wine, which would be more advantageous to them, and I had no objection to make.

"As usual," added d'Urville, the sailors "put on all sorts of weird and wonderful acts; there was a parade of mummers, a sermon and a feast. The finale consisted of singing and dancing."

We were not all that far from the scene of d'Urville's revels. At 8.20 a.m. on 9 January we were at Latitude 64°11′ South, Longitude111°17′ East, smooth sea, wind six knots from the ESE, speed 4.2 knots, visibility 100 metres, course 259°, steaming west about one and a half days from Casey. The radar told us there were twenty bergs within six miles, and that is why, with that restricted visibility, we were travelling at only four knots. Ewald Brune mentioned in passing that a German polar vessel, similar to *Icebird*, hit an iceberg in northern seas recently and went down with all hands. The incident was hushed up. Indeed.

The temperature on the fo'c'sle at ten was a pleasant, mild 0.6°C. We were well rugged up in our ventiles, and the slight shivering apparent here and there was not due to the temperature, but to the fearsome stories of what was in store for us that had been circulated in recent days. In particular we were told of the disgusting concoctions lovingly prepared by Uwe from the foulest ingredients he could find on the ship. Dozens of us were up there, crowded together in our motley, and waiting.

Soon came the ominous banging of a gong, and up the companion climbed two tow-headed (literally—their wigs were made of rope) dignitaries in flowing robes, with malevolent grins on their faces. King Neptune, to whom we bowed, seemed rather like our supercargo Alistair Baillie; his acolyte with the gong seemed not unlike the captain. They took their places behind a long table, presided over by Uwe with a great cauldron, a ladle and a satisfied look on his face. German military music blared over the loudspeaker.

First came a series of charges against specific offenders. The chief engineer was arraigned for polluting the sea, placed on a platform attached to a crane, a set-up we had been uneasily eyeing, and to our horror was hoisted up in the air, then overboard, and dropped to the icy sea, in which his legs were immersed. Harald saluted as he went down. Then, similarly, half a dozen other offenders were placed on the tray—they included Geraldine Nash and Peter Gormly, our doctor—and disappeared over the side. Peter sang "Abide with Me" as he went. We all found it a little startling.

Then for the rest of us. Spread on the fo'c'sle deck was an enormous cargo net. We were mustered on this, collectively abused by the Monarch, and informed that we would be deposited collectively in the sea. The slings tightened, we grasped each other and wondered how bloody serious these maniacs were. And then Neptune relented and received us individually, cleansing us with the administration of a draught of Uwe's, something with a strong base of curry. (Last time, we were told, Uwe used as a stock the bloodied water left at the bottom of frozen meat containers.) Uwe was merciful to me, kind soul. I was one of his pets. He slipped me a wink and slipped a mere *soupçon* of brew into my paper cup.

Finally we were dignified with new Antarctic names, and a rather elaborate certificate enshrining them. An alarming hour.

28

KNIGHTS OF THE EMPEROR PENGUIN COURT

Know All Men By These Presents: and to all Penguins, Seals, Whales, and Gooney Birds and all denizens of the frozen southern wastes in the land of the midnight sun—

Know Ye, That: STEPHEN MURRAY-SMITH, "Sea Elephant", has with my Royal consent passed the Gateway to the bottom of the world by crossing the Antarctic Circle.

BE IT FURTHER KNOWN: That he entered this land of icicles, blizzards and myriad snowflakes aboard the Good Ship M.S. "Icebird" on 3 January 1986 at 140° East longitude.

That I, Australis Rex, Ruler of the Southern Winds and Sovereign of all the Frozen Reaches it touches do hereby declare this hot-blooded Neophyte to my Royal Domain to be a True and Trusted Salt Brine Encrusted REDNOSE.

And so on.

29

Back in the cabin I write my first feature for the newspaper. On the general issues, as they seem to be emerging to me, of Antarctic research. Text follows, as they say.

Australia holds the key to the world's cellar—or at least that is one way of looking at this country's scientific responsibilities in Antarctica.

The issue arises from the current debate, both in political and scientific circles in Australia and on board this Antarctic vessel *Icebird*, on the significance and direction of strengthened Australian drives in this formidable continent, of which Australia claims ownership of some 42 per cent. This claim covers theoretical possession of 35 to 40 per cent of the world's fresh water, an ironic circumstance seeing that the world's two driest continents are involved.

While Australian motives are no doubt in the last resort political, not least because the financing of Antarctic development depends on political arguments put to the Australian electorate, many scientists see the Antarctic Treaty, of which Australia was a founding member in 1959, as the world's most successful international accord—an accord which unifies scientific and political objectives in a vast, internationalised area in which military and strategic considerations are significant only by their absence, and where the quest for knowledge for the benefit of the whole world is held to be the only true goal. "The Antarctic Treaty," says Patrick Quilty, the science deputy-director of the Antarctic Division, "is a damned beautiful thing."

The argument is that only by scientific work of the highest international standards will we achieve that respect and recognition which will allow us to continue to exert strong moral and political influence in the Antarctic Treaty. It is accepted, at least by informed opinion aboard this ship, that Australia has slipped in the Antarctic prestige stakes. In the 1950s we held second or third place. Today we are down to sixth or seventh.

This scientific argument overlooks some other important Antarctic issues, such as the spiritual and aesthetic significance of this land, its historical ties with Australia now stretching back one hundred years, and its proximity—Antarctica is much closer than most Australians imagine.

Yet Australian scientists are now subjecting our work in Australia to close scrutiny. A marker here was the establishment in 1985 of the Antarctice Science Advisory Committee, under Professor John Lovering of the University of Melbourne. [Now vice-chancellor of Flinders University, South Australia.]

Some leading Australian scientists, both in governmental and academic circles, criticise current Australian Antarctic research as predominantly "curiosity-minded". By this they mean that it is unco-ordinated and unplanned in the wider sense, that it has evolved on the basis of earlier commitments, rather than having its direction and significance periodically examined, with clear priorities established.

To this other scientists, such as Dr Quilty, reply that "Curiosity has to be the motivating force behind any research," and that our polar science is essentially moving in the direction of applied economic and social significance. Quilty instances the glaciology program, which he says is of enormous world interest: "The work we have done in the field in association with the Americans, the Russians and the French is close to providing the data which will establish whether or not the icecap is stable, or whether most of the world's cities will one day find themselves seventy metres under the sea. Some say that such changes can happen very quickly, in geological terms, perhaps in just a few thousands of years."

Quilty also points out that, for instance, the current Antarctic Division investigations of the harvest potential of krill in southern waters—the world's major untouched protein resource—suggest that there has been an overestimate by a factor of four. Our cosmic ray programs, he says, are the most advanced at either pole and, while not yet of visible economic significance, are of great interest in the developing field of high-energy physics.

Despite their internal arguments the scientists both on board *Icebird* and back home agree with each other that science in Antarctica is suffering because of the inertial force of our long-term logistic and building programs down here, feeding off their own growth. This is creating a position where money is increasingly being diverted from direct scientific applications to the provision of more and more service personnel, and this undermines the fundamental scientific purpose of our being in Antarctica.

This view overlooks the fact that we also have to 'maintain a presence' in Antarctica for political reasons, a purpose which some foreign observers aboard this ship see as incompatible with our adherence to the Antarctic Treaty. It also overlooks the problems of establishing complex installations in these difficult surroundings, and the past starvation of Antarctic programs which now has to be compensated for.

The scientists' complaints, however, are now being accepted at least to the point where the Antarctic Division is seeking 'small is beautiful' solutions to the issue of establishing a chain of summer stations, such as is projected at Cape Denison (Commonwealth Bay), and some of which are likely to become permanent.

(*Australian*, 11 January 1986)

30

9 January 1986

We are heading back to the coast, into Casey. There can be few more exciting or beautiful experiences than entering pack-ice. The sea is glassy. The brash ice gives way to growlers, little bits and pieces of decayed ice, then to small floes, snow-dusted if they are flat, icy-pinnacled if they are more contorted in shape. Below, light green through the water, you see the ragged floor of the floe, often many times its size. The ship ploughs on. It shudders as it hits and deflects the floes. In our bow wave, often now some distance from the ship, pieces crumble off the side of the floes and they subside into the water, like pieces of icing picked off a cake by children's fingers.

Gradually the calm surface becomes more and more choked with floating ice. A leopard seal, disturbed, flexes its snaky neck to glimpse the intruder. In the distance, ahead of us, the ice is thicker. It merges into what seems to be a continuous horizon of white rocks.

The fascination is of the mixed elements. To find a grove of trees on the moon would hardly be more strange than to see these clean, random solids sprinkled across this glassy water. From a distance the sea takes up the color of the floes, and looks like a continuous ice-sheet. The floes of the pack-ice create a random beauty. We are more used to beauty organised and coherent.

We push through the ice, three or four feet thick, and as we do the great spatulate bow of our ship presses down on it, breaks it, thrusts it aside. Floes caught a glancing blow, and with leads behind them to retreat to, will spin round on themselves, with perhaps a crack or two right across their clean shirt-fronts. But those truly caught by our cruel weight first seem unmoved. Then they split, burst, disintegrate into a boiling mass of a million fragments. They swirl in the whirlpool of waters, turn upside down to expose bases discolored with the algae on which the krill feed, undersides where marine organisms find an unlikely home. Bomb-bursts of the same brown-green ice swirl to the surface.

And the pattern of this tumult is never repeated. This is where 'compulsive viewing' was invented.

LATER

We were hove to in the pack today for four hours, our bow hard up on a big floe, dense fog all around. Ewald was not prepared to go on.

31

At Casey, 10 January 1986

Still aboard the ship but, from what I've seen and from what I've read, why do Antarctic stations have to be so ugly? The physical sweep of the Casey panorama from here, a few hundred yards offshore, is utterly magnificent: pale brown rocks and darker moraines shrugging the overlying snow off their shoulders; ice cliffs and shelves, mushroom islands with their creamy toppings and, away offshore and out to sea, that wonderful frieze of Iceberg Alley, that mile upon mile of icebergs stranded on a bank, so that we had to overrun our course and skirt the bank on the way in here.

A study in black and white: the valley at Commonwealth Bay, Douglas Mawson's Boat Harbour to the left and his expedition hut of 1911–13 centre right. The katabatic winds channelling down these slopes make it the windiest place in the world.

This desiccated seal carcase lies by the edge of Boat Harbour, Commonwealth Bay, where men of Mawson's party dragged it prior to their departure in 1913.

Building works at New Casey, overlooking a grand prospect: the *Icebird*, the abandoned Wilkes station and a stately row of grounded icebergs.

The Wilkes station, near Casey, was built by the Americans and subsequently occupied by the Australians. Buried in snow and ice, it presents an enormous environmental problem.

Looking at those ice islands one glories in this placid, sunny, bountiful day, which has enabled so much unloading to be done well ahead of schedule, and the cutting edge of which you feel only if you observe the barge workers in their fur hats and mittens, or stay outdoors long enough to feel the 'chill factor' as the little breeze lays its talons on your flesh.

But raise your gaze, and look ashore at man's inhumanity to Antarctica. Look at the tawdry, reach-me-down, straggling, stepped buildings of our present base here, and a few hundred yards away up the rise the products of the plastic civilisation which is now replacing the tin civilisation: children's toy blocks of color-coded housing, red for living, blue for power-generation and so on, scattered it would seem at random along a ridge. How public service architects, builders and engineers love ridges! Maximise the impact! When you've finished playing with your earth-movers, stick your 'construction' on the ridge. The skyline is free, and up there your genius will forever force itself on the viewer.

A welcome recruit to the ship's company has just boarded, Ron Lewis-Smith, a Scottish botanist who was dropped off on an earlier trip and has been down here a month or so, a senior member of the British Antarctic Survey and a veteran of ten Antarctic visits. "I must say," says Ron in his quiet way, "Casey station is the ugliest I've ever seen, and that's saying a lot." He adds, with studied understatement, "In fact all your Australian stations stand out." [Ron, an official British observer under the Antarctic Treaty, released on his return to Australia a report on Australian environmental vandalism in Antarctica which received international attention and caused a lot of political embarrassment and Antarctic Division resentment.]

Yes, yes, I know there are the best of reasons for the dispersal of buildings over, it seems, all available ground: drift snow and the risk of fire among them. And these plastic buildings dominating the ridge above the harbor up there to the west would look quite dinky if shoved across a table as models at a committee meeting in Canberra, or Melbourne, or Hobart. Perhaps the Russian and American stations, and the Chinese station, and the rest of them, are excrescences also. But it's hard not to see an Australian national purpose at work.

"You do seem to go a bit hard at making your mark," says my

new Scottish friend. "Wander around on shore and try to find the science all this is supposed to serve." I thought, not for the last time, of the trendy New York church in Peter de Vries's *Mackerel Plaza*, with the "small praying area" up one end. And I pointed out to Ron the Boxing Kangaroo flag the *Chicken* is flying as it plies its way to and from the shore. "I thought it was just a joke," said Ron. "Of course it is," I answered. "But it's more than that. A lot of us Australians see it as a kind of national flag. It expresses one of our attitudes to the world. It probably expresses our attitude to Antarctica too. It's not flying on the *Chicken* by accident."

Yes, we've gone a long way towards buggering up one continent. There's no reason why we shouldn't start on another. Like Chips Rafferty and Paul Hogan, we have a lanky reach. And, with two million square miles to play around with, why economise?

Economise? The present building programs are going to cost a hundred million dollars, perhaps more. And on top of that, of course, is all our previous investment. "There's no doubt," says Ron, "that you're going to end up with the most elaborate bases in Antarctica."

And we don't even want them any more! Well, we don't *need* them if we're talking about purely scientific work, *à la* the Treaty. But otherwise? I'll come to that.

How much has been put into Casey, say? At today's values, sixty or eighty million? In one way I'm not very concerned about this. If we're spending a hundred million dollars on our Antarctic bases, well then they're worth to me, for what they represent, at least as much as the new Parliament House in Canberra, which is costing more than ten times as much. And they've got nicer people living in them. If the Swedes or New Zealanders pooh-pooh this kind of investment—well, they can do things their way, we can do them ours. But must we do them quite like this? Casey, the old station *and* the new, is a blot on the landscape, the first of our offences against that Antarctic Treaty to which we pay so much lip-service. It's an environmental disaster of the first order, and if the Antarctic Treaty were any more than a gentleman's agreement put together by most ungentlemanly persons we shouldn't be allowed to get away with it for a moment.

Seriously, what *could* be done if we wanted to approach this matter of putting our roots down in Antarctica in another way? If we weren't all caught up in the technological imperative, if it were possible to step off the high-tech roller skates, if the vested interests of so many politicians and public servants, and for that matter academics and trade unionists, were not involved, we could go back and take some kind of lesson from the past. As Russel Madigan points out, his dad's hut at Cape Denison is still standing after seventy-five years, while the estimated life-span of the new Casey station buildings is thirty-five years. Mawson's hut is built of humble timbers and was hammered up in three weeks by a bunch of enthusiastic amateurs. Scott's huts are still standing. So is Shackleton's. For heaven's sake, Borchgrevink's hut at Cape Adare, of interlocked wooden planks, is still standing, and it was built in 1899. Only a few years ago, and even at Casey, odd bods around the station were bashing up good and useful buildings in their spare time. And wood is user-friendly; if you want another bunk and have a few planks and a hammer, then you have another bunk. If you want to hang your windproof up, find a nail. What about the fire risk? they will say. Well, the old huts survived in the days of kerosene lamps and coal-fire stoves, even if they did have the occasional scare. Perhaps today, with fireproofed wood and safer heating, they would do well. If you see pictures of similar outposts in similar latitudes in the Arctic, you'll see that that's the way they are built. They look pleasant, comfortable, on a human scale—not this gross maximalism we have here.

It is, of course, a laughable suggestion. Think of how the neighbors, the French at Dumont d'Urville, the Russians at Mirny, would smile! But do we really have to show the Antarctic that we love it by raping it? Today I suggested that for half the money we have put into Casey we could have a spectacular polar research vessel moored securely all the year round in a cove where the pressures of the ice in the open-sea reaches couldn't harm it. Our scientists could live and work in comfort, even luxury. There would be no need for wireless masts and heavy-duty cranes on shore, for vast transshipments of oil, for road-making and powerhouses which are backed up by stand-by powerhouses. A couple of helicopters on board, and a small vehicle park on shore with some emergency accommodation, would fit the bill. When we had finished with the site we could move on. Kapitän Ewald didn't smile. "A very good idea," he said. "Perfectly feasible." In fact it's no more than Scott did with the *Discovery* in 1940.

There's one big problem for us Australians. Animals mark their territory by depositing turds at the corners. We are dropping our turds too. A ship is not a turd-dropper. If we don't leave a visible mark on Antarctica, we're not really here. These fantasy buildings we are putting up are for aggression-display, not accommodation for scientists. In Australia if you're filthy rich you're a folk hero, and if something's really gross, it must have some merit. The best comment on our Antarctic building program would be the comment a Polish wit once made to me about the appalling Stalin Palace of Culture in Warsaw, supposedly a gift from the Russians to the Poles. "Tiny, but exquisite," he murmured.

"I'm so glad you didn't go ashore today," said my high-tech science friend Lee at dinner tonight. "If you think the station didn't look too good from the ship, just wait till you get ashore."

32

An Australian Antarctic base has all of the squalor and none of the novelty of a penguin rookery. I climbed down into the larc and we roared the kilometre into the shore, then heaved and shrugged our way over submerged rocks and up through a road cut through banks of snow to the foot of the Casey station. One wouldn't normally talk of the 'foot' of a station, but Casey's different. Take a dozen or so boxes, rectangular, perhaps twice the size of the familiar ship's 'container'. Set these up on steel scaffolding so that they are about five feet off the ground, perhaps twelve feet apart and ascending a hillside for a couple of hundred yards. Then, on the inland, windward side connect them with a walkway of planking and stairways. Finally (so to speak) take a lot of very large galvanised iron water-tanks, cut them in half vertically, then place the halves horizontally on the windward side of the walkway, and do your best to seal the lot against the weather. The result, either as a visual spectacle or a living experience, defies Heath Robinson's most bizarre dreams.

I am talking, of course, of the 'old' station, occupied at least until 1988. Casey's design has, in fact, aroused a lot of international interest. One of the bugbears affecting all previous Antarctic stations had been the problem of snowdrift; if the summer thaw was not sufficient to get rid of the winter accumulations, then the stations gradually disappeared—or the necessary clearing involved great outlays of time and labor. Casey, this caterpillar snaking uphill suspended above the ground, provides an answer: the blizzards blow the drift both *over* and *under* the building, which remains freestanding. At the cost of some vibration in high winds, it works. Still, the experiment has not been repeated, and the new buildings we are erecting in Antarctica are blasted and dug deeply into rock foundations.

The Casey design was in part a response to the problems met at Wilkes base, a few kilometres away across the bay to the east. Wilkes was established by the Americans as part of their Operation Deepfreeze II in 1956–57, in preparation for the International Geophysical Year of 1957–58, during which forty stations were established on the Antarctic mainland. In 1959 the base was transferred to Australia, but it proved unsatisfactory and the building of 'old' Casey started in 1965, being completed in 1969. Wilkes still exists, buried beneath snow and ice, its huts still full of 'antique' stores and equipment, an Antarctic Pompeii.

Jim Bleasel had told me that Casey was the "most Antarctic" of the Australian stations. It has the lowest temperature record (−41 °C) of any of our stations and, although the average windspeed at twenty kilometres an hour is only half that of Mawson, blizzards strike with little warning, and gusts of 300 kilometres an hour have been recorded.

As I climbed down from the larc, with a foothold on one of its great wheels, and stood back, I got my first impression of an Australian base on a busy resupply day. "My dears, the people, and the noise," as the epicene general is said to have described the First World War. The road, ground into slush and mud by the stream of trucks and larcs revving their way uphill in low gear, was a real hazard. The station 'oic' was darting here and there on a three-wheeled motor scooter. Between me and the sea were great piles of discolored snow, hiding God knows what memorials of past endeavors, and containerised huts holding out-offices and stores, seemingly dumped just where they first came ashore, years ago.

Fortunately Graeme Manning took charge of the tourists before they were flattened and took us into the Casey Club, the bottommost of the 'wind-shield' buildings, scene of many manic revels and, in its time, of a few dramas, about some of which we were shortly to learn. On the walls photos and mementos of past years, but no time to study them as we dropped our packs and went off up the walkway to visit the thirteen 'rooms' which opened off it: the mess, the bathrooms, the surgery, the oic's office and bedroom, the bunkrooms where occupants made heroic attempts at privacy within their tiny space ration, the busy radio room, the labs. "Good for social life and morale" says Graeme of this enclosed, interconnected little world, though others say that it's bad, that you can almost live a whole Antarctic life here without going outside.

Then outside to the great enclosed shed, a three-storey dome, in which the met balloons are filled with hydrogen, under stringent safety conditions, and released through the roof, and then across curious striated rocks to the radome—the smaller dome which houses the radar apparatus to track the balloons—and from which, being on the windward side of the station, we get the best view of its curious structure.

Then a trudge up the road, jumping rivulets of melt-water, until after a kilometre we found ourselves on the building site of 'new' Casey. It was more than a brief walk. It was the crossing of a divide between the old way of doing things in Antarctica and the new. The whole of the crest of the ridge overlooking the bay, an area of perhaps five acres or more in extent, was one great construction site. Concrete culverts, hundreds of drums of fuel, dumps of cement, excavations, ditches, tips of broken boxes, splintered wood, discarded ironwork formed the backdrop wherever we looked. Sited amidst this were the buildings so far completed, the most prominent being the store, the power-house and the huge central 'living quarters' building. Crisscrossing the site were great, above-ground pipes for heat-reticulation purposes.

The living quarters or 'domestic' block, when we entered it, caused our mouths to drop open. In appearance from the outside it is one huge shell, ten metres high, twenty metres wide, sixty metres long. Try those dimensions out on your suburban block. The cladding and roof are of double strip steel panels filled with foam plastic and attached to the main steel structure. Inside it was one vast, echoing cavern which would have made a generous home for a few airships. Concrete stairs ascend to a mezzanine with big bedrooms and bathrooms. In the rest of the space there will be a theatre, a library, a medical centre, mess rooms, kitchens. The core of the building is a great common room, reaching to the ceiling. Its bow windows look over what will be, if they ever remove the rubbish, one of the world's finest views, to the sea and islands and Iceberg Alley. Not all the talk we heard on the way down about our building program in Antarctica prepared us for this. It would be a bit like finding the resort on Hamilton Island in the middle of the Sahara Desert. Some say that, on the plans, is provision for an outdoor skating rink and a squash court. Whether that is true, or whether they actually get installed, doesn't matter. What is significant is that the scale on which these buildings are going up gives credence to that belief.

The supervising engineer is an impressive chap, J. R. Archibald, six years with the Antarctic design group, thirty-eight years old, a Swinburne graduate. He's got thirty-nine engineers and other staff down here helping him out this summer, and an on-site computer to solve the daily problems. I wondered what Douglas Mawson would think of it all.

And, for that matter, of the store, another great cavernous building reaching to the skies, within it huge doors guarding airconditioned rooms in which every conceivable item of Antarctic equipment is laid out on shelving mounted on rails, on the close-stacking principle you see in some libraries. A large crane driven into the store is reduced by the scale into a toy.

It was all so bewildering in its way, such a treacherous attack on what had been my mental image of Antarctica, that it was some days before I could collect my thoughts in the course of writing an article for the *Australian*. But of course I did have some thoughts too. It all seemed well designed, well built, civilised. With our expansive claims in Antarctica, why shouldn't we build well there?

If we want to get away from the yobbo image, which is what our old Antarctic traditions have degenerated into, why should not our expeditioners be treated better than pigs?—there's no doubt that old Casey is a sordid slum. (But should we have allowed the politicians and the bureaucrats to delay by ten years the removal of our men and women from that slum?)

The visit did have one interesting effect. Our foreign observers were as taken aback as I was: what we saw could only be interpreted one way, as a massive statement by Australia that it was in Antarctica in a big way, and there to stay. It is true that Gabriel Riccardi, observing the way cooling water from the powerhouse is to be used for general heating, said, "Your heat conservation solutions here are brilliant," but in general they were not pleased with what they saw. The day before Russel Madigan had said to Gabriel: "Well, what are you Italians doing here anyway? You've got nothing to do with the Antarctic. If you want to get into polar studies why don't you go north?" Gabriel was silent for a moment, swallowed hard, and said, "Politics."

33

Penguin Island, 12 January 1986

Nine o'clock of an unpromising evening: cold, flurries of snow, a chill breeze. But the excursion to Shirley Island is still on, and a larc-ful of takers is mobilised. First, in the cabin, the irritating climb into heavy boots, sweaters, windproofs; two pairs of gloves; fur hat. Then down to the deck for lifejackets. Doc Newman, the larcies' captain, kind-hearted and sharp-tongued, says, "These jackets are no good for a bloke as big as you. Try this . . .", and produces one of the larcies' own, superior, self-inflating type.

Down the Jacob's ladder, a breeze when the sea is as calm as it is tonight. About twenty of us, all looking like that Michelin man made out of rubber tyres, and none more than me. We stand crowded together, hanging on to the lifeline strung down the centre of the larc. "Everything's fine but where do I go?" shouts the driver. Finally away, with a great gout of wake and thundering engines, and the ship recedes into a misty distance. Out here in the middle of an Antarctic bay—ice nodules drifting past us, snow-covered islands and cliffs all about us, dark snowfalls set against a line of light all around the horizon, Wilson's petrels skimming the surface—it does seem a long way from anywhere. I sometimes think that our Italian and Swedish and Spanish visitors must wonder what the hell they're doing here, so far from their own beds.

But Shirley Island, a kopje of metamorphic rocks set on this cold coast, is near now, and we can see the sea-ice which, a day or so ago, we could have walked over from the mainland, but which is now banned as unsafe. "Leopard seal ahead," someone shouts, and there in the shallows near the ice-edge there's a wicked head above the water, thrashing something about in its jaws: a penguin. We have been told this is the way the leopard seals flay them, before getting down to the serious matter of eating. As we pass there is bloody flesh in the water, and on the nearby rocks and tossed-up ice-floes there are little gatherings of the Adélies, shocked into silence and immobility, huddled into mutual protection as we are huddled on the larc, and gazing apprehensively down on the water rather than on us. We are just in time to see a homecoming Adélie, perhaps conscious of the peril, come porpoising in to the little cove, and then perform the Adélies' great circus act, always winning admiration, of projecting itself out of the water in a vertical, standing position, to land upright on the edge of the ice several feet above the water it has left.

But first we have to get ashore, and our driver is looking around. We nose into shallow water, engage the wheel-drive, lurch along the shallow rocky bottom. We run our bow into the overhanging ice-edge and, using the bow platform as a step, easily step ashore. Very neat!

We pick the harder snow, for there are icy pools concealed, and step over there onto the rock. We look around us. The island rises to perhaps 150 feet. We can see a lot of it, perhaps forty acres, and scattered over the rocks are the separate penguin colonies, each with a couple of hundred adults. Scattered around on the snow are the disconsolate single birds, observing domestic life from a distance, with the detached interest but not, I think, with the cynicism of the bachelors of my acquaintance.

We disregard them as they disregard us. First we gather on the shoreline to observe the nature-red-in-tooth-and-claw drama so conveniently presented for us. Our sinuous leopard seal is now close inshore, only feet from our feet. First he lies doggo in shallow water, just under where the penguins are anxiously craning their necks to see what could be in store for them. Just the round of his back showing: "Pretending to be a rock," says our naturalist. Then he starts cruising, like a fox round a chicken-coop. Round and round he goes, the Adélies on the little bit of ice that he is encircling stupified with anxiety and rage. Every now and then he comes right to the water's edge where we are standing, raises his lion-shaped head, and gazes right at us. His open mouth is red and his teeth, his fangs rather, are wicked. One Antarctic doctor, we were told, crossing some sea ice, in a second had a leopard seal break through the ice beside him and fasten those fangs in his thigh—though I'm not sure this isn't an Antarctic folk story. No wonder our briefing notice on board said: "Beware of the Leopard Seals."

We tire of all this and switch channels, turning our backs to the sea and walking up the sloping rock to the nearest of the rookeries. Little notice is taken of us unless we get within a foot or two, when a swift, swerving hook of the beak comes our way. For these adults are preoccupied. Nearly all have one or two black-downed babies in their care, pressing together for warmth. The chicks are woebegone-looking creatures, now a foot or so high, altogether lacking the sense of dignity and occasion their parents display, unkempt and unhappy, like children who have been kept out too late.

One of the reasons, perhaps, that our presence is tolerated is that, within the colony itself, so much is happening. Never a dull moment, as we used to say in the army. *Here* is a Burlington Bertie, fixated on a nest-and-chick-bound bird, who saunters around with a nonchalant air, picks up a pebble and deposits it, and others like it, time and time again, perhaps all day, at the feet of the favored one. *There* some unfortunate chick has wandered a few inches beyond its allowed territory: squawks and growls from the affronted neighbor, pecks and stabs, and the bewildered baby can't work out in what direction safety lies. *There* two big birds, claret stains on their waistcoats, are fronting up to each other with menacing brays and flapping wings. Weary of well-doing, grandma would have said, and half a bottle too much inside their sleek bellies. Around and about, like spotter planes, glide the brown-and-white skuas, those scavengers and mosstroopers, the ultimate Antarctic survivors, who have made their accommodations with man and hang around the kitchen back at base like sundowners waiting for a handout. They have even been found at the South Pole itself.

(I heard a charming story today. Geologists out on a traverse from Casey were astonished to see two big Emperor penguins, 200 kilometres inland, trudging resignedly along towards furthest south. Since there was no way they could have survived, our gallant men picked them up, placed them aboard the caravan train, and brought them back to the coast. I'm told the Emperors accepted it all very calmly, almost as of right.)

The smell, once you get close to poke your lens into a family relationship, is rather sickly. Indeed you can smell it well out from the island, as you come in. So I wander away from it, down to the shoreline again, and sit on the ice with my video-camera (not mine—I wish it were) and decide to become a David Attenborough. I craftily wait for the penguins to come in underwater to their favorite landing place, and in twenty minutes at the cost of a wet arse get some wonderful shots of the spectacular jet-propelled landings. (These were very popular when I got back home.)

But the cold was seeping through my ventiles and, with the snow-flakes falling and the light growing duller I started thinking of my own comforts: a lighted cabin on board ship, a hot shower, a night-cap and a soft doona. As I crunched my way back across the snow to the larc I wondered about a creation that has made these very successful animals, the Adélie penguins, subjects of this utterly and ultimately bleak and unpromising homeland.

34

Murray Levick, the naval surgeon with Scott's second expedition, published his book *Antarctic Penguins* in 1914, a pioneering but still very useful account of the Adélie. Levick observed the birds very closely over a period of months when he was at Cape Adare with the Northern Party.

Levick starts with making the point that the reason there are no penguins in the Arctic—though there are penguins on the Galápagos Islands, at the equator—is that the penguins are quite defenceless on land, and would fall easy prey to the bears and foxes of the northern regions. Once upon a time, when tropical forests covered what is now Antarctica, the penguins' ancestors were sea-birds that flew above the waters, while the seals' ancestors "ran about on shore like dogs". With a changing climate the seals had to take to the water to survive, exchanging legs for flippers, as the penguins exchanged wings for flippers.

In October the Adélies can be seen trudging steadily south to their rookeries from the edge of the ice shelf, sometimes 400 miles and more north, where they have been forced to migrate during the winter so as to find open water where they can feed on the krill. They choose open, windswept ground to breed, for it is only in these conditions that they can find snow-free areas and pebbles with which to build their nests, thus giving their eggs some protection from the cold. The birds, which are about twenty-eight inches high and weigh about twelve pounds, complete their nest-building by the end of October, sometimes a thousand feet above sea level. Early in November two eggs are laid—they are excellent eating—and the hen sits on the eggs for perhaps a fortnight, before being relieved by the male. She may by then have been a month without food, and be down to half her original body weight.

Late in December the chicks appear, and grow with astonishing rapidity if they are not picked off by the skua gulls or killed in one of the many calamities which can strike at penguin colonies. Now the color of the rookeries changes, from the bile-green excreta of the fasting days to the brick-red of plenty, with the water open close to the rookeries and the parent birds waddling with difficulty up to the nests to disgorge, down their chicks' throats, the krill with which they have stuffed themselves. The penguins during this season can show a remarkable degree of social behavior. Cock birds have been seen bringing snow to thirsty hen birds on the nest; serious fights may be broken up by onlookers; and, when the chicks get to a size where the efforts of both parents at the same time are needed to keep them fed, communal nurseries are set up, day-care centres guarded by senior citizens.

When the young birds at last have their sea-going plumage they are escorted to a suitable nursery slope at the sea edge and there are given their first swimming lesson. Levick's description of the way the older birds enter the water first and splash about with their flippers to encourage the youngsters, and of how they will walk in and out of the water to inspire confidence, could well pass for a description of young parents with toddlers on any Australian beach in the summer. The new generation of penguins, however, do have a powerful incentive to get going: once they are capable of feeding themselves their parents leave them to it.

In late February and early March, with the seas starting to freeze again, and with the annual moult over, the colonies disperse, the lines of penguins heading north and disappearing over the horizon to winter quarters in the pack. But, as they do so, the Adélies' cousins, the great Emperors which are conceded to be the true symbol of Antarctica, are moving south to winter breeding quarters. Bigger birds, bigger chicks, a longer period necessary for rearing, so the Emperors lay in sheltered bays on the coast as winter deepens, in May or June. The chick is incubated for sixty days by the males, with the hens joining in when feeding becomes necessary. By late summer the chicks are ready to fend for themselves.

The first visit to an Emperor penguin colony has remained the most famous, that by 'Birdie' Bowers, Wilson and Cherry-Garrard to Cape Crozier, at the east end of Ross Island, in the June and July of 1911. It was chronicled, of course, by Apsley Cherry-Garrard in the best-known of all Antarctic books, *The Worst Journey in the World*. It was a round trip of 130 miles from base, not a great distance in itself, but it was carried out in darkness, the party had to relay sledges, at one stage they lost their tent in a blizzard, and the temperature dropped to −61°C, which is −77°F. Cherry-Garrard wrote that they were beginning to think of death as a friend.

But they got their three eggs, and they got back after five weeks. Wilson had a theory, out-of-date even then, that the embryo of the Emperor penguin might throw light on the evolution of birds from reptiles. Bowers and Wilson perished with Scott not long afterwards, so it was left to Cherry-Garrard to deliver the eggs to the Natural History Museum in London—eggs for which, as he wrote, "three human lives had been risked three hundred times a day, and three human frames strained to the utmost extremity of human endurance."

At the museum Cherry-Garrard, after some trouble, was admitted to the presence of one he simply identifies as the "Chief Custodian". He handed over the eggs and was told: "You needn't wait."

35

And I tell you, if you have the desire for knowledge and the power to give it physical expression, go out and explore. If you are a brave man you will do nothing: if you are fearful you may do much, for none but cowards have needed to prove their bravery. Some will tell you that you are mad, and nearly all will say, "What is the use?" For we are a nation of shopkeepers, and no shopkeeper will look at research which does not promise him a financial return within a year. And so you will sledge nearly alone, but those with whom you sledge will not be shopkeepers: that is worth a good deal. If you march your Winter Journeys you will have your reward, so long as all you want is a penguin's egg.

Concluding words of *The Worst Journey in the World.*

36

If the walk up the road from Old Casey to New Casey was a trip from the Antarctic past to the Antarctic present and future, then our excursion from Casey Base to the former Wilkes station was a trip back fifteen and more years. This can be a longer time than it seems in Antarctica, or at least in Australian Antarctica, where there is no historical sense, and hence no chance of building morale on tradition; where only tenuous records of annual expeditions are kept; where few—with the occasional exception of a John Béchervaise or Phillip Law—seem literate or reflective enough to write up their own experiences; where personnel change from year to year and not a high proportion keep on coming back, so that from the moment the returning ship docks in Hobart memories, lessons, all the shared experience which had been so painstakingly brought together, immediately disperse. We may be building bases to last decades, but the rest is existential, life is lived from day to day, or at the best from year to year. Past endeavors vanish into limbo.

Ashore and straight into the hands of Greg Hodge, the Field Training Officer at Casey this summer. Alert, friendly, confidence and competence clearly a mark of his make-up, his job is to train expeditioners, especially the increasing numbers imported for summer stints, in the business of looking after themselves in Antarctica. The adventurous, bush types that were once common in Antarctica are dying out. "So," said an oic to me, "instead of encouraging expeditioners to learn by doing, we ensure safety by restricting activities." This, of course, is one of the resentments of those who *are* bush types. The use of field training officers in the summer is an attempt to meet this problem and to ensure that normally chair-borne scientists actually get home again to write up their reports. It's quicker and more efficient to carry out at least part of this induction in Antarctica itself, though some is also done at Bernacci, in Tasmania. (The name Bernacci, at least, is a link with Antarctic history. If Borchgrevink is held to be a Norwegian, not an Australian, then Louis Bernacci was the first Australian to set foot on Antarctica, at Cape Adare on 17 February 1899. He was certainly the first Australian to work on the continent and to winter there.)

And now came our introduction to those remarkable vehicles, the Hagglunds. Devised by the Swedes for military patrols along the Soviet border in Arctic conditions, they are tracked vehicles like oversized Range-Rovers which, with the enclosed trailer with tracks working off the same engine, can carry an armed patrol through most snow and ice conditions. Ours were fitted with satellite navigation equipment which could well be needed, in the event of a sudden blizzard, even within a mile or two of base. There was also, of course, radio communication with base.

The Hagglunds are fiendishly expensive but are now indispensable to Antarctic work. Anders Karlqvist was delighted to see how much the Australians relied on them; to him, I suspected, they were some kind of an answer to Australian bombast. We set out in a convoy of two Hagglunds—one the station 'search and rescue' vehicle, which we borrowed—and, taking turns to drive, rode up through the desolation of New Casey, past the melt-lake from which water is carted daily for the station, through Penguin Pass and then straight inland and up on the ice slope, on track for the old Lanyon Junction airfield. A mile or two up, at the moraine line, we swung off left and halted, about 600 feet above sea level.

It was a wonderfully liberating feeling to be out here in the Antarctic 'wilderness' for the first time, miles of snow and ice around us on every side, the wonderful panorama of offshore islands and icebergs below us, the bergs stretching out to and beyond the stark black triangle of Nelly Island, the home of the giant petrels, which we had skirted on our way in to Casey.

Then back to the Hagglunds, and we ground and slipped our way down the snowslopes and between many outcrops of naked rock. Although Wilkes is only a hop, step and jump from Casey across the bay (on which, when frozen, a golf-course was once laid out, with some sensational drives recorded) the land route to the old base involves an almost circular track. By now we would hardly have needed to navigate, even in a blizzard, for the outworks of man had started to appear: rubbish tips, wrecked vehicles, hundreds if not thousands of fuel drums. Finally into, or rather above, Wilkes itself. Before us at ground level the plywood roofs of buried buildings. Wireless masts at odd angles with sagging wires. In the background the great yellow radome.

It was an odd feeling for us as we poked around, trying to see what lay inside these icy catacombs and trying to envisage the activities that once gave them life. At Commonwealth Bay Mawson's hut was still standing, and we could penetrate to his bedside. There I felt far less removed from Mawson's time than I did here from a scene which was almost a contemporary one. Indeed our voyage leader, Graeme Manning, had actually lived and worked at Wilkes. He was not with us on this visit. "Thank you," he had said, "I am not anxious to see Wilkes again."

If the authorities had in mind that we should be learning some short, sharp lessons from our Antarctic trip, they were certainly doing well. Or, to put it another way, if you were constructing a psychological drama in which people were dumped from elation into depression in a very short space of time, you couldn't have done better. That wonderful argosy of stranded icebergs against a blue-steel sea that we had seen on our way in will stay in our minds' eyes for ever. But so will the sordid vision of the Wilkes base. We had all heard of rubbish problems in Antarctica, and we had all seen the mess around Casey, been told of melt-ponds so polluted with cement dust that they have had to be abandoned as sources of water, had heard of the fragile lichens on the exposed rock faces that had been wiped out by similar activities. We had been told that we mustn't pick up a stone in Antarctica because the environment is so precious. (Expeditioners, banned from their hobby of polishing stones, said to us: "It's OK, though, if you quarry the rock in big lumps and destroy ten tons at a time.") But the problem of *scale* had not been put to us. Wilkes did that.

Here were acres of accumulated rubbish, and God knows what else, buried in ice and snow, the detritus of fifteen years of squalid existence by groups of men. We were given the hint that it was really all the Americans' fault, but by this time knew enough to work out that we had been at Wilkes fourteen times longer than they had. But we had also been round long enough to have some sympathy for the Antarctic Division. We were beginning to realise that there were two parameters. One was the 'ice window': only in January and February could ships work close enough inshore to cart all this away. The other was that all the ships and all the people in Australian Antarctica were fully committed, and over-committed, already. We mightn't all agree that they were committed usefully, but people were not bludging around sitting on their arses and twiddling their thumbs.

To return Wilkes to its prelapsarian state was going to take seasons of work, special task forces, special equipment, special ships, trained and experienced crews ashore and on board. Where were they to come from, and who would pay? The Australian taxpayers who leave forty truckloads of rubbish behind at the Melbourne Cricket Ground after a Grand Final?

Of course it should never have got this far. Of course we can blame the piss-in-each-other's-pockets clauses of the Antarctic Treaty. But it's there. There'll be a bit of cosmetic cleaning up, but my guess is that it will be there until the day when it's decided that it's all got to be preserved as a Historic Site. Indeed, there's talk about that already. What a nice way that would be of getting off the hook!

This kind of thought and talk went on as we stood around the Hagglunds, drinking thermos tea and eating sandwiches. Then the loudspeaker inside the Hagglund came to life. They were calling us from base. Greg went to see what was wrong, and came back with a long look on his face. The *Southern Quest*, which had taken our Project Blizzard people to Commonwealth Bay, and was now on its way to pick up the 'Footsteps of Scott' expedition at McMurdo Sound, had been crushed and sunk in the Ross Sea near Beaufort Island.

37

I was at the abandoned Wilkes base, formerly American and Australian in turn, and some five miles from here [Casey], when a radio message came through to our Hagglund tracked snow vehicle yesterday that the *Southern Quest* has been sunk in the Ross Sea, and all aboard transferred to the United States base at McMurdo Sound.

Our party, itself surrounded by debris and every evidence of the destructive power of natural forces on man's artefacts, experienced a sense of shock, and a fellow feeling for those exposed without the protective devices that surrounded us. One is always conscious here of the malevolent powers of cold and wind, waiting for any momentary carelessness in order to attack.

After profound relief that no lives were lost with the *Southern Quest*, the reactions here to the calamity have varied. Antarctic expedition members are aware of the immense preparations necessary to ensure safe survival in the face of the conditions we face in the south, and I have seen plenty of evidence of this in recent days, in the intense logistical efforts to unload the *Icebird* while calm weather lasts. Many have been working up to eighteen hours a day. The attitude then of professional expeditioners and administrative personnel tends to be that of voyage leader Graeme Manning: "This is a lesson that private expeditions to these latitudes should be discouraged by every means."

Ewald Brune, the master of the *Icebird*, who himself has lost a ship in these waters, says: "Down here you must have the right ship for the right conditions. The *Southern Quest* was down to nearly 77° South, in seven- to eight-tenths pack ice, which a current or a storm can quickly close to ten-tenths. In such conditions a ship with at least a Class 1A ice-rating is essential. (This rating relates particularly to the distance apart of the frames and the thickness of the plating.) The *Southern Quest*'s rating, believed to be 3, is suitable for open pack as worked by fishing vessels like her in northern waters, but is unsuitable for more than six-tenths pack. If such vessels were registered as merchant ships hazardous voyages could be prevented by governments under the Safety of Life at Sea conventions. But ships such as the *Southern Quest* and *Greenpeace* are registered as yachts, and are therefore outside the regulations. Their presence in these waters is a potential danger to other, well-found ships, who may have to place themselves, and all on board, in positions of danger to effect rescues. Private expeditions penetrating into areas such as the Ross Sea will seldom or never have the financial resources to charter properly rated vessels, and therefore they should always seek to link their plans with those of properly mounted government expeditions, as Project Blizzard has with its Commonwealth Bay project."

On the other hand William Blunt, the leader of the Project Blizzard party aboard this ship, has defended the private initiatives. "Of course events such as the sinking of the *Southern Quest* inevitably mean a backlash against private initiatives in such places as Antarctica, and very properly raise such questions as to whether such expeditions are adequately insured for such contingencies as recompensing governments for rescue and repatriation operations. But," he added, "I wouldn't like to see a situation develop whereby means were found to prevent all non-government expeditions in Antarctic waters." Blunt pointed out that there have been three responsibly mounted and successful expeditions by private bodies recently, to Heard Island in 1983 and to Commonwealth Bay in 1984–85 and 1985–86. There has also been most valuable work done in small ships in such areas as the Antarctic Peninsula, below South America. "There will always be a place," says Blunt, "for nongovernment initiatives in Antarctica by experienced people who understand the limits and don't get into the wrong place at the wrong time."

There is little doubt that the increasing activity of so many of the world's governments in Antarctica, which is spurred by the prospects of the renewal of the Antarctic Treaty in 1991—and its possible revision—will mean increased official efforts to keep private venturers out of the area. Yet at the same time increased government involvement in Antarctica will strengthen the determination of citizens' organisations to intervene. Legal impediments to private expeditions, at least so far as Australia is concerned, seem impracticable at this stage. In any case they are probably undesirable. And there are no means whereby the Antarctic Treaty partners can apply sanctions against outsiders.

Australia is now being used as a springboard by an increasing number of official and private expeditions. The only solution is to improve the mechanisms for effective consultation between our government and private bodies. The development of tourism, fishing and mining in Antarctica is to be expected, and will certainly involve new pressures of this kind.

> At the United States Palmer Base on the Antarctic Peninsula tourists are reported to occupy 20 per cent of the station working time during the summer. The Antarctic Treaty organisation is already alarmed at this trend, and has urged all governments to develop more effective consultation with unofficial visitors, both to protect historic sites and scientific work, and to reduce demands on Antarctic bases which they are not equipped to fulfil.
>
> (*Australian*, 14 January 1986)

I could have mentioned, in this despatch, that virtually *all* Antarctic expeditions of the Golden Age—Borchgrevink's, Scott's expeditions, Shackleton's, Mawson's—were private expeditions. And that it might be a healthy incentive to our Antarctic Division if our government were to encourage non-government institutions, say the Academy of Science or the universities, to mount their own limited-purpose expeditions.

I could also have mentioned that many Antarctic Division people are critical of private expeditions which, as they put it, are "in the 'jolly' category." By this they mean expeditions which claim a scientific purpose in their fund-raising but in fact do little more than collect a few samples, useful in itself but not science, which involves the writing-up and publication of results. "There's nothing wrong with putting on an expedition for the purposes of adventure, but let them be honest about it, as the 'Footsteps of Scott' people were." (In fact, though, this expedition produced some important scientific material, which is also of great historical interest, on the physiology of 'man-hauling.')

Finally I should say that the vile treatment the 'Footsteps of Scott' people got from the US Antarctic bureaucrats in Washington and in Antarctica, and the hardly more excusable treatment they got from the New Zealand Antarctic authorities when they were in trouble, suggest that the world and Antarctica would be a better place if it were official, rather than unofficial, expeditions that were banned. If any evidence is required that the old Antarctic spirit is dead, and that that unfortunate continent is now firmly in the hands of soulless bureaucracies, then that evidence will be found in Mear and Swan's book, *In the Footsteps of Scott*. At least the Australian authorities, in this regard, do not seem to be as bad as the others.

38

Diary, 13 January 1986

Graeme Manning called me into his cabin before lunch to tell me the day's most startling news. Matters have been in an appalling state at Casey. Barry Martin, the new oic who arrived, as they do, at the first summer visit, the 'ice edge' voyage as they call it—no major resupply, but people and mail landed by helicopter—has been at his wit's end. Barry found on his arrival that things were bad, that there had been during the winter an effective takeover of the base by some of the Department of Housing and Construction people who had been kept on from the previous summer. They found recruits from builders who came down for this summer. The word "terrorise" has been used.

It doesn't sound a pretty story. The roots go back to last winter when the then oic, together with one or two of his senior staff, allowed himself to become isolated from his rank and file. It can happen so easily, it seems. A wrong word here, a suspicion of too much clubbiness among a few there, a decision to go out bivouacking in the old Antarctic way, then when the weather blows up a bit a call over the radio to be collected in the search-and-rescue Hagglund. Suddenly authority has crumbled—the oic's authority can only be based on his personality, anyway—and the tough guys are getting up in the mess at dinner time announcing that there will be a public holiday tomorrow, while the oic eats by himself, shunned even by his friends, in a corner.

Barry Martin has tried to reassert control, but things have gone too far. The party that has come in for next winter has been forced out of the 'club' to take shelter in their tiny cubicles. 'Let's see who can get drunk quickest' parties have been held on the home-brew. The women have been harassed. Four of the party brought in for next winter have asked to be taken home: "This is not what we expected in Antarctica." Greg Hodge and the doctor, Michael Sutherland, have done their best to support Barry's attempts to get back on top, but the rest of the incoming party have been cowed. The ocker clique, always a potential menace on an Antarctic base, according to Phil Law's book, have got on top.

One of the things this long-drawn-out bloody building program has done to our Antarctic bases is to create two nations on them. On the one hand there are the ANARE people, selected as carefully as possible, often with fairly advanced skills, a fair level of general education and some sense of working within an Antarctic tradition. Left to themselves, as they were in the days when expeditions built their own bases, there's a fair chance that they will get on together fairly well. But now, enter the building program. This is not in the hands of ANARE but of the Department of Housing and Construction. In the summer the builders will outnumber the expeditioners. The Antarctic Division, though it is represented on the selection panel for the DHC people, has no final say in their choice. The builders are often scornful of the ANARE wimps, as they see them, are tougher and more ruthless in their manners and behavior, and resent any implication, which may be quite a fancied one, that they are only there doing a job and are not really Antarctic people. Sometimes they are loners and roamers, working-class bohemians. It's not always easy to get established, family-based tradesmen down to Antarctica.

The dramatic decision has been made to send home all the building workers, except the few attached to the wintering party, immediately, without waiting until the last voyage of the summer. [Later this was amended so that three of the 'innocent' could stay on until next trip out.] About eight are to come aboard. The volley-ball court, where the ship's beer is stored, will be locked. The troublemakers will be split up among cabins. The bar may be permanently closed. Six months' building time, in man-hours, will be lost, but the triangular decision—Graeme, the oic, Hobart—has been taken. The big question is whether John Hannaker, the overall project manager for the DHC, who is on board on a round trip, will accept responsibility for the supervision of his own people, or whether he will feel constrained by Antarctic rivalries to side with them.

So far as I can find out, nothing as bad as this has ever happened in Australian Antarctica before. But the situation isn't entirely unfamiliar to me. I remember how, back in 1942, and after the 5th Independent Company had been campaigning up around Lae and Salamaua in New Guinea for some six months, pretty well cut off from anyone, the decision was taken to send home the 'undesirables' as soon as the American planes from Port Moresby managed to get through to us again. The ones who were sent home then didn't seem particularly 'undesirable' to me; indeed, if I had been repatriating 'undesirables' I'd have started with the force commander himself rather than the other ranks. But things here at Casey have obviously been pretty rough, and I'm sure I haven't been told the full story, though I'm grateful to Graeme for opening up with me as far as he has.

And he did go a bit further. Up on the top of a ridge above New Casey there's another of the stark crosses that one sees at every Antarctic base. Indeed up above Wilkes there are two above shallow graves, one an American's, one an Australian's. No-one knows much about them, except that one was run over and one died of carbon monoxide poisoning; but the one up at New Casey is well remembered.

Graeme Manning was the oic here in 1979. During the winter Graham Reeves went out with some companions to what they call the "RMIT hut"—one designed at the Royal Melbourne Institute of Technology—to read some instruments. While there one of the sudden Casey blizzards blew up and the party was marooned, though safe enough. Graham Reeves had a 'call of nature' and felt he had to visit the latrine, the 'tabernacle' they called it, thirty yards away. There was no fixed line between the hut and the tabernacle, but Reeves was fully dressed and there seemed no great problem.

But Reeves did not come back. A search party found him some time later, buried in the new snow. He was still alive. They carried him back inside the station and started to try to revive him, cutting off the ice-encrusted hair and beard. Peter Gormly, our doctor, thinks that this probably killed him. Too much manhandling of a patient in these conditions leads to cardiac fibrillation and death from heart seizure. The first rule is not to touch the victim any more than is absolutely necessary. Reeves's wife asked for his body to be sent home to Hobart. His death is still talked of with sadness and concern.

Now, halfway through last winter, that of 1985, it got around among people at the Antarctic Division that there had been a "bad-taste night" at the Casey Club, in which the then oic had himself played a role. Some of the turns were too unpleasant to describe here, but one of them was a Graham Reeves Death Dance, complete with evil-smelling anointment, ice-encrusted hair and spasmodic jerks. Graeme Manning was revolted, and after thinking about it for a fortnight sent a telex to Casey, in the name of his 1979 party, to express utter disgust. To this there was no reply.

Times have changed, of course, but when I heard this story I was glad that Sir Douglas Mawson was dead.

39

This was not the first time that one of our Antarctic bases had self-destructed. Macquarie Island did a few years ago, though the details have been hushed up. More dramatically, Davis did in 1981, when the first woman, a doctor, was placed on one of our bases. She was of a religious bent and perhaps overconscientious—before she went down she had, it is said, proposed to give all the men on the station a monthly massage—but she was a good expeditioner. The trouble was that some of the senior people on the base decided to make her life a misery, and there were gross incompatibilities of temperament in any case: the oic, for instance, formerly of Southern Rhodesia, being fond of describing the killings of black rebels in which he had participated.

Everyone has been familiar with the general situation since the mutiny on the *Bounty*. Anyone who has worked in a university knows how some departments work together reasonably well, while others are seedbeds of debilitating hatreds and sabotage. It can happen in any group situation, but never more disastrously than on an isolated Antarctic base. In this case at Davis, I was told, the whole station complement split down the middle, half rallying to the doctor's support, half joining the tormentors. Morale vanished and, of course, the work was affected. Davis 1981 is still talked about as a prime example of What Should Not Happen.

No doubt there are other examples, not so serious, kept under wraps. In *Antarctic Odyssey* Phillip Law talks of "drunken brawls, insubordination and various forms of violence". "I had seen," he wrote, "young men in their early twenties go to Antarctica as moderate beer drinkers and return fourteen months later as alcoholics." The beer ration on the stations is low, at two bottles a week for each man, but this has little effect on the grog problem when home-brewing is a major Antarctic cottage industry and bored men have plenty of time to drink the product. And no-one has dared to try to stop the home-brew.

Grog of course can be a problem, but it is also a solace and a cementer of social relations in a situation where, as one expeditioner said to me, "You can never be sure down here whether people are being nice to you because they realise there's no alternative, or whether they're being nice to you because they like you." Phil Law has pointed out that, though there are great problems consequent on isolation—no women, few luxuries, little variety in food, physical immobility among them—there are also great compensations for those who can seek them: a job to be done, wonderful scenery, exciting excursions, a sense of élite endeavor.

Law and his successors have worked hard on selection procedures for Antarctica. Psychological tests have been developed, in part based on those applied to submarine crews, which seek to identify the "blander, more casual, less aggressive" types likely to be successful in Antarctica. Testing may be useful, but it has its limits, as I reflect when I consider that at school a vocational guidance officer advised my parents to make me a company secretary, when in fact my first career was going to be with the Communist Party, and I realise now I would have made an awful company secretary. And the pool of applicants for Antarctic postings is, some say, drying up, so that, as Law admits, sometimes a risk has to be taken.

I find the situation interesting in many ways. Obviously we need to have better-educated, 'professional' types on the bases if we can get them, and if we are serious about our scientific work, which in itself is doubtful. This coming winter, on Casey, there will be *one* Australian scientist, with one Chinese, out of about thirty-three people. Even the much-hyped glaciological traverses have their critics. The glacier cores which *were* extracted last season, at the cost of great endeavors and expense, melted on their way back to Australia for examination! Some traversers have returned without completing their work, because of morale problems.

But, if we do ginger up our professional programs, what will happen under present circumstances is that an even greater cleavage will open up between the mechanics and builders, on the one hand, and the rest. I certainly wouldn't wish to live on such a base as Casey, with its infantile sexist pin-ups, childish 'games', low-quality pop music piped all over the station, and the emphasis on all the most vulgar, tedious and repetitive aspects of the Oz character. Gresham's Law indeed. Even the more civilised are frightened not to accept the standards of the yobbos. For the most part even the 'professionally' qualified engineers seem basically ocker types, as one would expect from our technical education system. I'm not arguing for a 'class' system. No doubt engineering at this level is an important factor in social mobility, and in any case there is much that is quite admirable in Australian egalitarianism. But crudities, the lack of inner resources, hostility to the different, resentment of the reflective, do rise to the surface here. They certainly triumphed at Casey this year, where they got away with putting a baby's chair in the mess for the oic, and labelling it WIMP.

People who know Antarctica well tell me that, for some reason, Casey is traditionally the roughest of the bases. Explanations vary: fewer scientists there; Antarctic Division policy to isolate the roughnecks; perhaps the very design of the base itself. But *Icebird* people tell me that, trip after trip, it is the larcies, with their deeply ingrained resentments at being taken for granted, and the Casey mob, that have the biggest chips on their shoulders. An interesting sociological thesis here for someone—though I wouldn't like to be a disguised sociologist or psychologist on an Antarctic base whose cover was blown!

An inevitable consequence of all this is that the ANARE people will be delighted when they at least see the backs of the DHC builders, whom they see as effectively in control of Antarctica at the moment, especially in the summer. But this raises three new issues. The first is whether, even if there were no builders on the bases, it would be possible to return to what is in any case partly a romantic vision of the past. The second is that, with the Australian government steadily (1987) cutting back funds for the completion of our building programs, the builders are likely to be there until the ice melts. The third is that, with our new and highly complex bases, a considerable maintenance and building component is now likely to be required permanently. If so, the Antarctic Division would probably like to have the funds to administer that component itself. If the Division made a move in that direction, the public service battles in Canberra would exceed in fury any Casey blizzard.

Brendan Doran suggests a title for this disquisition: "The Class Struggle in Antarctica."

40

So much drama, but little dramas as well as big ones. Coming out to the ship in the larc, after a day ashore. Doc Newman in charge. We slither down the slope into the sea and start trundling out into water deep enough to float in and to engage the propeller. Suddenly a great lurch and we're tilted over to one side, almost into the water, and are stuck there on a huge rock, unable to get off, neither fish nor fowl, and most undignified. Finally we managed to struggle back to shore to inspect the damage. Doc was quite furious: "A station here for twenty years and they still haven't got round to marking that bloody hazard."

A reminder of the pressure these chaps are working under. They're calm and efficient, because they realise they have to be to get the job done and to avoid accidents. Sometimes some little thing going wrong will release the pent-up anxieties, and we see behind the mask.

41

But the 'tourists' had few anxieties. Impressions flooded in on us as we scribbled our notes and took our pictures. We were in danger of not realising that the greatest marvel of all was right under our noses; that we had the privilege of observing, and for many of taking part in, the major annual resupply of an Antarctic base. Short of taking part in a great combined assault operation against an enemy shore, we wouldn't see the like of this again.

For the moment when the anchors went down in Newcombe Bay, and the launches and larcs and barges were lifted overboard by our great cranes, and the hatches were cleared to be rolled back, opening up the great caverns below, was a moment for which hundreds of people unknown to us had been working for years. Ships had been built, orders for well over a hundred thousand separate items had been placed, manufacturers had been cajoled, computers had been jammed with lists, draughtsmen had been designing, men and women had been trained, politicians had been briefed. From hundreds of tributaries, and by train and road and sea and air, the infinite variety of Antarctic requirements had percolated south, from all over Australia and from further afield, finally to stand in all the order of precisely marked and placed crates and pallets and drums and bulldozers and boats and baulks on the dockside at Hobart, complete and ready for loading at a given time on a given day. And while this was going on committees had met, committees on personnel and science and communications, on clothing and transport and finance and food, and more committees on the politics of Antarctica both here and abroad. And the object of all this was to bring us safely in clear water off Casey base on a given day, and to get our thousands of tons of cargo ashore at the tiny landing sites, so that once through that eye of the needle they could reverse their original concentration and now fan out to the hundreds of places on shore where they would finally be put to use.

For days before we arrived at Casey the ship had been humming with an air of organisation the purpose of which I only gradually came to understand. Phil Gard, the Antarctic Division's cargo-master, and Alistair Baillie, the ship's supercargo, were to be seen scrambling in and out of manholes giving access to ladders leading to the bowels of the ship. Geraldine Nash was not to be seen without a list in her hand or a notice to be stuck on a board. By the time Ewald was 'finished with engines' I had worked it all out.

Everyone on board had, from the moment we arrived, a place to go to and a job to do. This hopeless bunch of amateurs, these surveyors and physicists, carpenters and engineers, typists and clerks from head office in Hobart, this diplomat and that meteorologist, were going to unload—in near-freezing conditions and with gear that, if not makeshift, was at least a long way from sophisticated cargo-handling facilities—thousands of tons of stores.

And so they did. They stood on pontoons against the ship's side, clad in fur hats and heavy gloves, as great trucks were swung out menacingly above their heads. They stacked crates on those pontoons, signalled crane drivers, lashed down and rode their loads inshore, where in turn they helped unload. Apart from one day when a blizzard struck, and we awoke to find the whole ship under feet of snow, they worked unremittingly, some to the point of exhaustion, reeling back to their cabins so tired they could barely peel off their ventiles.

It was hair-raising watching it all. "If that lift breaks, or if that little claw gives way, those drums will fall from forty feet, and there'll be six people fewer for dinner tonight."

I suppose every safety regulation in the book was broken a hundred times over, starting with the fact that hardly any of the dozens handling cargo in such conditions was qualified to do so. But the Antarctic Division people would presumably say: "What else, short of bringing down another ship full of waterside workers, can we do? Every hour counts. Time lost here means time lost at Davis. Time lost at Davis is time lost at Mawson. Time lost at Mawson means that, at the end of the summer, one whole voyage has to be cancelled, or a ship gets beset, or even perhaps lost. The A-factor runs things here, not the Book of Rules. We may take risks unloading, but if we don't get the job done we risk not only work programs, but also other lives, further down the track."

So, yes, and against my nasty nature I was moved, very moved. I began to feel well of my own countrymen. All this immense labor, carried out without complaint, without shouting, in good humor, without congratulation. Could anyone else do it as well?

And now there were matters of state being hammered out on the bridge, literally as well as metaphorically above our heads.

42

Diary

Graeme Manning tells me he was pleased when the forty-knot blizzard struck and Ewald decided to get away from the anchorage and steam up and down the bay to be on the safe side, for it gave the opportunity for a 'public holiday' to be declared. "People are getting a bit rough at the edges," Graeme observed.

Apparently he and Ewald have 'had it out' on the bridge about the cargo-handling. Many irritations and misunderstandings emerged, as they always have (and always will) in Antarctica between the skippers of ships and the leaders of expeditions. The two roles are not only complementary but also overlapping, and no one person can occupy them both. But the conflict between them has wrecked many high endeavors.

Perhaps in retrospect the issues won't seem big ones, but down here, on the day and given the pressures at work, they blow up into anger and upset. In the way of these things they start off with specific allegations and develop into broader accusations.

The initial misunderstanding was that Graeme didn't know, when Ewald offered him the use of the ship's empty 'dumb' barge (the fuel transporter), that its capacity was the same as that of the unifloat (the huge powered pontoon that is assembled like Leggo). The two could have been used backwards and forwards from the shore, allowing the small barges to be stood down or used for other tasks. (These small barges, driven by amateurs from the Hobart Antarctic Division headquarters, have been so poorly designed by the Division's own engineers that they have been found not to meet Department of Transport specifications, and have only restricted certificates of operation.) This misunderstanding has cost us what may be a critical half day.

More alarming is that Ewald asked Graeme who, as well as being voyage leader, is also operations manager of the Antarctic Division, why the detailed recommendations he made verbally to the logistics section of the Division, following last summer's operations, had not been acted upon. These included recommendations that a dumb barge be built, to avoid the serious fuel spillages that occurred in pumping fuel ashore last year. When Ewald received no reply or satisfaction from the Division, his company made its own dumb barge and shipped it out to Australia. Graeme denies ever having heard of Ewald's recommendations, which were never circulated or discussed. I would have thought it would have been wise for Ewald to have put such a crucial suggestion into writing, but in any case there has been a SNAFU.

Then there is high blood pressure over the unloading operations themselves. The ship claims that it makes the crucial decisions on cargo-handling, but the voyage leaders want their say too. So Graeme criticises the ship's cargo-handlers as "cowboys", prepared to overload the barges in order to clear cargo out of the holds as quickly as possible. "It's calm," says Alistair. "They'll take more." "No," says Geraldine in her fur hat, walking around with her walkie-talkie, "we are only allowed this load on this barge." "Well, then," Ewald and Alistair reply, "the hold-ups are your responsibility, not ours." And Ewald claims that the ship's forty-tonne cranes are not being used—"we could clear the ship in half the time".

It's only fair to add that my own observation is that, despite these spats, the ANARE–*Icebird* relationship is a close one, informed on the whole by good will and intelligent compromise. And just as well: we'd be stuffed without the *Icebird*. Decades of duckshoving, years of political inertia and myopia, have left us at the mercy of the Germans. Little wonder that they will exploit that advantage if they can.

I am continually amused, during these logistical debates, at the close parallels between the problems of unloading thousands of tons of stores and equipment at Casey, and our own problems every year unloading a couple of tons onto the beach at Erith Island in Bass Strait. So many of the debates are the same. For instance, how many on board getting the gear out of the ship and overside? How many on shore unloading the gear as it comes into the beach, and stacking it? Much that happens here is different only in scale.

Upanchoring early this morning in the blizzard we lost an anchor and three shackles (ninety-one metres) of chain: some say

$80,000 worth, some twice that and more. Only sixty feet down, though, and Ewald hopes to recover it all with divers next trip. (He didn't.)

43

The sight of 30,000 bags of cement going ashore at Casey Antarctic base over the past few days, not to speak of 1270 drums of fuel, containers, seatainers, a forty-ton crane, trucks, tractors, bulldozers, semitrailers and a couple of thousand tons of assorted Antarctic impedimenta, gives the observer a lot to think about. Particularly the observer who has envisaged nothing more than the landing of some huskies and sledging rations. Are we building a new Maginot Line, isolating the Soviet bases perched along our coastline? Are we building secret silos for Australian ICBMs? Or has someone devised an ingenious corner in building supplies, depriving continental Australia of its material resources?

Obviously the first thing you do, on landing on an isolated Antarctic coast for the first time, is to put up a flagpole. All the more so if you are an Australian, sitting on nearly half of Antarctica with the guilty look of the schoolboy who has hidden the chalk. To put up a flagpole you need a carpenter, a rigger and someone to dig the hole. To service the pulley at the top you will need an engineer. You will also need a painter, a sailor who can handle ropes, and a seamstress to mend the flag when it gets tattered, as it soon will. You will of course need houses for these people to live in, a radio operator to send wedding anniversary messages to their spouses, a doctor to patch them up when the flagpole falls on them, a cook to feed them, a storeman for all the gear and someone to look after the generator which will warm them and light them. By this time the organisation is so big that you will need an officer-in-charge.

By now your base is a microcosm of the human condition. The flag continues to fly, and Australians at home and abed sleep more soundly knowing it is there. A country unable to organise a decent taxi service in its national capital now has an empire. (In terms of expense, isolation and dubious relevance, Canberra might be called the Casey of Australia.)

There is more to be learnt from flag semiotics in Antarctica. At Casey station three flags are flying: a German flag (our ship is German); the ANARE flag, green with a leopard-seal device, the leopard seal being a singularly sinister Antarctic character; and a tattered Oz ensign flown, in defiance of flag etiquette, in a position inferior to that of the ANARE flag. The threadbare nature of the Australian flag, the lowly status accorded it, could be ascribed to national diffidence and our wish to show that we are just one of the Antarctic boys: though we do claim vast segments of this thickly iced cake, though we do send Soviet stations squatting on Australian Antarctic Territory their annual radio licences, which are of course ignored, in essence we are not jelly-bellied flag-flappers, as Kipling once put it.

The game is given away, though, by the Boxing Kangaroo flag flown from the rigging of the *Chicken*, the ship-based launch which is the flagship of the mosquito fleet which has been ferrying all those stores ashore. Our wide-eyed and often ironic-tongued foreign observers aboard *Icebird*—a Swede, some Germans, two Italians, a Brit and a Spaniard—took the kangaroo flag for a joke. I told them that it also represented a chip-on-the-shoulder determination, the kind of thing those observers complain about when they say: "Why can't you be more like those nice New Zealanders?" Not knowing as much about them as we do, they see the Pig Islanders in Antarctica as models of good manners, nonassertiveness and modest scholarship.

The Commonwealth Department of Housing and Construction is, although formally it works under instructions from the Antarctic Division of the Department of Science, the major determiner of our activities in Antarctica. As things have been now for a number of years, as they are at the moment, and as they will remain for a considerable time, the Antarctic Division is here to service the aims and objects of the DHC, whose employees call most of the shots, dominate the bases in the four-month summer season at least, and are producing edifices that remind me of Hitler's boast that the constructions of the Thousand Year Reich would make good ruins.

The main building at the new Casey station, a kilometre up a road alternately dusty and icy from the old station, is ten metres high, twenty metres wide and sixty metres long. It's the proposed 'domestic' building, and it offers quite a contrast to the squalid 'dongas'—as the prefab sleeping quarters are called—of our old station. It is only one of a number of buildings on much the same scale being erected at Casey, and similar constructions are well advanced at Davis and Mawson, our other two bases on the Antarctic continent.

There is no doubt that these new station buildings are, and will be, superb. There will be nothing like them elsewhere in Antarctica. The 'domestic' building at Casey will include a library, a theatre, comfortable private rooms, elaborate recreation facilities, a magnificent community loggia with, through its plate-glass windows, a spectacular outlook. "Comfort, yes, but this is ridiculous," says a hard-bitten expeditioner just back from months on the icecap inland in a small caravan.

But the comforts and facilities are no more than are eventually going to be necessary to support a dignified human existence in Antarctica if—and this is now disputed—this is now the way we are to go. Present conditions are degrading on all our bases. Private employers in Australia attempting to impose them on their staffs would end up in court, if not in gaol. If we want a better standard of behavior in Antarctica, especially perhaps towards the increasing number of women who will be coming down; if we want to attract a higher level of scientific involvement; if we want to reduce the sad accidents which still sprinkle our Antarctic work; if, in short, we wish to make our investment here on present terms more cost-efficient, then this is the way we have to go. The Hut Point mentality of Robert Falcon Scott's day, when gentleman adventurers eating ship's biscuits and seal meat took on the Antarctic as a challenge to their courage, is long in the discard.

But there are many who regret its passing, and with some justification. Within our own Antarctic Division there is a cleavage between the 'new men' with their slide rules and their desk-top computers, and those who fear we are losing too much of the spirit of moral commitment which was crucial in our earlier polar activities.

A leading Scottish Antarctic scientist aboard this ship finds it strange, for instance, that there is no photo of Mawson, or even of Casey, in the community room at Casey base. (In fact there are portraits of both the Queen and of Lord Casey at Casey station, but their glass is cracked and they are tucked away in a storeroom.) There is general agreement that one unlooked-for effect of the huge building program has been to introduce to the stations a number of workers who are there primarily to perform contract functions and save a few bucks, men who in many cases at least lack much of a commitment to Antarctica as such, and who have accelerated the breakdown of the old Antarctic morale.

This may now never be retrievable. If things go on as they are now we may be witnessing the birth of a new era down here, an era in which we have, not stations, but Australian townships in Antarctica, distinguishable from Shepparton or Hay mainly because the children have to be taken to and from school in blizzard-proof buses. We are half-way to that position already, and at least it is one way to go. The Argentinians have adopted this position, that of actually colonising Antarctica, of arranging to have people married there, and babies born. The Chileans have had a Cabinet meeting in Antarctica.

This rebuilding of Australian Antarctica is not easy and it is not cheap. And one of its effects has been to increase the resentments of scientists, who see themselves as second-class citizens, and point out that the only reason we are supposed to be in Antarctica, under the Antarctic Treaty to which we subscribe, is to conduct scientific work. They point out that these new buildings at Casey, these Cyclopean edifices which now straggle along the Casey skyline like semitrailers outside a roadside café, do not include any facilities for scientific work. (The project managers say that two small scientific buildings, not yet designed, will one day appear on the site.) They point out that Australia is paying $42 million this year, for which we will see only eight professional scientists wintering in Antarctica.

I must say that I feel some sympathy for an Antarctic administrator who must decide, with limited funds, whether to send a desperately needed plumber for today's purposes, or a scientist for tomorrow's. There's a general feeling down here among the expeditioners that the scale of their efforts is not appreciated by the Australian public. I asked the senior DHC man here what he would need to complete the whole building program at our stations by the end of next summer, instead of—as at present reckoned—about 1993. "I would want ten ships," he said, "and a thousand workers. I would also want the exclusive use of every architect's office and drawing office in Australia for the next three months, in order to get the designs finished, the materials ordered and the crates on the wharf at Hobart next October."

Seventy to eighty people are working full-time in the DHC's Antarctic drawing office in Melbourne and, although the present estimated cost of the entire project is $70 million, in fact there is going to be no change from a final cost of at least 100 million 1986 dollars.

This is not a stupendous figure, given the importance supposedly attached to Antarctica by the Australian government, provided we want the product. But it is only fair to add that sceptical foreign observers here point out that the British have recently rebuilt, with scientific objectives paramount, three of their Antarctic stations at a cost of $3 million each, each project taking two years. And that the German company that owns the *Icebird*, together with an associated Danish company, have recently tendered to the Italians to provide a ship like the *Icebird* for their next expedition, plus a functioning base, the base to be erected by fifty workers in forty days!

So we are in danger of placing ourselves in the position of a general with an immense baggage train. We are in the clutch of ideas formulated ten years and more ago, no longer fully acceptable to us, but the implementation of which we cannot stop. We are, in other words, in danger of accepting the logic of static warfare in Antarctica. Such a war may suit some political aims, but it does not suit the scientific aims which are ostensibly the main reason we are here, and which in the long run are the main political argument we have.

Today it is clear that the future lies, not with fortifications, but with flexible, combined operations. The main 'useful' priorities here are offshore oil, the potential of krill harvesting and the uses of the fresh water locked up in icebergs. All of these demand a seaborne research mobility which we do not have, because the financial, political and industrial questions relating to the building of suitable vessels in Australia, or even the leasing of them, are too difficult for us to face.

The most promising landborne scientific work, apart from upper atmosphere physics, is likely to be carried out by small 'raiding parties' with a high scientific component (thus reversing current ratios), mobile and well trained on a 'get in and get out' basis. We mounted an operation like this with limited success last year, at Stillwell Hills, west of Mawson, and at the moment have another in the field between Casey and Davis, at Bunger Hills. Although promoted as a 'new' concept, these new tactics are in fact no more than elaborated versions of exercises carried out in the 1960s and 1970s, flying small parties in to and out of selected sites in small choppers.

These promising new, lightly mounted 'summer stations' now being actively promoted by the Antarctic Division do not in essence depend on the presence of fixed Antarctic bases, being Hobart-mounted. They could help us break through the fixed defences we have barricaded ourselves behind down here. The key may be to develop one of our bases down here as a major spearhead. This should be Davis, the only station with room to expand and, above all, able to accommodate a reasonably weather-reliable airstrip with a rock surface. Such an airstrip somewhere in Australian Antarctica is essential, if the investments we have made are going to make any sense in the future. At Davis it will cost perhaps $50 million, and there are environmental objections, but these must be solved.

The essence is, then, that we must get away from the mental concept of operating through fixed stations, and instead must see our Antarctic outposts as advanced headquarters, with considerable local autonomy, for extended operations both on land and sea.

Only in this way can we make a virtue out of what is now an embarrassment, receive returns from current outlays and retrieve something from the ridiculous strategical position in which we now find ourselves.

(*Australian*, 22 January 1986)

44

There are oddities to this shipboard life. One is the fact that, because of the vagaries of the ship's design, all movement is in the vertical dimension, up and down companion ways and stairs. Another is the desiccation of the atmosphere. Since Antarctica is a dry, low-humidity continent in any case (or, to be strictly accurate, a continent with 100 per cent humidity, but with little moisture in the air because of the low temperatures), there's no relief from the ship's air-conditioning by going outdoors onto what there is of a deck, or by keeping escape doors and ports open, as they are most of the time.

In consequence nasal passages and mouths dry out, and thirst, even on shore among the ice and snow, is a problem. An additional problem on *Icebird* is water. The ship's water is officially stated to be "non-potable", something to do, I think, with the tanks needing cleaning. The result is that thousands of plastic flagons of Hobart water are shipped each trip—apparently it wasn't easy to find a supplier for this unusual order. At first we were allowed to draw these flagons and take them to our cabins. Later we were told that we could only drink the water in the mess. Later again we were told that the tap-water was drinkable after all! All very familiar to anyone who has ever been in the army, but a source of irritation on board. The *Nella Dan* in its recent besetment ran out of plastic water, and that created quite a crisis with shipboard morale. The *Icebird* has completed four Antarctic voyages since it was first chartered, the water problem has been the same on each, and not once has it been reported for rectification on return to Australia.

It's rather odd, too, that the charter conditions of *Icebird* leave all matters of food and drink to the ship. Australians coming on board thus find themselves exposed, in the twinkling of an eye, to the tastes of Hamburg. Only the sweet Holsten beer, often barely chilled, is served in the *lokale* down under the mess room.

The food suits me. Eggs to order in the morning, for instance, with ham and bacon, and splendid home-made bread if you want it, toast your own. Oddly, only German muesli and another cereal, neither of which I like. I am surprised that no-one has raised a protest at the absence of Cornflakes or Weeties, but then Australians are a timid lot and closet whingers. No porridge: I should have thought a standard component of an Antarctic diet, if ever there was one. Nor can I understand the absence of the excellent UHT milk now freely available in Australia, and surely designed for just this kind of use—our milk is all mixed from powder. Surely someone in the Antarctic Division could be spared for a few minutes to think about these little matters, perhaps not so little.

These cavils aside, we are handsomely treated, and many are watching their belt buckles. I had frankfurts for lunch, scallops and rice for dinner. There is always some rich German soup, which I leave well alone. Tonight cantaloupe and ice-cream for dessert. Chips with everything, but plenty of other vegetables too. Yesterday for lunch there were 'chicken rolls', a long way from Canton.

So we are not hard done by. Uwe stands over the consumers to ensure that their plates are loaded and their faces happy. He looks so disconsolate when some special dish is taken only in a small serving that he is driving many to a corpulence which will serve them well if they fall overboard, where an extra layer of fat may extend life in this sub-zero water from four or five minutes to nine or ten — DO NOT SWIM. ADOPT THE WOMB POSITION — but in any case not for long enough for the ship to put about and pick you up.

45

Diary, Casey

There was a heated and unpleasant argument in the bar downstairs last night, when I went in late, probably unwisely, about 11.30. It's a bit of a bloodhouse at that time, even more than at others, but I was bored, and in any case my middle-class guilt suggests to me that I should do more 'mixing' than I do.

Doc Newman got stuck into me with all the ingrained resentments of the larcies, who feel they are among the few 'professionals' on board, that their advice is never asked, that they do the dirty work and get no thanks. Doc was full of pride at having landed his 1270 two-hundred litre drums in his two larcs, with four men, in three days: drums full of the special fuel which is used in the great sledge trains that go off on traverse. "I told Graeme we'd do it if he pissed off all those visitors we kept having to take ashore and bring home." (Graeme did piss us off.) From this proceeded scathing criticisms by the larcies of the divided control of the unloading operation: "We want one person who really knows what he's doing to give all the orders on ship and on shore. We used to have such a chap but they got rid of him. [This a reference to the 'cleansing' of the Antarctic Division after Jim Bleasel took over.] Now there are too many chiefs and no Indians. It's inefficient and it's dangerous." And so on.

Well, it certainly is dangerous. One of the officers said to me yesterday that "Sooner or later someone is going to be killed." I have just come in from watching Alistair Baillie slipping and sliding on the snowy tops of containers as they come down on the great cranes (backloading from Casey) signalling the crane-drivers, positioning the great boxes, juggling with slings and hooks, man-killing falls waiting on all sides, and I called out to him: "For Christ's sake, Alistair, look after yourself!" Alistair grinned, and waved his gloved hand: "That's what they all tell me. They told me it before I spent three months in hospital in Rotterdam, and they tell me still." The *Icebird* tries to keep cargo-handling crew members to the minimum, because for much of the time there's not enough for them to do. Because of the Antarctic Division's lack of specialised expertise in shipping matters, when writing the charter for the *Icebird* we let them get away with it. The result is that there are only six crew members available for cargo work, and that is why we have to draw, very dangerously, on amateur labor. There should be twenty crew working in shifts on the cargo. As things are at the moment it is possible for a crew member to work for twenty-two hours with only an hour-and-a-half off. Some have worked nine hours straight in the lower hold, in bitter cold and a foot of snow. The crane-drivers, straining their eyes in sometimes uncertain light, are a particular worry. Crew members have told me the position is "incredibly dangerous". (This is one of the matters I reported on to Barry Jones when I returned to Australia. So far as I know no action has been taken.)

Back to the *lokale*. Doc was working up to a denunciation of those who "don't belong". He did it elliptically. "Despite my criticisms this is really a great organisation and a wonderful bunch of people. They're down here to do the right thing, even if they lack the ability to do it. They're not going about the operation the right way, but they've got the right ideas. They *want* to make it work."

So far, so good, and few would disagree. But then the discussion veered, and the hops and other participants started taking over. First an attack on Greenpeace, then very quickly an association made with the Project Blizzard people too. One of them, Jonathan Chester, was sitting with us. "These bludgers, these con men, they are only interested in ripping off the fools who give them money. They come down here for their own interests . . ." The diatribe continued for some time. Jonathan, on my advice, left. Then a specific charge was made: that the Project Blizzard people, when asked to lend a hand with the cargo, asked for indemnity against injury. This proved that they did not belong. In any case they were "up themselves" and were a clique on board. A chap with a big beard from Casey, I take it one of the 'undesirables', gleefully joined in. There was a scent of blood in the air. "'Put in the boot!' I sez. 'Put in the boot!'", to quote the Sentimental Bloke.

It wasn't hard to see what was now happening. It's true the Project Blizzard people hang round together but, after all, they are friends, they've been through a bit together and, in any case, what profit would there be in consorting with people like the present company? But the resentment was just as much directed *via* Project Blizzard at the rest of us: those who drink wine with the captain or whisky in our cabins rather than beer in the pub, who communicate with each other in a different language, who are outsiders, despised eggheads, with no real manly work to do.

(First of all, to settle the charges against the Project Blizzard people. Lawyers always cause more trouble than they solve, and the Blizzards' lawyer had, in my view inadvisedly, raised this whole question of indemnity. In fact Graeme Manning was prepared to offer them indemnity if they worked. When Hobart was consulted it not only barred this, but idiotically ordered that the Project Blizzard people be confined to the ship, a directive Graeme very gallantly and correctly ignored. In a way the Blizzard people have had bad luck. They shouldn't be on the ship at this stage at all. We were supposed to be voyaging t'other way round, picking them up last call and taking them straight to Hobart. This would have given them the time they wanted at Commonwealth Bay, but our voyage plan was changed because of ice at Mawson.)

Brendan Doran, may the saints be praised, was with me at the bar table. In his admirable diplomatic way he pointed out that the Project Blizzard people were required by the government to sign indemnities themselves, they were not covered as everyone else was covered, and might properly ask to have the matter clarified. He also said that, if they seemed a clique, perhaps this was because they had been made one.

I had intended to keep out of the whole thing, but I was getting angry, and I finally let go. "The worst of the seven deadly sins was held to be that of Pride. Spiritual arrogance is a loathesome thing, and we all suffer from it. Why don't you look at the Greenpeace people and the Project Blizzard people and start from where they're right, not from where they're wrong? They have as much right to be down here as you. More so, in many ways. They're sacrificing quite a lot to come to Antarctica—you aren't, not in financial terms, anyway. Some of them have given up months of income because they have ideals. Shit, you say they shouldn't be here because they're not 'official'. Don't you realise that the trouble with us Australians is that we're frightened of individualism? Don't you understand that we're one of the most heavily governed and regulated countries in the world? Don't you realise that Barry Jones and the Department of Science went out on a limb to offer Project Blizzard a helping hand, seeing something worthwhile in their aims? Don't you realise that this kind of co-operation between officialdom and ordinary citizens is rare and precious in our country? And perhaps getting rarer? Don't you realise that in attacking the Project Blizzard people, who in any case so far as I know have no connection with Greenpeace, you're attacking yourselves? That if you succeed in putting the boot into them, one day you'll find you have to get permission to join your local Rotary Club? Don't you think ideas and ideals are important? I tell you this, if this country has a future in Antarctica it will be because people have *ideas* about it. You can work as hard as you like down here and it will all go to waste unless people are persuaded that Australians should take an interest in the place. *Everyone* who comes down here, for a long time or a short one, has a part to play, a different part, but all part of one long-term aim. Why do people try to isolate groups and persecute them? Why do humans behave like this? I've seen it everywhere I've been. You should be bloody ashamed of yourselves."

This all raged for an hour. Some of the bigger idiots pulled out, and eventually the others moved back from what they'd said before. Not, I think, that anyone was converted. I should have had enough sense not to get into beery brawls, but I hate this jealousy and resentment, yahoos trying to hunt down the gentler and more thoughtful. Or should I have practised what I preached and seen that these are really good-hearted blokes, always ready to give someone a hand, who have been working very hard, are on edge, have jumped to conclusions too fast?

Peter Gormly, "Doctor Death" as the boys call him, thought it over later, when I waxed indignant to him. "Listen, Stephen, argue with whom you like, if you get into a situation in which you wish to argue. But don't get into confrontation situations with last year's winterers, some of whom are on the boat. People in their situation, we have found out time and time again, have very special problems. For that matter," he added wisely, "we are affected too, locked up on this ship together for six weeks. More than you think. We don't realise it, but we can all become very odd."

Yes, well, I should have learnt that lesson before.

46

It was bitterly cold, probably minus five degrees, and we were rugged up to the eyeballs, stamping around on the icecap, fifteen kilometres inland from Casey, and as close as we were going to get to the South Pole, with only 1400 nautical miles, say 2500 kilometres, to go.

For the first time we were in the classic Antarctic situation of the white-out. The white of the snow-covered ice blended invisibly with the white of the air and the sky. No horizon was visible. But for the pull of gravity we could have been scuba divers in a milky sea. It was disorienting and disturbing. It was a situation which has led a lot of good men to their graves. We stayed close to each other, kept an eye on the Hagglunds, as we laughed at the battered sign: WELCOME TO LANYON INTERNATIONAL AIRPORT. CASEY STATION.

We were over a thousand feet above sea level and Greg Hodge, who navigated while I steered, was punctilious in setting the satellite navigation and checking the radar as we drove through the falling snow, nothing to see except the snow falling from the caterpillar tracks of the Nodwell ahead of us, and the occasional marker made of fuel drums welded together, some bearing signs: CASEY CITY LIMITS, or KANGAROOS NEXT 9 MILES. After an hour we stopped, and Greg ordered us out into a world which was both cold and hard.

Flat ice and snow running into nothingness in all directions. The possibilities for sightseeing were limited. Yet we were standing in a segment of Antarctic history, and Lanyon Junction had a lot to tell about the A-factor and the costs of trial and error on this continent.

The absence of air access to Australian Antarctica has always been one of our major problems. At the political level, for a start, it has made it impossible to 'sell' Antarctica to an Australian Prime Minister or to members of Cabinet by taking them down to see it. It even made it impossible for Barry Jones, Minister responsible for Antarctica for over four years, to visit our stations there—though, to add insult to injury, he was able to visit, by courtesy of the Americans, the South Pole in this period.

But these are not the main issues. For a start, we have been relying on two foreign ships, the *Icebird* and the *Nella Dan*, to maintain our Antarctic presence. Other nations, sceptical about Australia's claims in the Antarctica, have noted that we cannot even supply our own transport. Although these ships are under contract to us they may also be, in the northern summers, under contract to others; if damaged in hazardous circumstances in the north they might simply not be able to meet their charter obligations to us. And the accumulating experience of operating in Australian Antarctic waters goes to the benefit of other captains and crews, not to our own. Although it may be cheaper in the short run to do it this way, and though it may sidestep some industrial problems, it is the lazy, 'she'll be right' way out of our difficulties.

Again, however good the ships it is crippling to have to rely on them alone. In the season of which I am writing, that of 1985–86, the *Nella Dan* had been beset for fifty-four days, the *Icebird* had been nipped in trying to go to the rescue, and the *Nella* had to be extricated by the Japanese icebreaker *Shirase*. (The *Icebird* in fact got quite a fright. Shaped underneath like a box with splayed sides, the theory is that the pressure of the ice, as it builds up on one side of the ship, will tilt the vessel over and slide it sideways, up onto the ice on the lee side. In fact the *Icebird* is too heavy for this agreeable theory to work, and at one stage in her three-day besetment, with an iceberg bearing down on her at two knots, it looked as though she could be overwhelmed in the classic manner, by the ice climbing over the bulwarks like a monstrous invader, filling the decks and sinking the ship with its weight.)

As a result of the *Nella*'s extended besetment the Antarctic Division had to charter the navy's flagship, HMAS *Stalwart*, to resupply Macquarie Island and to change over expeditioners there. *Stalwart* was operating at the limits of her ability. (In other words Australia, with her Antarctic aspirations, does not even have a naval vessel which can get to Macquarie Island without problems, let alone Antarctica. Macquarie Island is a mere 1500 km south of Hobart and is actually part of Tasmania!) Then, on her last voyage of this season, *Icebird* cracked her main drive-gear, had a struggle to get back to Hobart, and had to wait for a part to be flown in from Germany. The *Nella* had to be rechartered. With the *Icebird* back in operation after a three-week delay, the two ships only just managed to complete their tasks in a hazardous race against the shutting of the ice-window. The twenty-two summer expeditioners at the new base of Edgeworth-David, in the Bunger Hills between Casey and Davis, were at one point in some possible danger, and as it was had to be helicoptered out fifty miles to sea in order to get to the *Nella Dan*.

In the following season the *Nella Dan* drifted helplessly and perilously off Commonwealth Bay in a Force 10 gale while a broken piston was replaced, and in January had to be rescued from another besetment by a Soviet ship. Plans to land a party at the Bunger Hills were abandoned. In the same 1986–87 season the *Icebird* was holed in three places when it struck an uncharted rock at Davis. By the end of these two seasons the inadequacies of relying totally on sea transport, and the desirability of the extra option of air transport, were once more firmly back on the agenda.

And finally, to cap it all, came the grounding of the *Nella Dan* at Macquarie Island in December 1987, and the controversial decision to scuttle the ship.

There is mounting anger, all the more so since the transport problems have been visible for ten years and more, designs for an Australian Antarctic vessel were prepared five years ago, and the

Antarctic Division has for years been lobbying for money for an air link in a campaign that has simply been ignored by government.

The arguments in favor of an air link, apart from those concerning image, are obvious enough. Emergency medical evacuation, for a start, though whether it would be possible to operate planes in the dead of winter is not clear. Discipline, too, would benefit: the opportunity to remove unhappy or anti-social expeditioners from the bases would give officers-in-charge a little of the clout they do not now possess. Lastly, our *raison d'être*, science, would be the great beneficiary. Senior scientists and observers, now reluctant to devote months to an Antarctic trip, could be flown in and out, and a fixed-wing capacity in Antarctica would add a great deal of flexibility to our research programs there. The Trans-Antarctic Mountains, for instance, in our eastern sector, have never been mapped because we just don't have this capacity. Meanwhile we have the irritation of seeing Americans and New Zealanders, with their access to an air base at McMurdo Sound, able to dive into what we regard as Australian territory for some juicy scientific pickings.

I found it extraordinary, too, that the question of heavy-lift, long-range helicopters had, so far as I could see, been talked about a bit but not acted on. Certainly not even the biggest of choppers could have made much impact on the building-a-city scale cargo in the *Icebird*'s hold, but to have had one on board would have immeasurably improved our efficiency. It's not hard to imagine a couple of such birds handling the bulk of our ship-to-shore cargo in days to come, when the building programs are over. The little choppers we now have in Antarctica have revolutionised our logistic situation, making for instance the early and late ice-edge voyages possible. If the RAAF's Chinooks can lift great iron anchors and two-ton capstans from the wreck of an old windjammer in Bass Strait, it doesn't seem unreasonable to suggest that they may also be usefully employed in Antarctica. But the RAAF wants to charge $5000 an hour for their use!

Thirty years now the discussions about an Antarctic air capacity have been going on, and still there is no resolution of the matter. If the foreign observers on the *Icebird* saw this as a reason for reporting back to their governments that the Australian game in Antarctica was one of bluff, who would blame them? Phillip Law raised the matter first in 1957 when, as director of the Antarctic Division, he proposed a rock runway at Davis. This is still the most desirable solution—I'll discuss it later—and we should have had immeasurable benefits had Law's views been acted on at the time, but I suppose Mr Menzies was more interested in Lord's than in Law. Phillip Law continued to raise the issue during his period as director, which ended in 1966.

Lanyon Junction—I couldn't find out the origins of the name, but I take it it is American—was our sole effort to establish an airstrip in Australian Antarctica. The icecap at this point is pretty flat, and graders smoothed it out, some transit huts were erected and markers put in place, and in November 1978 the first ski-equipped American C130 Hercules plane flew in from McMurdo Sound. There were five flights, in all, in two years to November 1980. They flew in summer expeditioners, scientists and tradesmen, except for one flight, in January 1979, which brought into Casey a mixed bag of politicians and pressmen.

As we stood around in the white-out at Lanyon Junction, the wind-chill factor, Greg Hodge told us, at about −15°C, and actually painful to take off our double glove-and-mitten layers, Patrick Quilty told us the story of the politicians' visit: "There they were, the whole bloody Parliamentary Public Works Committee. On take-off to go back to McMurdo the plane veered right off the runway and hit one of the markers. There was red hydraulic fluid all over the snow. I was acting director in Hobart at the time, and the message came through to me from Casey that they were in the air with their faulty hydraulics. 'My God,' I thought immediately, 'eleven by-elections. We can change the government.'"

The flights into Lanyon Junction ceased when the American National Scientific Foundation, which runs the McMurdo base with help from the US navy, ran short on funds for Australian free-loaders—and when the American pilot who had missed the runway on takeoff reported that it was in a deplorable condition! The next stage in the Lanyon Junction story was an attempt, following a report from the Melbourne University Program in Antarctic Studies, to construct a compressed snow-ice airstrip at the Junction, capable of taking wheeled Hercules aircraft. This would make the strip much more flexible. The original cost estimate was $6 million. A great snow-cutter machine was actually airfreighted in to Hobart from Germany—we saw it at Casey waiting for RTA. Some $1.5 million was spent on Lanyon Junction before Jim Bleasel cancelled the whole project. No wheeled plane has ever landed there.

A sad story of crushed hopes. It has since been decided that, in any case, the weather is so uncertain at Casey, and it would cost so much to keep a strip open, that the whole idea of intercontinental flights to Casey is impracticable. Feeder flights, to and from Davis, may however be possible if a strip were ever put in there.

The temptation is to be cynical about the wasted money and effort, and maybe there's plenty there to be cynical about. Yet nothing venture, nothing gain, and in cases like this we have no alternative but to make up the rule book as we go along.

A pity about those by-elections, though.

47

CASEY

Talking to Anders Karlqvist on the bridge, as we watch the snow float thickly down outside. It's a rarer sight in Antarctica than those back home may imagine. Most of the snow that accumulates down here hasn't fallen from the skies, but has been blown from one part of the place to another.

Anders—slight, tall, blue-eyed—has been phoning through a speech, at some enormous expense via a satellite link, to a meeting of the Swedish Academy in Stockholm on polar matters. He translates part of his speech to me.

Anders tells his colleagues that he finds it whimsical to be observing Australians, from their hot land, trying to adapt to living with the cold. Anders clearly believes that Australians know nothing about the cold. It's probably around 0°C at Casey this afternoon. In Stockholm, where dignified people in suits and carrying briefcases are matter-of-factly attending an Academy meeting, it's −14°C.

No wonder Anders permits himself a wisp of a smile.

Up on the moraine above Casey yesterday afternoon, swooning over stones with the geologists, Anders turned to one of them. "Do you know how to make a snowman?" The Australian, a little startled, said: "Well, I suppose you just take up some snow, and then more snow, and you pat it all into place."

Anders looked at his friend with wonder. He took a snowball and rolled it along the ground. Soon it was a yard across. Then he took another, and did the same. Then another. And then he put his spheres of snow one on top of the other. "There," said Anders, "*there* is the way to make a snowman."

This afternoon he said to me, softly: "Every child of three in Sweden knows how to do that."

48

After a seven-day stay at Casey station, Antarctica, this research and resupply vessel *Icebird*, under charter to ANARE, left its Newcombe Bay anchorage at four o'clock this morning, seven o'clock Australian Eastern Standard Time.

The *Icebird* is *en route* to Davis station, about a thousand nautical miles from here, and four days steaming west. We are standing well to the north of the continent to avoid pack-ice.

Some 2300 tonnes of supplies, including great quantities of material and heavy machinery for the current building program, and three-quarters of a million litres of fuel, were landed on Casey's icy shoreline by pontoon, barge and army larcs in an immense combined operation, interrupted by two blizzards, during one of which we lost an anchor.

Our voyage leader Graeme Manning, operations manager of the Antarctic Division, has commented: "I am very satisfied with this successful operation. Long hours of voluntary labor have been worked by Antarctic Division personnel, expeditioners and visitors. In addition to the landing of supplies we also managed to backload large quantities of surplus equipment and rubbish from Casey station." Manning says that fast ice, still present at Davis and Mawson stations, will present obstacles to the completion of our full program at those stations, and we may have to content ourselves with the transfer of passengers by helicopter and the pumping of fuel through a pipeline laid over the ice. "But," he adds, "our major task on this fifth voyage of the current summer season, the resupply of Casey, is now completed."

The *Icebird* has picked up from Casey twelve of the 1985 wintering party, who have thus completed fourteen months there. These include three expeditioners who have just returned from the most demanding of tasks our Antarctic work has to offer, in this case a four-month, 2500-kilometre traverse across the ice, 250 kilometres inland and parallel to the coastline, living in a small caravan hauled by a bulldozer. These traversers have told us that the return to Casey from such a trip as this presents the same problems of readjustment to 'civilisation' as does the return of the main wintering party to Australia.

(*Australian*, 18 January 1986)

49

The traversing work our expeditioners do is important for two reasons. The first is psychological. It would be possible for most of our expeditioners to go through a whole year in Antarctica without feeling any more snow on their faces than wets their beards on the way from their 'dongas' to the huts in which they work and to the mess. At Casey, totally enclosed, even that is unnecessary.

So the members of the party who do the glaciological traverses experience the Antarctic equivalent of life in the raw. Living in the closest physical contact, their qualities of tolerance and sociability are stretched to the utmost. They take turns in driving, cooking; all help with repairs, refuelling and the boring of cores from the glaciers, sometimes in vile conditions and always in difficult ones. To the traversers it's a real job, away from the confines, the irritations, the pettinesses of the bases. On the *Icebird*'s way home one of the traversers, Don Waugh, said to me: "Yes, I'd come back to Antarctica again, but only for the traverse. There's no bastard out there." It's no wonder that they sometimes look with some scorn, which they have to disguise, on those who stay behind. But the traversers enable those back at base to feel that, at least at one remove, they can participate in the big, difficult, even dangerous jobs still to be done in the Antarctic. The 'diesos'—diesel mechanics—who keep these caravans on the road really are the unsung heroes of our Antarctic work, some of them, such as 'Papa George' Hedanek, achieving legendary stature.

The traverses dignify, and help to justify, all the work we do in the South. One of the proudest Antarctic memories is of the first great traverse, that of September 1962 to January 1963, which covered 3000 kilometres from Wilkes to the (then uninhabited)

Russian Vostok station and back. The six men who took part, led by the New Zealander Bob Thomson (who is now in charge of his own country's Antarctic activities), ascended to 4000 metres and had oxygen problems. The Americans from McMurdo dropped 160,000 litres of fuel to the party to enable it to carry out its journey. One of the caterpillar tractors which took part has now been recovered, after much diligent searching—it was found in a Hobart butcher's garage—and has been restored, to be placed on display in the Antarctic Division's Kingston headquarters.

In the second place these traverses have a leading place in Australian Antarctic science. On our knowledge of the ice-cap, which is in effect one huge glacier up to three miles deep and shaped like a dome, on our knowledge of its history, characteristics, and the processes taking place within it, hang many assessments: of changes in the earth's atmosphere, of the future climate of the earth, of sea level, of fresh-water potential, to name but a few. Our glaciologists look at the movement of the ice-cap over periods of time, and delve into it with bores to extract cores which, when returned to Australia, are analysed for the composition of atmospheric gases trapped in bubbles within the ice. From this the history of changes in carbon dioxide and other concentrations can be reconstructed.

It is not, perhaps, very sophisticated science, but it is at least something we are good at doing. Our traverse teams in 1985–86 used four primemovers, two living vans, two generator vans, five fuel sleds, a laboratory van and store, and a mechanical drill and core box. Quite a sight on the move. Aboard were three diesel mechanics, a navigator–surveyor, an electronics engineer and a glaciologist.

The romance of the traverses soon wears off for those doing them. The work is repetitive, a bit like building a rabbit-proof fence across the deserts of Western Australia. And the traversers suffer from the universal Antarctic complaint of feeling that the efforts they make are just taken for granted. Time and again in Antarctica I felt that for the cost of a few telexes from Australia the morale down there could be greatly improved—personal congratulations from the Minister or Director when teams get in from a traverse, for instance, and for that matter birthday greetings too for the winterers. *Anything* that will make them feel that the bosses are interested in them *as people.* It's something that the Minister and the Antarctic Division just don't seem to be able to get around to, and it's one of the reasons that Antarctica is a people problem.

And when something of this kind is done, it's done badly. Winterers do get a medallion of some kind presented to them, before they leave their bases to return home. Those winterers who came back on the *Icebird* with us were not grateful for the kind thought. They were angry that so little attention had been paid to what should have been an important symbolic matter that, on the medallions, the word 'Antarctic' was spelt 'Antartic'.

Sometimes, too, the traversers meet with Soviet traverse teams, both parties hundreds of kilometres from home, delighted with company and prepared to break out the best of their grog to celebrate the occasion. But, when they part company again, our people are left to reflect on the way the Russians do things. They have a great Kharkov custom-built vehicle of great power, first cousin to an army tank, which incorporates living quarters. They have a driver–mechanic in charge of the vehicle, so that the others can get on with their proper jobs. They have a doctor–cook, a radio officer, a navigator, two glaciologists, a meteorologist and a magnetician. In other words, they have a team precisely trained for specific tasks. By comparison our teams are like volunteers picked for a picnic football match. If the Russians need a new gear-box a plane flies in and drops it by parachute. A discussion:

Antarctic scientist: The Russians are down here in a no-muck-about way. Like the Japs and the Yanks, they ask themselves one question: "What do we need to get the job done?" We Australians worry about policy.

Traverser: The Antarctic Division pulls the Australian way of life apart. We want to do a job too, but they won't let us. We're not down here to be laughed at, chaffed at or fucked about.

Another traverser: How can you fly like an eagle if you're surrounded by turkeys?

Presumably the Russians say, as they drive off waving goodbye

Platcha Hut, Vestfold Hills, near Davis.

from their encounters with our mob on the icecap, whatever the Russian equivalent is of: "What on earth was that? Bush week?"

50

I have solved an Antarctic riddle that has been worrying me for some time.

The riddle is this: why does the summer station at Bunger Hills, which is to the *west* of us at Casey, report to us that they have an *easterly* blizzard which we will shortly get at Casey? Surely, if it's an easterly blizzard, we should have had it at Casey before they did.

Then someone drew me a little diagram which shows me how delightfully simple the Antarctic weather pattern is. This is the diagram:

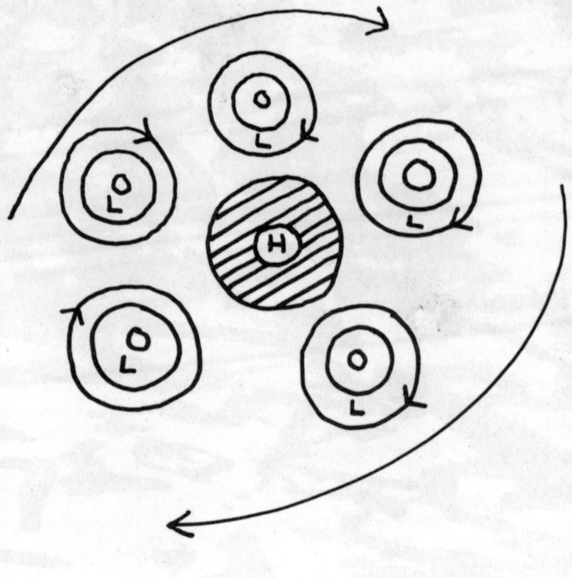

In the centre is the Antarctic continent. Over the pole is a permanent barometric high. But circulating around the continent in a clockwise direction is a permanent series of lows, themselves internally moving in a clockwise direction. So—all blizzards, at least on or near the coast, are easterly blizzards, just as all the weather is from the east. If the system were static, then Casey *would* get these blizzards before Bunger Hills, to the west. But, because the *whole system* is revolving, the lows affect places to the *west* of us before they affect us.

That is, of course, if you're at the *bottom* of the lows, as on the Antarctic coast we invariably are. But up north, say in the fifties latitudes, ships will be steaming through the *tops* of the lows, and hence getting their weather from the *west*.

Never too old to learn.

51

17 January 1986, at sea

Nita's birthday, and I'm very happy, for I've just come back from the radio room where I talked to her, and Joanna, on Inmarsat telephone at $17 a minute.

It would be hard to devise, for demonstration purposes, a more fiendish communications problem. On the one hand me, on a ship in the polar seas, 2000 nautical miles from Erith Island in Bass Strait. On the other hand Nita, on Erith Island, without power of course, let alone a telephone.

Solution? Ring, by some means so complex that the mind declines to consider it, but I understand involving Sydney, the lighthouse station on Deal Island. Deal Island is, like Erith Island, in the middle of Bass Strait, but separated from it by a mile of short-tempered sea. Hope that, by some concatenation of weather, fate and lighthouse hospitality, Nita is on Deal Island instead of Erith. She was. A happy party on Erith, systems working (without me?) and enough crayfish. Joanna is keeping a journal for me.

Telecom may regard the whole matter as unremarkable. I found it very moving, and hard to keep my voice steady.

52

AT SEA

Nothing left of the Casey experience now, except to reflect on our adventures there. We left at four this morning, and about breakfast time ploughed through some spectacular pack-ice, where I saw my first Emperor penguin standing, in its dignified way, on an ice-floe. Now we are in open sea, with a lot of bergs and growlers around, in and out of patches of fog. Course north-west, a 'slight to moderate' on our quarter. It's strange to find the ship 'alive' again.

Last night before we left, and as the late workers came in from their barges—Graeme on the ship's intercom: no more RTA material to come aboard; a blizzard due; battening down and clearing out—I offered Brian Turnbull in a nearby cabin a whisky, and this developed into a long and interesting 'bull' session with him, Lee Ranford, John Hannaker and John Stanhope, the Department of Science's lawyer. It was good for what I learned, and too for the good humor generated. Apart from Lee, I had hardly known these people before. I was surprised to find the DHC boss, John Hannaker, and Brian Turnbull, the admirable Antarctic Division liaison officer with the DHC, as concerned about the low priority of science in the building program as Lee and I are, and as ready to accept criticisms of the Maginot Line mentality behind it. (One wag told me the other day that ANARE stood for "Australian National Antarctic Rebuilding Expeditions.") They are very firm that these bases we are building, apart from serving the obvious and proper purpose of providing a more dignified environment without which standards of behavior won't improve, are only meaningful if they are to serve as advanced headquarters for Antarctic work, reducing the constant back references to Hobart for permission to do this and do that. That development has been one of the many curses of better communications. I can't see it ever diminishing, unless they leave the telephone off the hook. I can't see Hobart, for political *and* bureaucratic reasons, ever relinquishing power now to the bases. And, if Hobart did, I wonder how many of our oics would be prepared to accept it.

The DHC people also say that, together with this, must be a

more flexible Antarctic program involving field parties and, above all, the construction of a hard-rock airfield at Davis. They say it would cost $50 million.

Galley 'Mombasa' today. I reported *am Diensten* to Uwe at nine, and enjoyed myself dropping potatoes into a rotary peeling machine and shelling eggs. The tasks were not too demanding. At ten Uwe and Ernst, the chief steward, said I had to come down to the morning 'church service' in the bar. Here Ewald, Uwe and Ernst, with Ulli our kind-hearted woman steward looking on, made me play the incomprehensible Max game with them, while they kept my glass filled. Then Uwe dismissed me until five. A further indulgence, I gather, four being the normal time. I noted what I had noticed before: there's a real unforced democracy between all ranks on this ship, from the captain down, which would be unthinkable on an Australian ship. So much for national stereotypes. The evening stint as 'Mombasa' was, however, less of a sinecure than the morning one—an endless stream of great baking dishes, grease-encrusted from roast pork, a swaying kitchen and not enough hot water.

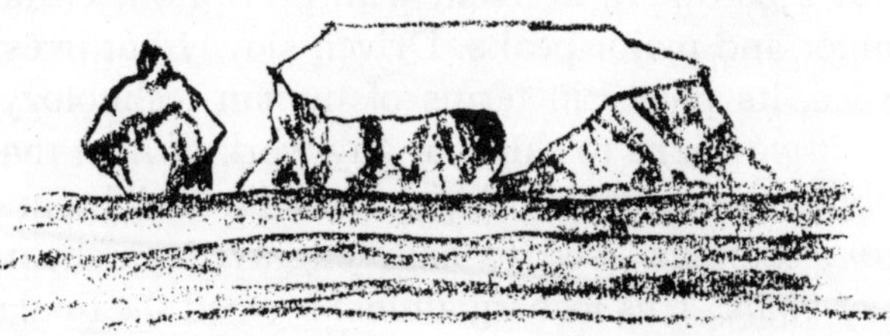

Between the slushy episodes, though, I took Peter Gormly's advice and went, along icy decks, to the ship's forepeak: "Get away from the ship's noises, Stephen, get up there at the bow, and use your eyes and ears. You'll never forget it."

Peter was right. It was like riding on a bowsprit, high above the ice we were ploughing through, ten-tenths most of the time but, fortunately, only one-year pack. We would have had a harder time in old ice. It was quite magnificent. I could have been riding a camel across a great white plain. And, for the first time, I heard clearly the *sound* of the ship's progress—the swish and clang of riven ice against the steel plates, an eerie gonging that came and went, a disembodied music that they never heard in the days of the wooden hulls.

Gormly joined me, to talk of ice, of the seals raising their sleepy heads from the floes, of storm petrels darting about and the skuas coasting alongside us, dark against the ice. "Look out there," said Peter. "That's a great sight: the swell moving through the pack-ice. It's like seeing solid ground moving. People who have lived through earthquakes talk of pine forests undulating like that." And, as we looked out, far into the mists on the starboard bow, we saw a phantasmagorical solid taking shape, an Antarctic mountain range appearing through the dark clouds—I thought of *A Midsummer Night's Dream* and "hot ice and wondrous strange snow". It was a terrifying iceberg. It was not terrifying because of its length, which may have been half a mile, but because, more than any of the thousands of bergs we have already seen, it didn't look like a berg, but like a piece of the Himalayas dislodged by some mighty cataclysm and slid across the plains of the Indian subcontinent into these foreign, southern seas. Perhaps 700 feet high, perhaps more, it was a cordillera in itself, with precipitous cliffs, hanging valleys, minor and major peaks. Driven slowly but irresistibly by the easterlies, its power in terms of human technology was unthinkable—it was hard to think of any work of man that it could not have obliterated without being deflected from its course. *Ultima ratio regum*, cannons used to have engraved on them, *the last argument of kings.* This iceberg almost seemed the final argument of God.

It was of small concern to us, though. We could slip around its edges, as we did, steaming for a smooth ten minutes through the *polynya*, the ice-free lake of clear water which such bergs have on their leeward side. But, even well clear of it, I looked back to its cloud-wreathed peaks and cliffs as a child looks back at a threat safely passed.

LATER

The iceberg I'm looking at now is far less menacing. It's a 'tabular', or table-topped, berg, a quarter of a mile long and 200 feet high. A work of art, really, with a delectable surface slope which exposes its top to us, and a slightly bow-shaped profile which, with its wrinkles and folded cliffs, conveys the suggestion of a dismasted, but still beautiful, clipper ship.

She sits there, seemingly motionless but in fact under way, shadows playing over her walls, enough sun getting through the grey overcast to make the snow-covered top gleam.

Ten thousand years, perhaps more, that ice has awaited its day, locked in the Antarctic ice-sheet. Every year it moved on its three or fifteen feet towards its rendezvous. Without form, and void, its beauty was all to come. It was a nothingness, locked in its vast, still prison.

Then, after centuries of waiting and slow descent, it came to its moment of destiny. Pushed out over the sea, though still part of the main, in a second it was racked with the pangs of division and of birth. With an appalling roar that echoed off the sea-cliffs far up and down some frozen coast it subsided into the sea. Great waves marched out. It rocked, and steadied itself, and became a new-born thing.

Pushed by the Antarctic winds, it began to work itself westwards and seawards. But already it was dying. Subtle chemical forces were sapping its strength, and it has perhaps four years to live. We see it as serene and unchallengeable, but already it is a monument to decay.

53

Patrick Quilty is the ship's iceberg buff. An unguarded remark will set off his rhapsodies, but they're more to do with money than with beauty. To Patrick there's gold in them icy caverns and cliffs. I never knew scientists were so mercenary. Here is a sample of Patrick's rhetoric: "Did you know that 350 cubic miles of icebergs are calved off the ice-sheet in Antarctica every year? This is half the world's total water needs. Change it into metrics if you like: 1450 cubic kilometres. Just think of it! Twelve to fourteen thousand cubic kilometres of water could supply 50,000 cities the size of Perth with all their water. I saw one berg which was 600 metres long and 400 wide and 150 metres thick: it was just the right size for Perth—32 million tonnes of water, worth $20 million: what a bargain!"

Looking at it another way, Antarctica possesses 70 per cent of the world's supply of fresh water. It can be thought of as the world's biggest and cheapest ice-making machine. Admittedly the blocks that fall into the tray are big ones, but they'll keep on coming for ever unless we humans change the world's climate.

This, of course, is one of the reasons why the glaciological traverses go out from places like Casey. The Antarctic icecap has been remarkably stable for twenty million years; and it is thickest, incidentally, in Australian Antarctic Territory, thus giving us the 'ownership', if you like, of most of the fresh water locked up in solid form on the continent. It moves seawards at rates that vary from a few metres a year in the interior to 200 metres a year at the margins. In ice ages the floating ice shelves around Antarctica will of course expand, helping to reduce sea level everywhere. About 20,000 years ago, at the height of the most recent 'cold snap', the sea level was about 400 feet lower than it is today. It has been stable at its present level for about 5000 years.

In prehistoric times the fluctuations in sea level were, of course, of concern to the human race, and sometimes no doubt were tragic. The Canberra archaeologist Rhys Jones, for instance, paints a graphic picture of the rise of the sea in what is now the Bass Strait area. Almost imperceptible though the rise may have been, over thousands of years, season by season the Bassian plain was subject to further intrusions by the water. Aboriginal migration routes to what is now Tasmania, and their hunting grounds, would slowly have been diminished. Somewhere, sometime, human populations were faced with momentous choices: whether to stay put on high ground and face the future on an island, or whether to retreat. In Bass Strait both choices were made. Those who retreated became the Tasmanian Aboriginals. Those who stayed became the first Flinders Islanders, and vanished from history about 7000 years ago.

Today, though, the effects of a rise in sea level would be much more catastrophic. Humanity can no longer pick up a few implements and a fire-stick and wend its way to warmer climes in the south or north. Our civilisation is a static one. For the most part out cities and factories, and much of our food-producing land, are on the continental littorals. If the ice-caps of Antarctica and Greenland melted, the water would rise to the twentieth floors of the Melbourne and Sydney business buildings.

Until recently the main concern about the possibility of the Earth's warming up was focused on the increasing amounts of carbon dioxide, largely from the burning of fossil fuels, to be found in the atmosphere. Hence the analyses by the glaciologists of the bubbles of 'ancient' air to be found in core samples from the ice: one recent deep boring has enabled scientists to measure the constituents of the air that was around 160,000 years ago. In terms of our admittedly slight scientific work in Antarctica, the glaciologists were kings. They were doing something useful. The other two groups of Antarctic scientists lived, by comparison, on handouts. The biologists and botanists were more or less regarded as parts of the landscape, and the 'upper atmosphere physicists' were regarded as Dr Brainstawms who were allowed on the scene as a concession to 'pure' scientific research.

This has changed overnight, as so often happens in scientific history. In the first place the role of the biologist/botanist will increase significantly, as the monitoring of ecological and environmental change and the drawing up of conservation policies mounts closer to the top of the agenda. But, more dramatically, the physicists have become, at least potentially, the key people in Antarctica. And this is how it happened.

In 1985 a British scientist, Joe Farman of the British Antarctic Survey, reached for the charts from an antique instrument, invented in 1931, called a Dobson spectrophotometer. By looking closely at what the observations had to tell them, he and his colleagues made one of the most startling discoveries of this century.

Farman was interested in the ozone layer. This lies between fifteen and thirty miles above the Earth's surface, so tenuous that, if it were compressed into liquid, it would be no thicker than a pencil. But the layer performs the all-important function of screening the Earth from ultraviolet radiation from the sun. If the layer were damaged there could be vast increases in cancers, eye cataracts and certain diseases, not to speak of the burning up of crops and, potentially, famine becoming a standard human condition rather than an occasional one. And the sea level would rise as the ice melted.

Farman says that what he discovered was beyond belief. "One day we woke up to the discovery that the ozone over the Antarctic was falling away from us." A giant 'hole' had appeared, covering virtually the entire Antarctic icecap. Through the lenses of the American Nimbus satellite the hole was swirling with disparate colors: purples, reds, blacks and yellows. Tracking back, Farman found that American satellites had been recording the growth of this hole for years. The information had never been passed on by the NASA computers, because they had not been programmed to pick it up.

In the first year Farman was studying the ozone hole it was appearing in early September, reaching maximum size in mid-November and disappearing in December. The hole reaches from 30,000 feet to 150,000 feet and is about the size of Australia. And it is appearing each year earlier and earlier.

At first some scientists argued that the hole might be due to natural fluctuations, but that view is no longer being heard. It is due to chlorofluorocarbon (CFC) and halon pollution, now emerging, it has been said, "as one of the most serious threats to life on Earth".

These pollutants possess one hundred thousand times the insulating properties of air itself and will, if they succeed in destroying the ozone layer, wrap the Earth in a heated blanket. One million tons a year enter the atmosphere. Ozone is particularly vulnerable to the CFCs: one part of chlorine will destroy 100,000 parts of ozone. Measurements taken in 1987 show the hole as bigger than ever, with 15 per cent less ozone present than in 1985, when Farman analysed the records, and more than 50 per cent less than when we now know the abnormal drops began, about ten years ago.

The causes? Aerosol cans with CFCs as propellants. Refrigerators. Air-conditioners—an airconditioned car puts two pounds of chlorine into the upper atmosphere each year. Plastic foam food cartons used in fast-food outlets. Fire extinguishers. Computer cleanants. The effect is believed to be most visible in the Antarctic because ice crystals in the stratosphere speed up the action of CFCs, but Swiss scientists report the depletion of ozone over northern Europe too, reaching as far south as their own country.

Panic stations, of course. International conferences seeking cuts in CFCs, with tardy and inadequate response by world governments, except the United States. Some third world countries want to expand production. Yet no-one now doubts that the world will warm up because of this pollution over the next fifty years, and many scientists fear above all that some natural action—a solar flare, a nuclear explosion—could trigger a qualitative decline in the ozone layer, a decline which could threaten the nature of human civilisation.

The blowfly, one of the causes of the crisis, may be one of its few beneficiaries.

And then, of course, there would be more icebergs, and thus more beauty in the world, but there could be no-one to see it.

It's not commonly realised that icebergs, like penguins, belong to the south, and not to the north, of the world. The only icebergs found in northern waters calve from a couple of big glaciers on the west coast of Greenland. Since there's no Arctic continent there's no Arctic ice-sheet to break off in great slabs. The ice around the North Pole is simply sea-ice. Submarines break through it, up to the surface. There are of course lumps of ice floating around in northern seas, and one of them sank the *Titanic*, but the stupendous sights of Antarctic seas will never be seen in the north. In the 1960s two icebergs were tracked for years in the Antarctic Peninsula area. One measured 68 by 47 miles, the other 65 by 33 miles. In November 1987 the American National Science Foundation reported that an iceberg 155 kilometres long, 40 kilometres wide and 275 metres thick had broken off the Ross Ice Shelf in the Bay of Whales area, eliminating the bay as a geographical feature. Its area was five times that of metropolitan Melbourne, and the water locked up in the berg would supply a city of two million people for 700 years. The biggest iceberg ever recorded is said to have measured 280 miles by 60 miles.

Patrick Quilty believes that, in ten or fifteen years, we'll be getting water out of Antarctica. "The Germans have been working on the technology," Patrick says. "They're very nearly there."

The technique may well develop this way. An iceberg will be identified that is the right size and shape and which is already being pushed by an ocean current in the right direction. It will be wrapped in plastic. Occasionally it will be nudged by a tug into another current, to take it closer to its destination. Later it will be towed. By the time it gets to its destination, say Adelaide or even Arabia, it will be a plastic bag full of water, like those children take goldfish home in. It will be manoeuvred as close inshore as possible, without tearing the bag. The water in it will then be pumped to reservoirs or artesian basins. In the course of doing this the ice-water will be used as a heat pump, utilising the temperature difference of perhaps 25°C with the surrounding sea water, and feeding electricity into power lines ashore. Perth would need say three bergs every two years, each about one-twentieth of a cubic kilometre. Nothing to it.

And, of course, the delightful thing is the environmental non-impact. Not even the most heavily-bearded greenie has yet been able to come up with a convincing argument as to the demerits of pinching the occasional iceberg from Antarctic waters, while the availability of berg water to needy areas will obviate the need for environmentally destructive dams and crosscountry pipelines.

My friend Ray Marginson, chairman of the Melbourne and Metropolitan Board of Works, says, "Nonsense." But we shall see. He may be splashing Antarctic water in his whisky yet.

54

AT SEA

The captain's table again, and some good stories from Peter Gormley and Ewald Brune on their medical adventures at sea: emergency deliveries, dead bodies found in cabins, and the like. Peter reminds us that the *Ships' Captains' Medical Guide* very sensibly ends with the prayer for the Burial of the Dead at Sea. A similar book is available in German, and Ewald writes down the resounding title for me: *Gesundheitspflege auf Kauffahrt-seisschiffen.*

Part of the Wilkes station, near Casey.

Acres of ice-filled buildings at the former Wilkes station.

Sitting on penguins: Stephen Murray-Smith on the Adelie penguin rookery on Shirley Island, near Casey. The time is about 10 p.m.

In the methodical German fashion Ewald acquired his medical qualifications as a ship's captain by studying fours hours a week at a hospital for two years. Alistair gained his by spending two weeks at a Sydney hospital. Both, I am very sure, better than nothing.

Ewald cracks a real Germanic *Witz.* Instructions are being radioed from on shore to a ship with a serious illness case. "Go to the medical chest and take twelve tablets of Number 35." "But there are no Number 35s in the medical chest." "Then take Number 70 and divide by two."

55

This is a very clever German ship. There is that air of slightly heartless competence about it that makes one wonder, yet again, how the Germans lost the war. (When I mentioned "the war" to someone on board a young man asked me: "Which war?") Ewald told me this morning, as we were engaged in the unAntarctic activity of peeling stamps off the hundreds of envelopes he receives as ship's postmaster, that his father was captured by the Russians at Stalingrad. A lucky man to get back, even with a couple of bullets in him, and to sire Ewald in 1951.

The crew, not large for a ship of this size and complexity, work long hours with much cheerfulness and informality, and all call each other by their first names. There is little Germanic bureaucracy, except in the radio room. Alistair, the young Australian mate, seems very happy on the ship, and they seem fond of him. Peta, the pretty Tasmanian girl who is always to be seen around in overalls and working boots, and does a full stint as an Ordinary Seawoman, makes good money and seems very content.

The officers put up with passengers on the bridge at all times, even when we get in the way, but I have never heard a complaint. The stewardesses seem only too pleased to accept special orders and to dart off to the galley to please someone's whim. Uwe takes a personal interest in everyone's appetite. They say that on the *Nella Dan* the niceties are more in evidence: glasses instead of the mugs we have to drink wine from; chairs instead of padded benches in the mess, tablecloths instead of laminex, white-coated stewards actually serving at table. But then the *Nella*—called after Phil Law's wife—is now an old ship, and no doubt has the problems of one. Here everything works, or nearly everything.

The Germans have overreached themselves in one area. There's a most ingenious lavatory and sewerage system. All wastes are treated and rendered innocuous on board by the ship's "Biocompact Biological Marine Sewage Treatment Plant", solids from which only have to be discharged every eighteen months. But, at the user end, matters are not so simple.

Evacuation of the pan is supposed to be effected when a knob is raised. Some infernal vacuum system, powered by a frightening force in the bowels of the ship, sucks the pan clean with a roar and a swish which has frightened Australians into standing well clear. It's easy to imagine parts of oneself disappearing too. But there is trouble with these bits of devilry. Every now and then the ship runs out of suck. Questions are asked over the 'bing bong' (the public address system) as to what cabins are affected.

Often Harald, the obliging chief engineer, himself arrives, singing "In diesen heiligen Hallen". Quite an honor. Like a good plumber he then sends for his mates. In turn they disappear in search of tools. The little bathroom built into our cabin disintegrates under their hands. Wall fittings are unscrewed and torsos disappear into unexpected cavities. Splendid, though muffled, German curses drift back. Then I am expelled from the cabin, later to meet a beaming Harald on the stairs: "All OK now."

But, sadly, too often it's not. We now have a new cabin companion, come aboard at Casey, a German himself and a very seasick one, Andreas. Andreas has been appointed, by Brendan and me, Shithouse Liaison Officer for Cabin CO2.

56

Diary

I started to write a humorous article for the *Australian* but, before I had written more than a couple of hundred words, people around the ship who popped in to the cabin had passed on to me so many funny stories, some of them black humor, that I gave up trying to have art improve on life.

The stories included:

Two of the 'undesirables' ordered to board the ship at Casey are not on board. On the other hand one person who is not supposed to be on board is with us.

A rock-crusher was sent to Mawson, but when it got there no-one knew how to make it work. In a year it only produced twenty tons of crushed rock. So the DHC last summer ordered a thousand tons of crushed rock for Mawson. By the time the stones had arrived on the dockside at Hobart the cost was $1 a bag for contents, $40 for packing and delivery. But by this time an expeditioner had turned up at Mawson who had been a quarryman, and he produced a thousand tons of crushed rock without ado. So what to do with the crushed rock at Hobart? The answer was to get it out of sight. It was shipped south to Mawson and used for filling. This enterprise involved three days loading at the Hobart end, and three days of charter time in unloading at the Mawson end. Operation Save Face, one presumes. (Query: how true are such stories in the first place, and how much do they gain in the telling? The fact that in any case they can be told is significant, I suppose.)

As we saw, cargo went ashore at Casey expeditiously, and disappeared up the road to the great new green store, also expeditiously. These inward stores, therefore, were pushed holus-bolus onto the high shelves of the compactus system as they came in. All in crates, of course. But the documents identifying what is in those crates were left in the containers, which were then sent back to the ship as RTA. Most of the papers are now irretrievable, and desperate efforts are being made to get copies radioed in from Hobart.

Ewald Brune is fuming over the loss of nine rolls of film he took during the besetment of the *Nella Dan*—and, briefly, of the *Icebird* too—a few weeks ago. The films were left with the Antarctic Division for processing, and cannot now be found. Base motives are suspected, and Ewald talks of the law. Why base motives? Others later filled me in (this voyage really is becoming quite a learning experience). There is said to be a solid, pro-*Nella Dan* faction in the Antarctic Division, opposed to a very-much-the-minority pro-*Icebird* faction. Jim Bleasel is said to lead the latter, one of the reasons for his personal difficulties there. The *Nella* faction disapprove of the new emphasis on better logistics planning and smartened administration—presumably they stand for the Old Antarctic Values as opposed to the New. (If what we have been seeing is 'improved', what in God's name was it like before?) They are said to be up to all sorts of dirty tricks. (The implication is that they wouldn't be past putting Ewald's negs down the chute.)

Yes, that's enough fun for one day.

57

Diary, 18 January 1986

Today I had one of the rarest of Antarctic experiences. I saw a great black iceberg, and I was one of the very few people on board to see it.

It was about seven at night and most of the people on board were at dinner, or down below somewhere. I was, as usual, on the bridge. Norbert, the first mate, was on watch. Far off on the port bow I saw this patch of black, and Norbert obligingly altered course for it. As we drew near, and then alongside, I realised we had struck an oddity indeed. Here was a great berg with a concave top. The huge cliff-face facing us was black from top to bottom. It was about 200 feet high, with striations of white where snow had cascaded down the face from the top of the berg. It was an unnatural sight in these waters, even an eerie one, a reversal of the order of things. And it was even odder to make the discovery myself. *I* had never heard of a black iceberg.

As we cruised close past we saw that there was a cliff-foot, a small ice shelf protruding twenty or thirty yards, and on this shelf we numerous boulders, a small moraine. Gradually I began to sort it out. Here we had a berg which, like so many when they start their lives, had grounded on a muddy shoal in shallower, coastal waters. As it lightened, and as the currents and winds took hold of it, it dragged its vast bulk across the bed of the sea, driving great rocks and mud into its texture.

Later, as melting and division took place, its centre of gravity altered, and with a great shrug it up-ended itself, so that the bottom of the berg became its side, embedded with rocks as a Christmas pudding is with fruit. Attrition continued, and as it melted the rocks fell down the cliff-face and formed this moraine at its foot. Juvenal called the black swan, a creature he had surely never seen, a *rara avis*. I understood now the force of his imagery. This was a rare bird indeed.

POSTSCRIPT

I had never come across across a reference to a black iceberg in my readings in Antarctic literature, but in the course of writing this book read Helen Rosenman's new, and first, translation of the journals of Dumont d'Urville.

On 21 January 1840 d'Urville was within sight of the Antarctic continent and, with his officers and crew, was seeking desperately for any sign of ice-free coast on which to land and collect evidence, indeed to prove that what they were seeing was in fact land, and not just a vast accumulation of ice:

> Soon the lookout thought he could make out a black patch at the edge of the sea and eagerly announced his discovery; several officers who had swarmed up into the rigging themselves, in their turn, believed they could see these hoped-for signs through the mass of floating ice islands that lined the coast. But then, as we got closer, the black patch they had seen suddenly disappeared. We saw that one of the floating islands was an earth colour, and this could have given rise to a misapprehension. We imagined that this was the black area sighted by the lookout.

58

19 January 1986, 2.30 a.m.

I rise quietly from my bunk, conscious of Brendan sleeping the sleep of the righteous civil servant, and of Andreas, our quiet and gentlemanly German from Kiel, Andreas of the marzipan box, hidden behind his curtain in the upper bunk. I slip downstairs to the servery in nightshirt and slippers.

I seek a solitary midnight supper of tea and toast—with the exception of breakfast, meals here never seem to happen when you're hungry. I take Morley's *Pictures from the Water Trade* with me, a witty study of the interactions between the author and the Japanese which, rather to my surprise, I find much to my taste.

But I find that the *Icebird* supports a flourishing night life. There are half a dozen late stayers in the mess, watching a hectic home video of the celebration of midwinter in the Casey Club. It's strong stuff—a bit strong for me at 2.30 a.m. I wince, and turn back to the servery and the toaster.

Two red-eyed denizens of the night emerge from some burrow complaining of being "burnt", which I discover is youngspeak for a hangover. Their spirits are dampened, but one of them finds the sight of a fat old man in a nightshirt sufficiently amusing.

But the turnup for the books is the wandering in of Brian Turnbull, bearded and burly. One of the pleasures of this voyage has been meeting some blokes like Brian—a Brisbane boy, a quantity surveyor, former oic of Mawson, now the Antarctic Division's contact man with the Department of Housing and Construction, a key position if ever there was one. John Hannaker, the DHC boss-cocky, has told me of the role Brian has played in reducing aggro between this awkwardly matched tandem pair of government departments.

Quiet talk at this hour, in a quiet ship—the video has finished by now—and it's a good way of learning. I learn again what I learnt a night or two ago, that beneath some fairly hard-bitten exteriors on this ship there is a deep desire to work, not for personal or departmental advantage, but for an ideal called "Antarctica". I learn that this is not always easy—for instance, when the DHC wants to charge $90,000 for a simple instrument box for the theodolite tracking of met ballons, a box which the Antarctic Division thinks should cost $15,000 at the outside, and which others say could be built on a DIY basis for the cost of a few swear words. I learn too of the intelligent appreciation, by many of those involved in the infinite detail of construction work, of the larger, 'philosophical' implications of what they are doing. I am impressed and humbled. I am glad I stumbled down those stairs.

59

At sea (but revised January 1988)

Barry Jones was asked, in an interview with *Playboy*, whether he thought Australian soldiers should have training in polar conditions.

"I think they should be able to kill people anywhere," Barry is said to have replied.

The trouble is, of course, and as Barry knows, that under the Antarctic Treaty military operations are barred in Antarctica. This doesn't seem to prevent military involvements, though. The French base of Dumont d'Urville is partly manned by conscripts, given the choice of military training in France or Antarctic service. The American navy is heavily involved in Antarctic logistics and administration. The Argentinians and Chileans make no bones about military and naval involvement. The New Zealanders use their army to build their stations. Even we Australians use an army detachment to operate the larcs on these re-supply trips. The Russians, who eschew any services involvement in their operations, have commented on this Australian 'military presence' in Antarctica.

For all that it really is quite extraordinary, given the strategic significance of Antarctica to Australia, that our air force and navy are so totally excluded from that continent. There is no naval vessel, not even a hydrographic one, that can go near the place. Simple prudence would suggest that *real* naval operations in the Antarctic region can't be ruled out in the future, and that we should have a couple of ice-strengthened ships both for this purpose and for emergency use in our present situation. It's an uncertain world. But the Department of Defence, in the true tradition of the thinking that led to the fall of Singapore, states officially that "There is no requirement for defence activities to support our territorial or economic interests in Antarctica."

I'd be taking careful note of that piece of deluded nonsense if I were working on the General Staff of some countries.

As with the navy, so with the air force. We should long ago have had an air link with Australian Antarctica. I'm even told that the RAAF would like to be involved, but is excluded—the Department of Defence has a policy that the services are not used to support 'civilian' operations except on a trial basis. This seems a foolish policy but, even if we accept it, it should not prevent the army's building an airstrip at Davis and the RAAF's inaugurating its use for a year or two. Here is a real operational situation, invaluable for training, which could help recreate the 'national efficiency' our leaders are always talking about. Locked into their petty concerns, the politicians and bureaucrats cannot get around to the modest amount of lateral thinking that might solve, not just one problem, but many. Instead, every year, we suffer the national humiliation of going cap in hand to the Japanese, the Russians or the Americans for help to get us out of a mess we have got ourselves into. It's bloody pathetic.

I've even heard it suggested that the Australian army should build and run our bases for the scientists. Our scientific involvement has, however, at least until recently, been so low that it might be difficult to get away with this. I've also met the argument, strongly put, that the logistical and organisational aspects of our work in Antarctica should be contracted out to private enterprise, leaving the Antarctic Division free to concentrate on its proper role, that of scientific work. Jim Bleasel's argument against this is that our Antarctic Division runs the building and logistics part of our programs in the south much more cheaply than private enterprise does for the Yanks.

The contrast with the British is interesting here. The Australian Antarctic Division has a seven-person executive: director, deputy-director, policy, operations, resources, medical, science. Of the persons occupying these positions only two have carried out research programs in the field, have serious Antarctic experience. The rest are public servants with quite short service with the Division. Yet this executive group makes the decisions which operate Australian Antarctica and which intimately affect the scientific work there—ostensibly the only reason for our presence. Shipping schedules, for instance, are vital to scientific planning, but the decisions are taken by seven persons, only one of whom is a scientist—and none of whom, to our cost, is a shipping expert! So low is the status of the scientist concerned, who is supposed to be responsible for the co-ordination of all our scientific work in the south, that he is not allowed to attend meetings of the Antarctic Science Advisory Committee (ASAC), even as an observer.

Turn now to the British Antarctic Survey. This is *run* by scientists. The director, Dr David Drewry, is one of the world's leading glaciologists, and the executive members represent the environmental sciences, the earth sciences, the life sciences and the atmospheric sciences. *One* administrator sits on the executive. The Survey has about 400 personnel, runs two ships and three aircraft and, as an independent research institute within the Natural Environment Research Council, reports directly to the Minister for Education and Science. The BAS operates four Antarctic stations, two (Rothera and Faraday) on the Antarctic Peninsula, one on Signy Island in the South Orkneys and one, Halley, on the ice in the south Weddell Sea. A fifth station, on Bird Island off the north end of South Georgia, maintains a BAS presence on that sub-Antarctic island since the closure of the main station at Grytviken following the Argentine invasion of 1982 and the (scientifically unwelcome) persistence of a British military garrison, which occupies the former BAS station. The annual budget of the BAS is about £12 million, with salaries for scientists about half those paid to Australian scientists. For their £12 million the British have an annual output of about 200 scientific papers. For $42 million we Australians get about one hundred.

It is true that the British bases are not logistically maintained by private enterprise, but it is easy to see why Australian scientists, with a paranoid tendency to see themselves as hardly more than tolerated in Antarctica, sigh—not for freedom from bureaucracy, which being rational souls they see as inevitable, but for a different form of bureaucracy. They point out that, after all, the Antarctic Division is—or was at this time—part of the Department of Science; that it is the US National Science Foundation that conducts American affairs in the Antarctic; and that the American stations are run by private contractors, the National Science Foundation merely providing the scientific superstructure.

Jim Bleasel of the Antarctic Division would deny that scientists are necessarily, even usually, good managers. He would also deny that 'Antarctic hands', whatever their worthy achievements on the sixth continent, are good managers either. Indeed, he could well argue that he was brought into the Division because they weren't. Jim would argue that his fourteen years experience as an engineer and project manager in remote locations is a better qualification to run Antarctica than participating in a glaciological traverse—though he is a strong supporter and defender of these traverses. To the charge that the Antarctic Division is now no more than a career public-service department, increasingly a whistle-stop on a career path, he would answer that the Division will always be more than that but, if that were so, it would be part of the price paid for the transition from amateurism to professionalism, from crisis management to preventive maintenance.

This is not always fair to those who have laboured mightily in the past for Antarctica, and to many of those in the Antarctic Division today. Not only has Bleasel not carried with him in his innovations and enthusiasms many of his middle-level and senior staff but, more seriously, he has sometimes given the impression that he is not very worried about this. The point, it seems to me, is that the Antarctic Division will always be an area of government where on-the-job pride and experience will have to mesh with 'on top' management expertise, and part of the job of management is to make sure this happens. I hope it is happening, but I am not yet convinced.

Perhaps it is significant that our Antarctic Division is very much a lone operator. Government, clearly, is not very interested. There are no powerful and broadly-based advisory bodies, or independent polar institutes, to inspire effective criticism and debate from outside. Our media pick up Antarctic crises, but have little interest in keeping in touch with policy issues and in informing the public about them.

One result of this is that the Australian achievement in Antarctica has been material rather than conceptual. We have had our successes in logistics and building and engineering, in solving problems as they come along, but we have not done this within a framework of longitudinal thought. What *have* we learnt in forty years? What do we really know of the totality of the natural, historical and cultural resources we command, or claim to command, in Antarctica? What are our most important environments down there? What priorities are we going to give to which of them? How do we rank them against the resources of Antarctica as a whole? What long-term management plans do we have? Can we save money and extend knowledge by working more effectively with other nations rather than, as at the moment, against them?

At the moment the answer to these questions is the silence of Antarctica itself. But they are being raised, and they will increasingly be raised. They lie behind the discussions of new forms of Antarctic administration. They relate to such problems as the personnel issues on the actual stations, the uneasy relations between different government bureaucracies with interests in Antarctica; problems which range from communications and logistics to the levels of scientific work at present being carried out by us. A new ship for Antarctica is welcome, and so are other resources as they come along. But this is only tinkering. The issues go beyond money, which is relatively easy to get, and into the hard areas which cost nothing but thought and the drawing together of good and experienced minds.

You can understand our segmented approach driving people mad at times. On a previous voyage *Icebird* hit a rock on the approaches to Mawson. She was using Australian navy charts and the rock, although it had previously been reported, was not marked on the charts. The captain of the *Icebird*, with visions of his vessel at the bottom of the Antarctic seas, demanded an explanation. He was told that the Australian navy only marks on its charts perils that it itself has investigated. Since our navy does no serious hydrographic work in Antarctica, and has not the facilities to do so, it does not mark on its charts the findings of others.

Since then Captain Brune has switched to using Soviet charts: "The most reliable," he says.

60

Diary, 19 January 1986

Ewald's birthday party this morning. The talk turned, as we sat in his cabin, to the problems of having our own Australian research ship. Lee Ranford and Patrick Quilty were there. We share the same sense of humor, and enjoyed the Germans' satire at our expense. "Forty million dollars," one of them says, "to build a decent ship like this in Germany. Eighty million dollars here. But we'd lease the ship to you for $14 million a year, less over a long period. Don't forget, you need stewards for the stewards in Australian ships. And would your Australian officers pick up a paint brush or work their guts out in the hold, as ours do? You're out of the market."

We've got to remember, though, that the *Icebird*'s owners are very smart operators, real entrepreneurs of the sea. In a way they're running a sophisticated tramping operation, and they have to be. I admire their astuteness in realising that people like us have to be worked on. They're generations ahead of Australians in their awareness of public relations. They appear to run a non-union ship. She's said to be out of favor back at home in West Germany. They *have* to live on their wits. No doubt we're lucky to have the *Icebird*, and no doubt in our situation it's cheaper to buy milk than keep a cow. At least in the strict financial sense.

AFTERWORD

Even before the loss of the *Nella Dan* at Macquarie Island in December 1987, its replacement was under serious consideration. There was intense commercial rivalry to obtain the contract for its replacement—so there is good money in Antarctic charter work, after all! The Australian government announced on 16 December 1987 that $124 million would be spent on a ten-year charter of a new supply and research ship for Antarctica, probably to be named the *Sir Douglas Mawson* (why the "Sir"?), and to be jointly owned by P&O and the West German company that runs the *Icebird.* It would be built in Australia, would fly the Australian flag and would be in service for the summer of 1989–90. It will be staffed by Australian officers and crew. It is clear that, despite the digs we heard on the *Icebird*, Australian unions, faced with massive unemployment in the shipping industry, will 'come to the party' on Antarctic manning problems.

And the future of the *Icebird*? My guess is that this will also be forced into Australian ownership, partly because of government insistence and partly to afford liquidity to the *Icebird*'s owners, who will probably retain a minority holding.

So we will then have two Australian Antarctic ships? Yes, in a sense. They will fly our red ensign, and orders will be given in English, rather than Danish or German. But they will not be owned by the taxpayer. They will remain entrepreneurial, in the same sense as the *Icebird* and *Nella Dan* have until now been entrepreneurial. This *may* be the best way to go, but it does mean that our Antarctic bureaucracies are going to have to sharpen up their capacity to deal with entrepreneurs.

61

Diary, 20 January 1986

There was a bad night on the *Icebird* last night, I discovered from my spies at breakfast. Ewald put on a grand birthday celebration for all in the bar, and huge quantities of a villainous punch were concocted, and presided over, by Ernst, the chief steward.

All went well while Ewald was down there in the *lokale* with the mob, but after he left it became increasingly willing. There was a fight. A larcie fell outside his cabin, hurt his head, and was removed to hospital. Then someone gravely insulted Geraldine, who was trying to help—told her to fuck off, or something like that. Graeme Manning and Geraldine are far from amused. Geraldine has been advocating a dry ship from now on, certainly a permanent ban on free grog, and even no more women in Antarctica. Apparently she didn't get the support she expected from the other women on board, half a dozen clerks and the like from the Antarctic Division, and she feels that women down here can't exert a good influence if they don't stick together.

All this has led to the day's being taken up with various views on low life, ranging from 'oics should have the powers of special magistrates' to 'boys will be boys—all you're seeing here in public is what these people get up to at home in private.' From 'you've got to get the best out of people by looking at their good sides' to 'why let bastards ride roughshod over you?' Peter Gormly says that Antarctic stations are well-behaved if the 'responsible' people get on top early. Graeme Manning tells the story of how, when the last ship sailed out of Casey in 1979, four pot smokers came to him, said they had a year's supply, and what was he going to do about it. Graeme called a meeting of all on the station, declared himself without a vote, and after four hours of talk got an 18:0 agreement that (a) there would be no public smoking, (b) there would be no proselytising, (c) there would be no smoking affecting duties, and (d) that he would be the sole judge of offenders. There were none.

We are about 150 miles offshore as we skirt the northern edge of the pack on our voyage westward to Davis. Plans chop and change hourly. The *Nella Dan* is about twenty miles ahead of us, also steaming west. First we were to rendezvous with her, pick up some chopper parts for Mawson, drop off our Davis passengers by station chopper at Davis, load the Davis chopper, steam to Mawson, mend their chopper, do what unloading we could and return to Davis. A few hours later we were told that, because of the fast ice at Mawson extending twenty or thirty miles out to sea, we shall not go there at all, but transfer our Mawson cargo to the *Nella* at Davis, unload our Davis cargo there, and return home. If this is so it will be a big disappointment.

This evening a private dinner party, eaten on our knees, in Peter Gormly's minute cabin. Guests: Anders Karlqvist, Pat Quilty and me. Subject: what complaints do Anders and I have?

Well, we said, as guests we could hardly claim the right to make complaints but, if they were interested, we felt that—although we had been treated with every consideration—our possible roles had not been looked at very imaginatively. What we were trying to do was as important as unloading a bulldozer or two, and that applied to the other observers on board, too. The Mawson cancellation was going to affect the useful work we could do—had that been taken, at any stage, into consideration? Even if the decision to omit Mawson were then adhered to. Anders felt his desperate need to see science and talk to scientists was not understood. I said that it would have been useful for me to be allowed to witness some of the planning sessions on board, to get an idea of the pressures and to understand better what lies behind the chopping and changing, the adhockery, which most of us on board feel we are at the mercy of.

(Current comment on board suggests that the real reason we're not going to Mawson is that the enquiry on the besetment of the *Nella Dan* has been going on since we left Hobart and that, although its findings were bland, Jim Bleasel is not going to risk more trouble by having *Icebird* down at Mawson too late in the season, on Voyage 7; and that therefore he's shortening this voyage.)

And if, as Peter Gormly says and is no doubt true, many on board are puzzled at the very presence of people like Anders and me, then—we said—some way should have been found for us to explain our roles to those interested, as we are perfectly willing to do. (One well-used piece of Antarctic slang is *jafa—just another fucking academic.*) I have in fact got on well with many on board, and make new friends every day. But, Anders and I said, being 'popular' on board, or even 'understood', is not the highest of our priorities. Our first priority is doing the jobs we have to do.

62

I didn't know it at the time, of course, in fact had no inkling of it, but that lunch was the prelude to the most moving and beautiful visual experience of my life. We've all stood and admired wonderful prospects, the memory of which stays with us even as it fades. But what happened to me between 9 p.m. and midnight on 20 January 1986 has trailed clouds of glory about my life ever since, has taught me that it is possible for an atheist to have, in his own way, a transcendental experience, and completed any conversion I needed to humility in the face of the natural world. It was an experience which has not faded. Its joy was tempered only by a sadness that those I would most have wished to share it with were not with me. It was the entry from the open sea to Davis.

As I went up on the bridge after dinner that quiet evening the sun, though declining, was bright, the skies open to the west and the rays flooding down on us at low declination. Hours before, turning south, we had broken through the pack that lies off Antarctica like a tank-trap, and then had clear water. But now we were approaching the coast again. Far in the distance the grey wash of the Antarctic icecap. Against it, brilliantly picked out by the sun, close-packed lines of grounded icebergs, but still tiny from this distance out. As we steamed steadily in through a placid sea the first small pieces of decaying ice rocked in our wake. A few minutes more and we were in open pack, and the floes were getting bigger. We could no longer afford to ignore them, and started wending our way at reduced speed to reduce the worst of the occasional impact. And, all the time, looking ahead, we could see ourselves approaching the great rampart, the walls of ice a hundred feet high, the outer defences of the Antarctic coast which, it clearly seemed, we could never hope to breach.

Within an hour of sighting the first insignificant ice fragments we were up amidst the ramparts themselves, barely moving, at two knots, as we started to thread the needle. There was an air of tenseness on the bridge. Ewald, seated in the steering chair and wearing dark glasses against the refraction, as we all were, conveyed an apparent air of nonchalance as he munched his sandwiches. But he was wary. His eyes never left the ship's path ahead. Jörg was hovering behind him, surveying ahead with binoculars, responsive to every muttered order from Ewald to check chart and echo-sounder. Ewald's hand on the little black knob, like a gear lever, the ship's steering wheel, would move momentarily left, momentarily right, as he manoeuvred the *Icebird* as delicately as a jeweller with a watch mechanism.

And we—a crowd now on the bridge—we were silent. Not because of the finesse of the operation we were witnessing, but because things were drawing together, we were involved in a total process of human temerity and natural forces opposed, as Manning Clark would say we were learning 'what it had all been for'. We were insolently thrusting, time and again, our bow and then the whole ship between great bergs that towered above us. Leaning out from the flying bridge, it seemed, we could almost scrape their sides with a boathook, like boys along a picket fence.

The sun, as it declined to the horizontal, flooded the bridge with its sideways light but, more to the point, lit the bergs and the floes,

The *Nella Dan* steams out to sea from Davis station to conduct marine research in Prydz Bay.

Station outbuildings and 'donga' lines at Davis.

Emergency food cache at Davis station, a precaution against a disastrous station fire.

receding into an infinite distance, with a golden, refulgent light, turning the ice into a fairyland and investing it with a warmth that belied the freezing temperature outside the bridge doors. Ewald speaking softly into the phone that linked him to Peta, forward lookout in the bow. And now the ship had its *Doppelgänger.* We were so close to the soaring ice walls we were now coasting past, and the sun was so low as to be the candle in a shadow play, that our image accompanied us along the icebergs as we went.

The normally noisy mob was quiet, *kaum einen Hauch*, philistine tourists silenced by the soaring columns of Chartres or Salisbury. All the luck in the world had suddenly turned our way. A hard winter had preserved the ice. A cold summer had helped. The weather was benign. The sky had cleared. And the time, now near midnight, was right for these wonderful sun effects. "You could come fifty times to Antarctica," I heard someone say, "and never experience this again."

And now we knew there had been a pass through those bergs, only a couple of hundred yards wide, it is true, but a pass. Perhaps Ewald knew about it. And now we were through, and the long line of the Vestfold Hills—modest things, looking like dark sand-dunes from here—became more prominent. Small, rocky islands appeared to contrast with the bergs. For some reason they looked as though they were covered with bushes. On one of them was a cross. As the sun sank still further the bergs started throwing shadows on each other. I was speechless with wonder.

And now, ashore, we could see at last the stark block buildings of Davis. There was a flare, fired to welcome us as we threaded our way in. The land-fringing shelf-ice was ahead of us. We had come a long way to be stopped a few hundred yards from our goal.

63

Davis, 21 January 1986

Watching ice-breaking is even more compulsive than watching the ship break through pack-ice. There is a difference. With the latter the ship brushes aside the offending ice in its way, seeking to avoid what it can and to give the rest of the growlers and floes glancing blows which will send them cruising off to one side, lazily at first, then gathering speed as the full weight of the ship's bow is conveyed to them, until in a paroxysm of split and upturned ice, gouts of seawater and boiling whirlpools, they settle again to a new life, undisturbed this time until their inevitable death.

Pack-ice comprises the pebbles and stones we kick out of our way. But ice-breaking is the assault on a solid sheet of fast ice with cold chisel and maul. This ice lies there, as innocent as all get-out, between the reasonably open sea we are in and the little Australian township we can see there ashore, only a few hundred yards away, a township that is waiting for our fuel, our building materials, our stores. It is infuriating. No-one ashore is prepared to risk a station vehicle on the ice. Even if they were, there is a narrow ribbon of open water between the land's edge and the fast ice which those vehicles couldn't cross. We can't use the larcs, because they are not ice-strengthened and, if they broke through the surface, they might be holed and disappear for ever. We can't, of course, use the barges. The best that we can do to cross this insignificant gap, which might as well be a minefield, is to rely on the station's one helicopter.

Flown with d'Artagnon panache, the chopper dips and banks round our ship and the *Nella Dan* all day. (The *Nella* is lying on our port side, a couple of cable lengths away, like us with her bow stuck into the edge of the fast ice and her engine-room telegraph set to 'Dead Slow', holding here there.) It darts in like a honeyeater to hover above our foredeck, to drop its pendant, netted load in a cleared space which doesn't look large enough to take a wheelbarrow, to pick up another, then to back out gracefully for its next foray. We marvel at the skill and stamina of the pilots, working to the limits of their allowed hours. They and their machine are pleasant reminders of home. Vowell Helicopters, run by our old friend Bill English, has sent them down here, and we have probably seen the chopper and its pilots in Bass Strait many times, on lighthouse runs.

So we shall assault this puny barrier. "It's slushy on top—it will go to pieces if we look at it," some say. So we back off a couple of ship's lengths. The skipper is on the open bridge wing at his auxiliary controls. He is bulky in his padded jacket and trousers, his patterned mitts, for although the sun is shining brightly there is an air temperature of minus one, and the smallest breeze chills the face and fingers to actual pain in a few minutes.

Stop engines. Half ahead. Full ahead. We lumber through the water like a bull working itself up to a charge. We hit the edge of the ice. The ship shudders. The superstructures on their rubber blocks disconcertingly oscillate violently. We are all hanging on to the nearest support. The bow of the ship rides up on the ice—it is wedge-shaped, not sharp—and, for a moment, nothing happens. There are a few seconds of stasis. Then, across the face of the fast ice, a black crack opens. Like a lightning flash it zips across the surface. And now, close under the ship, great blocks are being carved from the mother sheet. They sink, then explode upwards, sometimes with such force that they project themselves onto a floe top.

The ship is, for a few moments, remorseless. It is confident in its 6000 tons and its seven knots. Then its confidence falters. The bow drives further up on the ice sheet. This time the ice withstands the pressure. There is another pause, a what-shall-we-do-now pause. The captain accepts defeat. Centre rudder (this places it in a protective housing). Stop engines. Half astern. Full astern. The water below our counter boils. We back away from the ice sheet, nudging as we do so the broken ice in our wake that is already beginning to freeze together again.

Ten minutes have passed since the last attack, and now again into the breach. But this time we vary the assault. We don't strike where we struck last time. The armored bow drives in to the right or the left of the previous wound in the ice. Now we shall do better. The ice now has a moat of open water, the moat we made in our previous pass, to expand into. So we make ten yards more than we did last time.

But this ice sheet is not weak, after all. It has fooled us. Those brown, slushy patches we see on top are merely superficial. Below is four to six feet of case-hardened, steel-blue water-rock. As lumps break off and roll on their sides we see its strength, reflect on overconfidence, consider the A-factor again.

So we have far to go. The tactics are ancient: divide and conquer.

This enemy will not be defeated by *force majeure*. It is not going to be beaten into submission. This fast ice is locked into position between the coast and the rocky islets offshore. So we are not trying to break straight into Davis. We are trying to open up an alleyway through the whole obstruction, parallel to the shore, from the open water where we started to the open water a half mile or more ahead. This, we hope, will weaken the confidence of the ice sheet. If we succeed, current and wind will clear the channel we have made, sweep the detritus out into open water. The ice sheet will waver, will split, the cohesive forces within it will surrender. Surrender will do no good. It will become a retreat, then a rout. The alien invaders will have won.

What a splendid theory! It doesn't work. The breeze angles in behind us. The ice we have so painstakingly demolished over a long day of using the ship as a battering-ram now is rallying, is pressing on our heels, threatens to cohere once more. It may even, if we drop our guard, turn the tables and imprison us, a bee in amber. Then we wouldn't be able to get the necessary way on to break out. So it is we who retreat.

The master race has a glum face tonight.

64

Davis is our furthest south and, at Latitude 68°35′, the southernmost of our Antarctic stations. Well within the Circle, its peculiarity is that it is perched on the edge of one of the largest areas of ice-free land in Antarctica, a 400-square-kilometre block of peninsulas, islands, lakes, hills, fiords which, if forested and in temperate climes, would be the playground of millions.

The Vestfold Hills, as they are known, were discovered and named in 1935 by Klarius Mikkelsen, of the Norwegian ship *Thorshavn*, owned by the persistent Norwegian explorer and whaling-master Lars Christensen. Christensen saw the exploration of the Antarctic coastline in the light, as he put it, of Thor banging away at the giants with his hammer. It was an apt metaphor.

The area was next visited by the remarkable Australian Hubert Wilkins in 1939. Although working for an American, Wilkins claimed territory he touched on for Australia, as we shall see. In 1954 an Australian expedition under Phillip Law landed, very close to the present site of Davis, and hoisted the flag. Davis station itself was established in January 1957, in preparation for the International Geophysical Year. It was closed in 1965, to allow resources to be concentrated on the building of Casey, but to leave any station unoccupied in Antarctica is risky—under the Antarctic Treaty anyone who wishes may walk in and take over—and Davis was reopened in 1969.

The Vestfold Hills are defined officially as an "Antarctic oasis", an oasis being defined as "a substantial ice-free area separated from the ice sheet by a distinct ablation zone". What this means, in the case of the Vestfold Hills, is that they are free of ice for a number of intersecting reasons: the deflection of flow from the Antarctic icecap by the great Sørsdal Glacier flowing to the south and east; craggy terrain which facilitates the removal of fallen snow by wind; a possible local retreat of the ice-sheet; the fact that, rock having been exposed, its heat-retaining qualities discourage the accumulation of snow and ice.

Whatever the reasons, and scientists are wary of making final conclusions about them, the fact is that the ice-free areas of Antarctica have delighted explorers and scientists since they first came across them at the beginning of this century. They delighted the explorers because they were different and unexpected, a change from the eternity of ice. Scott, finding one of these 'dry valleys' in 1903, said "in some respects a more beautiful scene it would be difficult to imagine". Scientists welcomed the oases because in them, and on the occasional exposed rock-faces of the mountains of Antarctica, they could get out their geological hammers and, where lakes were present, whatever scientists use for shrimp-nets. To both scientists and laymen exposed rock was welcome as places where huts and, later, buildings could be erected without the prospect of waking up one morning to find oneself well out to sea on an ice floe.

The lakes of the Vestfold Hills have been called "the jewel in the crown of Australian Antarctica". There are some 250 of them, and they are in fact unique in the world, presenting a range of environments from the hypersaline, with water that doesn't freeze even down to $-30°C$, to water that is completely fresh. The marvels they are assumed to contain are still little known, their environmental management in its infancy, their relationship to other environments of the Antarctic continent little studied. To limnologists, and to many others, they are one of the wonders of the world.

To us, on the ship, Davis remained for some time an unknown quantity. We could see it there, and I was grateful that, unlike Casey, it didn't sprawl over a skyline. Davis seemed smaller and tidier than Casey, and so it turned out to be. But was the lesson of Davis to leave the same kind of sour taste in our mouths as Casey did? We had time to contemplate this on board, for the helicopter was more than fully engaged in ferrying incoming and outgoing expeditioners to us and the *Nella Dan*. So we watched the ice-breaking, and attempts to lay a rope across the ice by chopper to pull a fuel line ashore with, and like the people in *Casablanca* we waited. We were, however, cheered up by one circumstance: we were going to Mawson after all. The oic there had put his foot down and demanded his stores, working no doubt on the old army principle of 'once they're so close don't let them get away'.

65

Diary, Davis, 23 January 1986

Off the ship at last! Down to the foredeck, and packed into the tiny helicopter with Bob Beale and Paul Wright, from the *Sydney Morning Herald*. We were hemmed in by piles of great containers, and I watched the clearance with no little interest as the rotors turned. A giddy swing over the ice, and a swoop down to the pad behind the main buildings at Davis. No time to look around. Survival gear dumped aboard and up again, course south-east, juddering over the frozen inlet of Heidemann Bay and then over the burnt-out landscape, studded with craters and potholes and frozen tarns, of the Vestfolds. The land from this height looked as though it had been seared with a flamethrower to the point where only ashes and slag remained.

Chattering along now over Ellis Fiord, lightly frozen into weird serrated patterns, and losing height as we drop down over the Mule Peninsula, some ten kilometres out from Davis. Good God, this looks like the beginning of the world, or perhaps its end. Down there in a hollow under a cruel, rocky ridge is a little, orange, pyramid tent, Antarctic pattern. It looks as absurdly out of place as the moon-buggy did. But it's where Patrick Quilty has been hiding out for the last couple of days. We leave it behind us as, losing height, we touch down on desolate rocky ground, featureless and, if we did not know there were friends about here somewhere, frightening—all the more so as the pilot barely allowed us to get our feet on the ground before he was off again and disappearing into the sky.

As we gazed around at this brown landscape of clinkers and bulldust, no trace of white to be seen, two heads rose out of the ground nearby, one bearded, one handsomely moustached, both in full polar gear. Not Moomimtrolls but Patrick Quilty and Colin Walker, in real life a plumber at Davis, climbing out of a hollow to welcome us. The chill breeze soon drove us back down into the hollow, a shallow tarn, actually, looking—with its shallow brown water and half-submerged rocks—like a farmer's dam at the end of a drought.

Pat and Colin escorted us to a bank of friable yellow earth, almost dust, by one side of the pool, boulders strewn along its ridge. The soil collapsed at our footfalls, with gouts of dust rising to our knees. In this moonscape, burdened already with heavy boots and gear, I felt that I should be wearing a space helmet.

We were on Marine Plain, and at almost every step were treading where no man or woman had trodden before.

Marine Plain is on the Mule Peninsula, the southernmost of the three great fingers of denuded rock which comprise the Vestfold Hills. The plain lies by the side of Burton Lake, one of the biggest of the lakes in the Hills, a very salty lake, in periodic connection with the sea, which will certainly be of interest in the investigation of the evolution of organisms away from a strictly marine environment.

The plain itself is a considerable geological puzzle, the com-

Davis.

ponents of which are only slowly being sorted out. To fly, or walk over, the plain is first to be impressed by the sharp, rocky ridges that surround it, ridges characteristic of the whole Vestfold Hills area and consisting of ancient, Precambrian rock. One or two hundred feet high, they can be scrambled up, with much exertion and a little risk. But the really curious thing about these hills, at least to the casual observer, is that they are crisscrossed by what look like tyre-marks, a bit like a racing circuit after a *grand prix*. Parallel basalt intrusions, twenty to fifty yards apart, create great black streaks against the brown rock. They are so consistent, so regular, so nicely ruled that it's hard at first to accept that some artifice has not been at work in their creation.

Patrick Quilty is not moved by such commonplace observations. The really remarkable thing about this place is not so easily grasped.

Lying within these walls of rock is a low depression, only a few feet above sea level, and shaped a bit like a knucklebone twenty square kilometres in extent. Apart from about twenty little, shallow tarns, the nondescript surface is covered by millions of stones, small rocks to big boulders. Walking across the plain becomes a dance, as you try to direct your great Antarctic boots so that you won't trip. But Quilty is scornful, too, of the stones. What he's interested in lies beneath them. What he calls the Pliocene sediments, that yellowish dust we stirred up when we landed, which erupts at every pace, and which gives off, appropriately enough for those who are thinking that the floor of Hell must be like this, a sulphurous smell.

This thick, dry powder is composed of the skeletons of diatoms and is a foot or eighteen inches deep, except where it is piled up in deeper drifts around the fringes of the tarns. And it shouldn't be here. It's as friable as talcum powder; it lies over bedrock scoured by ancient glaciers; on it rest the countless rocks also deposited by glaciers. How could something so vulnerable survive these cruel forces? It's as though an egg could survive in a rock-crusher.

This diatomaceous earth is in fact an ancient seabed. It is formed largely of the tiny shells which lie undisturbed where the creatures died and, although the rock below has been gouged by glaciers, the rocks on the surface were probably deposited, quite gently, when sea-ice above the shallow inlet melted. At first it was thought that the deposits were of about the same age as the freeing of the Vestfold Hills from their ice cover, perhaps 18,000 years ago. Then, by ingenious dating techniques, involving comparison with similar sediments from McMurdo Sound in the Ross Sea, it was realised that this was a unique Antarctic site, an intact seabed four million years old.

The plain has been, for a number of years, the scene of an occasional scientific foray from Davis, sometimes over the sea-ice and up the fiords, sometimes by crosscountry trek and the crossing of Ellis Fiord at its narrowest point. The interest in the area has largely been geological. But in early February 1985, just a year before Patrick Quilty greeted us as we stepped out of the chopper, he was on a quick trip to Davis from Hobart and decided to take a closer look at the Marine Plain. He had pricked up his ears when the word reached him that it might be two hundred times older than had been thought.

Poking around, like a good Australian, in the slopes by our little tarn, Patrick found a dolphin, which is a bit like finding a buttercup blooming at the South Pole. At the time, though, he didn't know

what he'd found. What he picked up was an odd shape, size, color. Looked at more closely it had the honeycomb texture of bone—a big piece of bone. Then, in only the hour or two he had available, and with increasing excitement, he collected more fragments. Patrick's not a vertebrate palaeontologist, so he didn't know what he had found, but he did know enough to suspect that the bone fragments came from a mammal, that it was probably a marine mammal and that, given the new dating for the Marine Plain deposits, it was probably about four million years old. He also knew something almost as good as knowing—he knew who was likely to know.

With his bones back in Hobart in twenty plastic bags Quilty got in touch with the world authority on such matters, Ewan Fordyce of the University of Otago in New Zealand. The find has now been identified as not only a new species of dolphin, but also a new genus and probably a new family as well. I hope, when they get round to it, they call it after the irrepressible Pat. I like the thought of an Irish dolphin in the Antarctic.

The find, however, meant more than this. So far it is the only record of a vertebrate animal covering the last forty million years of evolution in Antarctica which has come to light anywhere.

All the way to Davis in the ship Pat, when he had time left from talking about icebergs, had been spouting about his dolphin. "The big question, Stephen, is whether it was just a fantastic piece of luck, a chance in a million. That's OK, I'd be quite happy with that. But I'm going out there again when we get to Davis. This time I'll take a day or two. *If* we find more material we'll know we're on to something really big."

When we arrived Patrick got ashore on one of the first chopper rides. He didn't waste time. He found a delightful well-mannered and enthusiastic assistant in Colin Walker, grabbed a tent and some bivouac food from the store, and flew straight in. They got their tent up on its tripod poles, and then hiked straight across the rocky plain to the tarn where we found them the next day. "This is where it was," Patrick said to Colin. Colin wandered off a bit to one side, and came back holding something. "Is this the sort of thing you want?" he asked.

And so Patrick knew that it was naming day in his Antarctic Eden. He felt, I have no doubt, as Edward Hargraves did when he picked up the nuggets at Ophir in 1851: "I shall be a baronet, you will be knighted, and my old horse will be stuffed, put into a glass-case, and sent to the British Museum." Other bits and pieces, including a vertebra from a large seal or a small whale, soon came to hand. And there they were, lying on the ground in front of us. We took off our gloves and fingered them, to an *obbligato* from Patrick: "You bloody beauty. These put last year's finds into perspective. A lot of damned good science is going to be done here by a lot of people. Some of the world's best scientists are going to be queuing to get here. You're the first to see the start of a whole new era of Antarctic research."

Heavy stuff, and followed by heavier: an Antarctic lunch prepared for us back at the bivouac by Colin. The dolphin skull and jaw, now recognisably assembled in line, lay on the tent flap at our feet. A billy boiling on a primus. Colin rooting in the tucker box and holding up with pride little silver bags. "Here, take your choice. This is Stephen's—beef casserole." New Zealand, freeze-dried. Tear the top off. Pour in the boiling water. Hold in the hands for a couple of minutes. Eat with a fork.

Perhaps I won't be an Antarctic explorer after all.

66

Marine Plain, like the incoming to Davis, has been one of those Antarctic experiences that stay in the mind. I tried to sum it up in a despatch to the *Australian*:

> The landscape looks as though it has been charred and blasted by the exhaust gases of a thousand space ships. Craters, battered boulders and the detritus of millions of years of frost attrition on rock cover the landscape. Low hills looking like cinder heaps obstruct the horizon in all directions. At every step you tread where none has before. Clouds of the yellowish dust rise as you walk. It is eerie yet greatly exhilarating. It is the ultimate abomination of desolation, yet it holds important clues to life on earth.

67

Science in Antarctica; Patrick Quilty and his diatoms; the *Nella Dan* and marine research in Prydz Bay, in a corner of which we in the *Icebird* were lying. Yes, it is time to talk about oil.

Phillip Law thinks we are witnessing the end of the Scientific Era in Antarctica, that we are entering the Resource Era. Science will of course continue, but the emphasis will move to the reaching of agreements on the exploration of Antarctic resources, and the distribution of the profits. In fact the Resource Era has already commenced. Krill and fish are being taken from Antarctic waters, and the matter of sealing is being examined by the Russians. The Treaty powers have been meeting on the mineral issue since 1982. The object is to establish an agreed 'minerals convention'. Eleven negotiating sessions have now (mid-1988) been held, and a convention on minerals could shortly be concluded. This will seek to regulate any future mineral exploitation rather than to encourage it.

But it all sounds ominous and, if the conservationists are right, it *is* ominous. It is unlikely that there will be any turning back. The New Zealand government, which is if anything on the conservationist wing of the debates, has said that neither a total ban on minerals development, nor even a lengthy moratorium, can be regarded as "an attainable alternative".

Politically it is fascinating. Those most keen to mine in Antarctica are not the seven nations which claim segments of the continent; it is the Japanese, the Russians, the Americans, the Brazilians who are amongst the countries anxious to move in. But the claimant states, including Australia, want special treatment and royalties. To admit this is to admit that there is some basis for the existing claims, and this is something that the nonclaimants have—until now, at any rate—refused to do.

Rare minerals such as platinum may be the first target, but oil is high on the agenda. And what we regard as Australian territory will be high on the hit list. So far only a little over half of Australian Antarctic Territory has been surveyed for sedimentary basins, but two large basin systems have been identified. These are the Wilkes basin, lying under the ice at the eastern end of our sector and to the west of the Trans-Antarctic Mountains, where the world's largest coal reserves are thought to exist, and the Aurora basin, inland from Casey. The Wilkes basin is about 1400 kilometres long in north-south direction, and up to 600 kilometres wide.

We do not yet know a great deal about the age, thickness and composition of these sediments, though it is suspected that the Wilkes sediments are between three and six kilometres deep, and the Aurora sediments perhaps two kilometres. They are overlaid, of course, by 2000 or 3000 metres of ice, but that is no insuperable problem and it is considered likely that the sediments are of sufficient depth, and of the appropriate age, for hydrocarbons to be present.

In addition there is a significant sedimentary basin of some five kilometres thick in the Prydz Bay area, off Davis.

We may be sure these prospects have not escaped other people's eyes. In 1972–73 traces of natural gas were detected in the Ross Sea. In 1974 the *Wall Street Journal* reported a United States Geological Survey estimate that forty-five billion barrels of oil and 115 trillion cubic feet of natural gas were recoverable from the continental shelf of west Antarctica, the oil almost equalling the proved oil resources of the United States itself. By 1979 the estimate of oil in the Ross and Weddell Seas area was fifty billion barrels. The Russians agree. In 1984 the first confirmed oil traces were reported, from off the Antarctic Peninsula. Drilling in Antarctic waters, possibly in Australian Antarctic waters, is possible within the next ten years.

The development of Antarctic oil has been compared with the mining of lunar gold. But it is now thought that there may be 200 billion barrels of 'oil equivalent' in basins already identified, perhaps a third of this in, or off, Australian territory. At the moment the nations are not free, under the 'voluntary restraint' agreements of the Antarctic Treaty, to prove or to extract what is there. Nor is it yet economically attractive. Prydz Bay oil would probably cost $60 a barrel to extract, more than twice the present world price. But the vultures are gathering. Seismic techniques used in Antarctica to gather data on the geology of the seabed are now far more sophisticated than is needed for 'pure' scientific purposes. The Russians and Americans have advanced Arctic oil technologies which can be transferred to the south. It is not the immediate rewards that the nations are jockeying for. It is for a favorable lie on the rails when the winning post comes into sight.

So—the end of the Scientific Era in Antarctica? Responsibility for Antarctica was removed in 1987 from the Minister for Science, Barry Jones, by the Hawke government. (In fact, in the Ministerial reshuffle of that year, Antarctica was initially overlooked entirely.) Some will see this as a symbolic stage in the development of politics in Antarctica. Others will see it as merely expressing the traditional contempt of Australian governments for the area, the work done in it, and the people who do the work.

68

Davis, when I got around to wandering about it, was a welcome change from Casey. For a start no squalor, no idiot canned music, a sense of order and purpose. To be fair the current building program at Davis, though ambitious enough, fell far behind the frenetic scene at Casey; and, although the chopper was doing what it could in ferrying small items from ship to shore over the ice, nearly all the materials and supplies we had for Davis had to remain in the *Icebird*'s holds.

I wandered down the donga lines, traditional Old Antarctic, which don't exist at Casey: cramped, insulated, interconnected boxes, hardly more than children's cubby-houses, where the expeditioners sleep and live much of their private lives. Escape hatches in the roofs in case of fire. Easy to see why people would want to get away into the open air for day or overnight trips: TAKE A RADIO AND ADVISE YOUR DESTINATION, ETD, ETA AND PERSONS IN YOUR PARTY. CARRY A RUCKSACK, SLEEPING BAG, BIVVY BAG, SPARE CLOTHES, FIRST AID KIT, EMERGENCY CHOCOLATE RATION, MAP AND COMPASS. DO NOT PRESUME THAT AN OVERNIGHT JOLLY WILL AUTOMATICALLY BE APPROVED. Then along the parallel line of station offices: surgery, labs, stores, oic's office, even a gym. And, down at the end, well away from everything else, a new sight: many tons of wooden crates piled up on a platform in the open air above the bare rock—stores that would enable the people on the station to survive if, in some appalling holocaust, the whole station were obliterated by fire. Unlikely, since fire precautions, including automatic alarms and extinguishing systems, are at a high level of sophistication and priority on an Antarctic base, but an interesting example of prudential thinking.

The dongas and the service buildings, though now outmoded and about to be replaced, at least have one feature which our new buildings on the bases will not have when they are completed, and about which there is a fair bit of controversy on all the stations. They have little windows, double-glazed and often not much more than a foot square, which can be pushed open in clement weather. It doesn't sound much but many say that it's psychologically important, that to open a window is a small victory for man over the machine, and that it helps people to feel that they're living *in* Antarctica, not sheltering from it. There have been many requests that there should be at least a few windows that can be opened in the new, 'permanent' buildings, but the planners in Melbourne have turned them down.

Down along the donga lines there's a reminder of the Soviet paranoia I used to know so well, and would like to forget: a sealed container stuffed with the gear of a Russian scientist who recently worked for a period with Australian scientists at Davis. He got in touch with his own base to ask permission to visit Hobart briefly in pursuance of his work. The next thing to happen was that a

Soviet helicopter landed out of the blue at Davis, the scientist was bundled aboard, and nothing further has been heard from him.

Further along is the radio hut, usually the busiest place on an Antarctic base, crammed with banks of equipment, teleprinters chattering and expeditioners knocking the snow off their boots as they stamp in and out for their 'radphone' calls back home. Outside one of the little windows in the radio hut at Davis is a small platform for Fred, said to be the only tame skua on an Antarctic station, who is usually to be seen there waiting for the next handout. "Don't give him meat in your fingers—he'll take the finger as well."

But the *pièce de résistance* of Davis is the new living quarters, not as large as the similar building nearing completion at Casey, but actually being used. It is here, and only here, that you can get the 'feel' of future living on an Australian Antarctic base, and the feel is good: plenty of room for expeditioners, especially in the long winter, to move around and to make their own decisions and to feel that they are individuals as well as members of a community. A large, well-equipped, open-plan kitchen, and furthermore a French chef, Roger from Paris, and lamb chops for lunch. "They seem to be very happy with your cooking, Roger." "If not, they can change the chef."

A large mess-hall, with the usual 'help yourself if you're hungry' corner. A loggia, with indoor plants—strictly speaking, there should be no imported plants in Antarctica, but the sight of a few green leaves can mean a lot to those sentenced to the monotones of rock, ice and sea. A humidifier, for the humans as well as the plants—the dryness of the air is a medical problem, the doctor says. A handsome lounge, with armchairs placed for the best views over to Nelly Island and Iceberg Alley, magazines scattered around. A bar corner—"Help yourself to the home-brew." It's good stuff, too, black like the Prague beer I used to love at Ů Fleků, and stored in its hundreds of bottles in the passage between the outer and inner entrances of the living quarters. (I asked for and was generously given a couple of bottles of beer as souvenirs—it was generous because the shortage is not of beer, but of bottles.) A small, cramped library, mainly paperbacks and hardly any Antarctic books. A film theatre, with racks of videos and old films.

All very civilised, walls adorned with mementos of past years, of visits from other nations. And there, in a prominent place, a framed photograph of Steve Bunning.

69

Steve Bunning, a bearded, handsome, kind face. In late October, three months ago, he went out down the lines on a typical station chore. A water-tank was leaking. Steve climbed inside, with a ladder, an electric light on a lead, and a tube of plastic sealant. There was an explosion, and he was found lying on the floor of the tank. He had burns to 70 per cent of his body.

No-one knows just what happened. It's thought that perhaps he stepped back from his work onto the electric light, smashed the globe, and that the fumes in the tank were ignited by the naked element. The most serious aspect was that he had inhaled the fumes and that his lungs were seared internally. There was a limit to what the station doctor could do. A general emergency radio call went out to all listening.

The Russians at Molodezhnaya were the first to respond. They grounded their aircraft and asked for instructions. There was now enough light to fly, but there was no landing ground except the sea-ice lying offshore. It was not known whether it had the strength to take the impact of the landing of a large transport plane. Inevitably more lives were now going to be put at risk.

The trouble with the Soviet offer was that their line of communication was with Mozambique, and no-one at Davis wanted Steve Bunning to end up there. So the Americans sent in a C130 from McMurdo. The expeditioners at Davis worked desperately for seven hours to bulldoze a runway on the sea-ice for the ski-equipped Hercules. The plane landed, and did not go through the ice. Steve was placed aboard, on his way via McMurdo to a special burns unit in Christchurch. Two hours after take-off he died. At home were his wife Glenda and three children, aged fourteen, eight and four.

It was a shattering experience for the expeditioners at Davis, completing their year's stint and, like Steve, looking forward to getting home. I was told that one of the reasons for the subdued atmosphere when I was there was that Steve's colleagues had just not recovered from the experience. This small group, so many months together and alone, had had part of themselves wrenched away.

It is the nightmare of every Antarctic base. It isn't supposed to happen, but it does, and often in the most unexpected way, as with Steve.

On the noticeboard at Davis was a message from his brother.

Dear Don and the Men at Davis.

Enclosed is a copy of what I had to say at Stephen's funeral service, as you requested . . .

Thank you for all your support. Thank you for your concern for Stephen and his wife Glenda and indeed all his family. Thank you for your magnificent effort to save Steve and your efforts since to make sure that although he is lost, he is not forgotten.

I have just finished reading Steve's diary and I almost feel like I know you all and could find my way round the base . . .

Steve's old High School has decided to dedicate and name an annual memorial award to the top woodwork student in Year 10 in his honour. Glenda is going to present the award at their speech day . . .

If there is a lesson to be learned it is don't wait till it's too late to tell those that we love! Just how much!

Later I wondered if those Americans who had risked their lives had received a medal, or even a personal letter from the Prime Minister, for their trouble. Later still I discovered that they received neither, though an official letter of thanks was sent to the American authorities.

70

Diary, Davis

The sun has been out all day, but the wind rose this afternoon, making faces burn and fingers freeze. Because of the wind we are no longer pumping fuel through the pipeline over the ice, and will pull out for Mawson after loading passengers RTA. Desperate last-minute attempts are being made to open crates on deck, extract essential items and get them ashore on the chopper, but the wind when it rises above a certain velocity grounds the chopper, which can't risk being blown about when it tries to land in the tiny space available on the foredeck. The pilots are certainly the heroes of this action at Davis.

The *Nella Dan* will be back from its marine research in Prydz Bay at noon tomorrow, and we will leave shortly after for Mawson. Davis itself, as someone said at dinner, is like a run-down mining camp. To adapt my friend David Martin's *bon mot*, if I had to choose between Casey and Davis I'd take Venice. Still, Davis is a big improvement on Casey, and the surroundings are unusual and interesting. Indeed Michael Madigan and others, who walked inland through the Vestfold Hills yesterday (there are emergency huts scattered here and there on lakesides), tell me it was quite enchanting, though not in any flowery-dell sense!

This morning I had a look for myself, but from the air. Jonathan Chester and I were offered the privilege—a high one, considering how busy the chopper is on station duties—of an aerial tour of the Vestfold Hills. First we flew over the proposed airfield site, along the shoreline north of the base. From the air, at least, it would be hard to envisage any site *less* likely to cause environmental damage, or more easy to build an airstrip on. It would hardly need more than some levelling, some tamping, a bitumen surface and a snow sweeper. The DHC people talk about a cost of $50 million, but others say the Army, if allowed in, could do it for a small fraction of that. Ship time from Hobart to Davis is about ten days, but average air transit time would be, allowing for delays, two and a half days. Direct flying time from Perth would be about nine hours.

The scientists on the whole are opposed to the strip. Patrick Quilty, for instance, is uneasy about fuel spillages on the rock, and the effects of kerosene fumes on the lakes which are, with Marine Plain, the scientific glory of Davis. He believes that Lanyon Junction at Casey remains a better site, and that many of the arguments against it have been cooked up—or, shall we say, have been based on faulty statistics. I accept Patrick's concern about the Davis strip, at the same time as I suspect that behind many scientists' objections to such projects is their desire to keep people out of Antarctica. This is partly because they don't want Antarctica damaged, but also partly because they don't want outsiders in their intellectual territory. As I found in that heated exchange with the larcies in the *lokale* on the ship, there's a lot of dog-in-the-mangerism in Antarctica.

The logistical, human and political arguments for an airstrip seem to me to be irresistible. Just to make some of the human ones: a fortnightly or monthly service to Davis from Perth or Hobart would enable expeditioners to take periodic leave to keep their affairs in order (and reduce the Antarctic divorce rate); it would enable expeditioners to be brought in and sent out according to circumstances on the station; it would make it easier to attract good people, particularly tradesmen, who now do so much better in northern Australian mining townships; and it would enable people like Rob Easther, the new oic here, to have his wife and newborn baby with him, a baby he hasn't seen and won't see for another twelve months. I think it's bloody ridiculous that this kind of sacrifice should be expected of him, or anyone else including his wife, these days. I suspect that Rob thinks the same.

From the airstrip site we swung inland, down the north coast of Broad Peninsula and then north over Partizan Island—the Russians did some exploring and naming here—and Long Fiord and peered down at the site where one of the Hagglunds recently went through the ice and sank, fortunately without dire consequences. The Davis diving team under Paul Butler had already managed to drag it back onto land. Already the true nature of the Vestfolds as a fiordland rather than a range of low hills was quite apparent, and our cameras were clicking busily. In its complexity of variegated rock, frozen inlets, scattered lakes, little islands it was a self-contained world of its own, infinite variety. No-one living on its fringe, as the people at Davis do, could feel themselves imprisoned.

Then right along Long Fiord, heading inland along one of the only two routes from Davis which give access to the icecap, then sharp starboard and down to Trajer Ridge, the other route inland. From here over Crooked Lake, the biggest in the Vestfolds, and a sighting of Mossel Hut below before we swung down Ellis Fiord, skirting Marine Plain, did some turns over the sea elephant colony south of Davis, indolent heads arousing themselves from somnolence to mouth soundless imprecations at our intrusion, and then a drop down to the pad at Davis. A wonderful half hour.

Followed by a cup of tea in the living quarters, and then a discussion with the new station doctor, Gillian Deakin from Sydney, and no relation to Alfred, largely on the subject of women in Antarctica. I picked up the topic again this evening, sitting in the 'smoking' section of the mess waiting for the Davis postmaster to arrive with offerings of philatelic rarities. The blokes who had some Antarctic experience behind them were reasonably fair-minded but on the whole opposed, on the grounds that 'women mean trouble'. One had a story of a woman, drunk on duty at an Antarctic station, who allowed her 'boyfriend' to read private telexes passing through the station to Australia. Others protested, and were attacked by the boyfriend. Another had a story of a woman who got pregnant to a ship's officer on the way down to Antarctica and had to be sent home. Another woman didn't like the 'slushy' duties, played up to some of the men, and had to be repatriated also. An oic on the way down in the ship courted a married woman on board, arousing resentment (and, no doubt, jealousy). There were the old stories of difficulties with separate lavatories and quarters. There is no doubt some bottom in these stories, but Gillian Deakin is probably right when she says that the real problem with many station types is that they've never had social relations with any women except their mothers (she hears a lot about mothers), their sisters and their girlfriends, and just don't know how to handle the situation. Allied with this is the resentment of some, perhaps many, that the presence of women undermines Antarctic *machismo*. I must write a feature article on all this.

Davis has been lucky in its oics. Paul Butler in 1985 [and again in 1987] and Rob Easther for 1986, both still on the base though Paul is to come back with us, are gentle, gentlemanly and thoughtful men, with an air of authority which comes from internal assurance and not from any assumption of rank. Paul Butler, incidentally, believes that the bases could operate satisfactorily without a doctor during the winter months. An odd coincidence. Yarning with Rob in his office I was telling him about our many summers on Erith Island in Bass Strait. "Yes," he said, "I visited you there last year." He was on the yacht *Domino*, one of many that cruise through in the summer months. Then Paul Butler walked in and was introduced. "Oh, yes," he said, "we've been in touch before. I was with a diving party which went out ten years ago and used the hut on Erith Island. I rang you up about it from Sale."

Brendan and I have been amused that the United Nations flag is flying here at Davis, as well as the Australian, German, Danish and ANARE flags. There's also a colorful signpost in the middle of the base, with fingerboards pointing to MURMANSK (in cyrillic letters), HAMBURG, MARSEILLES, GERANG GERANG 5240 km, CASTLE HILL, ANGLESEA, STRATHFIELD, DONALD 5288 km. Others are in Chinese, Japanese and even Hindi. A United Nations signpost, perhaps, but Brendan and I are amused that, in flying the UN flag, we are in effect flying the flag of our enemies, who want to remove this continent from the Treaty powers.

Talk too, during the day, with one of the senior DHC people, who had an interesting tale to tell. He knows a chap at the University of Sydney who's doing a thesis on the establishment of an airstrip and motel at Davis. The financial backer for the investigation, he says, is Dick Smith, though it's all been kept pretty quiet. Surely a good idea. If we want the Australian taxpayer to support our work in Antarctica, if we want Australians to think our territorial claim in Antarctica justified, then ordinary Australians have a right to see the place. It would be expensive and there would be many controls, but that's no problem. American national parks ration entry to prevent the destruction of what people come to see. Guided tours of the Vestfold Hills, with adequate safety precautions, would be the ultimate in tourist oneupmanship. [Certainly Australian businessmen are already (1988) meeting to discuss the tourist dollar in Australian Antarctica.]

71

Diary, Davis

An excursion to Sea Elephant Beach, something I have been longing to do. Quite a caravan: the *Chicken*, a larc and the small catamaran we have on board for the diving operations at Davis, but which we can't get ashore. If we can pull it up on Sea Elephant Beach we'll leave it there until the ice breaks out and it can be retrieved.

It was a long trip to the beach, almost a circular one outside Gardner Island, which is still frozen in to the mainland. But it was a wonderful opportunity to observe the penguins on the floes, and up on the slopes of Gardner Island, where sometimes they stood in groups on icy crags, from which there seemed no possibility of retreat, they in their turn watching us dispassionately as we threaded our way through the floes, sometimes finding ourselves in a *cul de sac* from which we had to back out with much energetic manoeuvring.

Once near the beach we in the *Chicken* had to stand off, for it draws too much water, but we watched the combined operation with interest. First the larc got ashore, up the black sand, easily enough. It then unloaded the catamaran's trailer and threw a line to the cat, which tried to pull the trailer into the water. Not powerful enough. So we had to link up the *Chicken* to the cat, pull the trailer into the sea, then the cat got itself up on the trailer and the larc pulled the whole caboodle up on the beach. Then the larc came back out to sea and brought us on the *Chicken* ashore. I go into such detail because the operation bore out my Bass Strait axiom that *anything* connected with the sea takes five times as long as any sane person, reasoning *a priori*, would think possible. An additional complication in this case was that no-one was prepared to actually get their feet wet, understandable perhaps seeing that the sea temperature is below zero.

The wallow was quite remarkable and smelled disgusting, so much so that several times I had to stop to retch. Well up the beach and presumably on bedrock, the sea elephants have developed what I suppose architects would call an 'integrated structure' for themselves, no doubt over thousands of years. The sea elephants on Macquarie Island and Heard Island have *real*, muddy wallows, but this was quite different. Take an area about fifty yards square. Pour concrete over it to a height of four or five feet. Then impress into it, while still wet, the body shapes of fifteen or twenty young male sea elephants, weighing between one and two tons each. Leave to set.

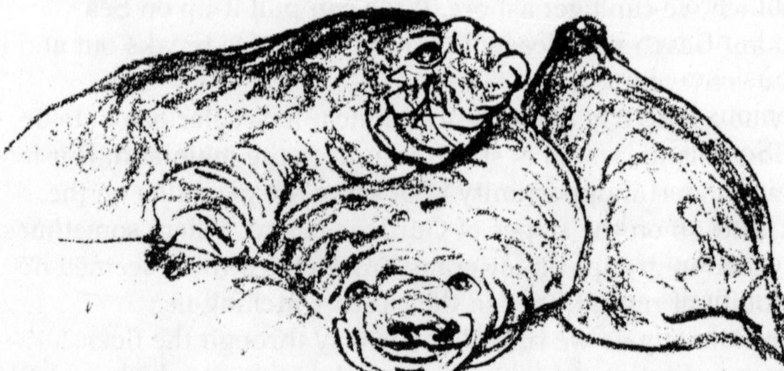

Of course it wasn't concrete, but it was a brown substance of the consistency of concrete, presumably the product of centuries of exhudations and rotting skin, bound together by shed hair. Lying in the hollows were the beasts, unmoving, watching warily with their great eyes. One or two of the more mature were more aggressive, rearing up with their trunk-like probosces engorged, roaring as they swung their heads to meet each new intruder, bright red mouths gaping to their widest extent.

The colony has a special interest. It is the southernmost occurrence of the elephant seals, in fact widely outside their classic habitats, the sub-Antarctic islands. The biggest population, of about 300,000, is on South Georgia, but Macquarie Island has about 100,000, and they are common also on Heard Island. Hunted until as recently as 1964 for their oil—though Australian exploitation finished in 1919—the world population, estimated at 600,000, is still recovering.

During the summer hundreds of immature male elephant seals haul out on the beaches near Davis, though the ones we saw are the only group at present here. Ron Lewis-Smith says that females sometimes appear also, to pup on the ice offshore, but that the cubs, so far south, invariably die.

On our way back from the wallows we passed by the *Nella Dan* and were waved aboard. I was anxious to see this famous ship, veteran of twenty-five Antarctic summers, and no less anxious to meet its famous skipper, Arne Sorensen. The marine science program manager for the Antarctic Division, Harvey Marchant, took us in hand and with tireless and voluble enthusiasm showed us his trawls, his tiny laboratories and the ingenious buoys which record currents on the seabed. Then we met Sorensen, inspected the bridge (a doll's house beside the *Icebird*'s), sat in the observation lounge above the bridge, where you must get a big-dipper ride in any kind of sea, and admired the cosy and traditional fittings of the ship: panelling, wooden bunks, brass gewgaws and the big saloon with its white tablecloths and murals by Hannelore Lauritzen. A "remarkable woman," we were told, one of the family that owns the *Nella*, head of the Danish branch of the World Wildlife Fund, accomplished artist, and actually occupying a suite on board on her first visit to the Antarctic, at the age of about seventy. I was sorry not to see her. And perhaps she might have given us a cup of tea, which no-one else thought of, though great was our need.

The day, though, was not yet over. The first thing we discovered on returning to the *Icebird* was that we were not, after all, going on to Mawson. 'Flexibility', a word now becoming a joke on board, has triumphed again. We are to transfer Mawson passengers to the *Nella* and return to Hobart. Hope deferred maketh the heart sick, and I felt I couldn't care less.

And, to end the day, the larcies' picnic, for which see below.

72

What is spoken of here as the 'A-factor' has defeated man's ambitions on this continent yet again, and the MS *Icebird*, on the second last voyage of this summer to our Antarctic bases, is now turning back.

Unseasonable fast ice, extending offshore at both Davis and Mawson, has frustrated all efforts to land the building materials and heavy plant we carry, and which we had hoped to be able to land in time for their utilisation in the last weeks of this year's intensive summer building programs.

At Davis this week we broke through, after a day's hard charging, to within one and a half kilometres of the shore, but for most purposes this may as well have been fifty. Fast ice here at this time of the year has not been experienced in Antarctic memory, and is ascribed to a marked cold spell last July, together with a colder summer than usual.

Whatever the reason the ice, instead of being rotten and easy to break through as we expected, proved to be nearly two metres thick and of a steely toughness which would have blunted our bow were it not already blunt and ice-strengthened. It was agonising to feel the ship's impact, 6000 tons at seven knots, and to find that within half a ship's length we had been forced to a halt. It all had a flavor of Moby Dick about it—in this case Captain Brune and the Great White Icesheet.

The problem is that, while passengers and light items of cargo can be unloaded by the one helicopter working here, in a virtually non-stop, twelve hours a day and more operation, we cannot use the rest of the unloading gear on board and on shore. We would normally be using larcs and barges. On earlier voyages this season it was possible to run the versatile Hagglund station vehicles across the fast ice to the ship's side, and to haul sledges back to the shore. But at this stage there is a forty-metre water gap along the shore line, which prevents access from the land to the ice. Nor are we certain that the ice does not have soft patches in it. So the promised land is tantalisingly beyond our reach. We do, however, have an umbilical cord—a pipeline laid by helicopter across the ice, through which we have pumped 350,000 litres of fuel ashore.

At Mawson, to which until today we were next destined, the position is worse, with twelve kilometres of fast ice offshore, although the ice in Horseshoe Harbor itself is breaking up. The *Icebird*'s ship's officers are confident they could break through, but Antarctic Division planners in Hobart have decided that the time involved in testing this proposition is not worth the risk to the successful completion of the *Icebird*'s next voyage, the last of the summer. So the possibility of an early winter freeze, and additionally the sobering effect of the besetment of the *Nella Dan* earlier this summer, have resulted in the decision to pull us back without proceeding to Mawson.

"I am naturally disappointed," says our voyage leader Graeme Manning. "Much of the plant and material we are carrying is needed urgently at Davis and Mawson, and the fact that we must now take it back to Hobart with us to deliver on the next voyage not only affects the completion of our current programs, but may present difficulties with the loading of cargo already being assembled in Hobart for that voyage." No voyage leader, Manning added, likes being defeated by A-factor. "But if you can't roll with the punch you have no place in Antarctica."

We have also had the almost unprecedented situation of having

Australia's two Antarctic vessels alongside each other in the same harbor. There is some rivalry between the ships, one Danish, one German, and the *Nella Dan* has a large sign displayed reading: WE ARE RED, WE ARE WHITE, WE ARE DANISH DYNAMITE. The *Icebird* ignores this impertinence from a ship which, battered after twenty-five Antarctic seasons, looks puny alongside the modern *Icebird*.

The *Nella* will sail tomorrow for Mawson with essential passengers transshipped from the *Icebird*, which it will put ashore at Mawson by helicopter, returning then to Australia and paying off for the season.

There have been ship-to-ship visits and the opportunity to inspect the scientific gear on the *Nella*, which has been trawling for marine specimens and has been retrieving three elaborate current-monitoring lines lowered to the seabed near here a year ago. One of these has been lost, probably owing to the failure of electronic release gear on the seabed. At $40,000 this is not something to delight the scientist or the taxpayer, but regarded as a normal attrition rate, to be accepted in Antarctic conditions.

The proximity of the *Nella Dan* last night inspired one of Antarctica's most bizarre parties which, with the sun still shining brightly and even warmly in the windless evening, was still going strong at midnight. The tightly knit army larc detachment, which services our work in Antarctica in a remarkable but little-heralded role, is normally split between the *Icebird* and the *Nella Dan*, and mates may be parted for as long as five months. But with both ships here cartons of Australian beer mysteriously appeared from some source, the larcs moored together in the open water beside the *Icebird*, and rugged-looking men in full Antarctic gear had an affectionate reunion.

There were some women as well, persuaded to climb down a swaying Jacob's ladder. Two electronically guided model speedboats appeared from the larcies' wanted-on-voyage gear, and for some hours these buzzed around the calm lake alongside, skilfully avoiding floating ice and zapping the penguins which were unconcernedly fishing nearby. Other Adélie penguins, electrified by the sight, stood on the edge of the ice-sheet, flapping their wings in amazement.

(*Australian*, 27 January 1986)

73

It was indeed a party, with rock music blaring out over the ice until the early hours of the morning. I was most flattered to be invited down by Doc Newman to join it. But the party had an unexpected sequel. Some time after I returned to Australia I had a phone call from the Department of Science. "We've had a hell of a time with the story of yours in the paper. Every animal protection group in Australia has written to the Minister, and also to the army, protesting at our sadistic treatment of Antarctic wildlife. What are we going to tell them?"

After I had finished laughing I thought about it. "Tell them that it all depends on the definition of the verb *to zap*. In this case it didn't mean that penguins were actually being hit on the head by model speedboats. It just meant that they were being annoyed as they went about their lawful concerns. In any case they are perfectly able to look after themselves."

The power of the press. I think the 'zapping' was the only point I made in any of my many despatches to the *Australian* that aroused any public comment.

74

Diary, at sea

A couple of hours out of Davis, homeward bound. This morning before we left was beautiful: snow gently falling, and with no gear working and no helicopter everything was laid under that Antarctic silence which many say is the true characteristic of the continent. "The silence roared in our ears," wrote Borchgrevink, "it was centuries of heaped-up solitude." A couple of cable-lengths away the lines of the *Nella* were fading as the snow settled on her. Only one disappointment: Doc Newman was persuaded to give up his attempt to get into the *Guinness Book of Records* with some polar barefoot waterskiing.

My heart is light. I suppose I shall never see Antarctica again, but I have seen it once, and there are many other things to do. Antarctica has certainly taught me a lot, sharpened up both cynicism and respect. I hope my mild cynicism hasn't earned me too many enemies back home, though. Someone in the Antarctic Division has complained about my saying that 30,000 bags of cement went ashore at Casey: it was said to be a gross exaggeration. Graeme Manning has checked the figures, and finds that it was between 40,000 and 50,000. I have also been criticised, I gather, for saying that we issue radio licences to Soviet stations on our territory. "Tell them," said Brendan, "that they ought to sharpen up their contacts with our communications people."

I'm irritated, though, that they don't see that I have been giving them tens of thousands of dollars worth of free and favorable publicity, and that, as regards criticisms, (a) most of my views are shared, indeed anticipated, by senior people in the Antarctic Division, and (b) that, even when they are not, and seem like digs, they are in the interests of the Division. Only the truth can make us free. Don't they see that, behind it all, I respect and believe in our commitments here? That is the real message of what I have been writing. But I'm buggered if I'll write publicity handouts for a government department.

John Stanhope came into the cabin, while I was writing the above, with a hair-raising story there hasn't been been too much said about. Seven went out the other evening in the *Chicken*, to tour the icebergs at Ewald's invitation. They broke every rule in the book by leaving no destination or route report, and no passenger list. They cruised far out among the bergs which I regarded with so much wonder as we came in to Davis. Ewald was steering adroitly among the floes when the unexpected, the unexpected that everyone tries to guard against in Antarctica, happened. Lying just under the surface, invisible, were the remains of a floe, in the last stages of dissolution but still a savage piece of ice. The *Chicken* rode up on it at just the wrong angle, and rolled over till the gunwales were level with the water. John, who was hanging desperately onto the side, said his face was virtually in the water. It was the end, said John. Another inch or so, and the *Chicken* would have filled and been on its way to the bottom. Ewald had no time to grab the mike and radio the ship. Even if they had managed to swim to and pull themselves up on a floe, they would have died within a few minutes. John said he is still badly shaken by the incident.

One 'jolly' I'm glad I wasn't on.

Axel the Funker (radio officer) told me today, when I tried to ring Deal Island for news of Nita and the family, that "Australia is engaged". The phrase sums up a lot of our national problems.

75

AT SEA

In Antarctica the smallest room is rarely that. The 'sanitary' huts are important foci of community release and communication. Expeditioners at various bases are proud of the idiosyncrasies of their own systems. Grizzled men in big boots, sitting around tables on the *Icebird* on its way home to Australia, beer bottles in their hands, wax sentimental about the dangers they have survived in a sitting position. Scientists suggest a comparison between the floor areas of the latrines on a station, and the floor areas of the laboratories. The laboratories win, but not by much.

By common agreement the traditional dunnies at Mawson, our oldest Antarctic base, are one of the glories of the continent. They have even been the subject of a serious contribution to Antarctic literature. At a 1962 international conference on Antarctic logistics, with the Russians burbling about the design of their polar vehicles, and the Americans pontificating on the construction of Antarctic airfields, the Australians are said to have presented a paper on the art of cold crappery. Or, specifically, about the Mawson thunder-boxes.

These are now off the secret list. Take a forty-four-gallon drum or, rather, take four of them, and sink them half-way into the ground. Put a concrete base around the exposed part of the drums. Insert a flue. Place kindling and briquettes inside. Urinate elsewhere. (This is a strict rule with all our Antarctic latrine devices—it accounts for the snow-free areas around the stations.) Sit. (But be careful—one expeditioner froze his penis to the steel drum. It was an hour before his friends heard his howls, and came running with warm water.)

Once a day pour a litre of aviation kerosene into the device. Then place a heavy steel plate, with an insert damper, over the drum, first removing the seat. Throw in a match and stand clear. Twenty-four hours later, sweep out the handfuls of dust and reload.

Phillip Law is said to have claimed responsibility for this technological triumph. The claim is disputed, but Law did later get an honorary doctorate from the University of Melbourne. And the Mawson bog is certainly known as the Law Hut. But this may be due to Antarctic irreverence. In any case, as well as the great Law Dome on the icecap, there are also four Law thrones.

Two of the thunderboxes remain in use at all times, while two are burning off. The user has the illusion of squatting amid volcanic fumaroles, which is comforting for the geomorphologists. Sometimes the analogy goes too far. On one occasion, when the drums were in use, petrol was accidentally poured into a replete drum instead of kerosene. The explosion sent the fifty-pound capping plate through the roof of the hut. In any case the hut catches fire every few years, thus giving an opportunity to test the station's disaster plans.

Loyal Davisites, however, denigrate the Mawson system and think their own a great step forward for mankind. The inventor is unrecorded. As you enter the Davis hut you see over the door the sign INCINERATOR BUILDING, a sign that properly belongs elsewhere but which is perfectly appropriate. As at Mawson, there is an ominous smell of hot metal in the air. Four cubicles confront the visitor, who has already been warned to choose a cool one. On lifting the seat a second flap, at what would normally be water level, also rises. Below are burning ashes. Having read the stimulating literature to hand one rises, closing the seat. Gas jets now ignite automatically and burn for fifteen minutes. Once a day the residues are vacuumed out.

It's ingenious and, as an expeditioner says, "nice on a cold morning". But, as a system, it is also not without its perils. A station electrician, fixing a faulty connection, failed to notice that a client was about to depart. The free gas in the hut ignited, and the electrician went through the side of the building. Antarctica hath ten thousand doors for men to take their exits.

By contrast to Mawson and Davis, Casey is a disappointment. Normal flush toilets have now been installed to replace the older chemical toilets, which figure in Antarctic mythology because of the number of sets of false teeth lost down them after parties. The new toilets are remarkable only because the discharge pipes have to be electrically heated to make the outflow to a biological filter possible. The outfall is an area to be avoided when the summer thaws set in.

Expeditioners returning to Hobart on the *Icebird* then have a new shithouse system to adapt to, a system I've already written about but which has not improved as the voyage has continued. One of the ship's engineers, fed up with the whole business, has rechristened the ship the MS *Scheissbird*, and is washing his hands of it and of us when we get to Tasmania.

76

Diary, 26 January 1986

Four p.m., and tremendous singing, and the sounds of a bush band, from down in the bar. I don't want to sound sanctimonious—though of course I do when I write this—but for most people on board there are only two ways of passing the time: getting pissed or, if the bar is closed or inclinations otherwise, sitting in the mess in semi-darkness watching a video for what is now the second or third time around. This afternoon is *Dimboola* again. Some, it is true, spend a lot of time sleeping. Russel Madigan has a neat little compact disc player and some classical music.

I've spent my adult life fairly closely involved with Australian literature and Australian history. I expect a reasonable proportion of my fellow Australians to be interested in the same topics also. Partly this is for the poor reason that I am interested and think they should be, but partly it's because in any case I think they should know something about their own country. I realise of course that Australia is just an existential way of life for most Australians, which is no doubt largely because the schools and universities have ignored it, but there are I suppose about eighty or ninety Australians on board, and I have been interested in observing over these weeks how many appear to share my interests.

The total score is that Jonathan Chester's brother subscribes to *Overland*, the limnologist Ian Bayly from Monash once wrote us an article on Lake Pedder, and we once published a poem of Bob Beale's. Someone on board today finished *Power Without Glory*, and Peter Gormly has read the recent Buzo novel and doesn't think much of it. And no doubt I'm being quite unjust to the many on board who read a lot in their own time and own way—Gormly, for instance, takes the London *Sunday Times* and, he tells me, buys a lot of books. Others are, judging by the noise from below, interested in such areas as bush music.

The Australian passengers on the *Icebird* are, I reckon, a fairly representative cross-section of Australian society, working class to upper-middle. (The skew from the norm would be that everyone here has some kind of a skill.) Not many seem to me to have 'intellectual' interests; perhaps I was lucky to get the score I did from my little survey, and shouldn't have expected more. In any case it is a snobbish preoccupation to have; it smells of Pride. Yet I feel that matters would have been different on an Italian, Russian or German ship.

Good-heartedness, I argue with myself, is in any case far more important than 'intellectual' interests. Here the Australians on board score high. So far as I can see they are, to a person, shrewd and decent people. I'm sometimes surprised how apposite and sophisticated their generalisations on Antarctica are. The rank and file remind me often of my own students, the mature-age tech college teachers and the like from the western suburbs of Melbourne who come into my evening classes tired after work: they know little about Oz history and nothing about Oz literature and many, if they read the newspapers at all, merely flick through them in the staffrooms: but they are competent, anxious to learn and understand once they are sure they are not going to be bullied or patronised, respectful of ideas when placed before them. It takes them some time, however, to accept the fact that I respect and admire *them*, and see them as teachers as well as learners.

There's plenty of room for misunderstandings, though. Over a meal in the mess, the conversation inevitably about the cock-ups, and probably concerning nothing more sinister than the water problems on board, I remarked as a matter of course that Australians were a lot of gutless wonders who whinged away with their mates but never confronted authority to demand redress. Days later I learned from some helpful spy that the remark, overheard, had caused deep offence to the 'element' on board—who had borne out the remark by whingeing about it but not asking me what I meant. Later on, when I had the chance, I did develop my theme, and I think I was forgiven. But it was another indication of the sensitivities on board, that the readiness to 'type' others ran both ways. Perhaps, as George Orwell once suggested, the 'class' divisions are mutually satisfactory to both parties.

It is certainly possible to have the most delightful and interesting discussions on board, some of the best I have ever had. Over mutton dinner tonight I had the fortune to sit with a witty group able to disagree with me and with each other with humor, passion and mutual enjoyment: Alistair Urie, who works in upper atmosphere physics; Brendan Doran; Ian Bayly; Lee Ranford; Greg Hodge; Peter Kerr and one or two others. You wouldn't find anything like it in the staff club at the University of Melbourne.

I sounded off at breakfast today to Graeme Manning, Peter Kerr of DHC—with whom I share a certain brand of cynical humor; he's always fun to talk to—and others about the cultural desert our bases present. "No books, no collections of Antarctic experiences, no station magazines come out of our bases. These products used to be a staple of polar expeditions. Think of the delight, later on, to those who wrote them. Think of the Antarctic Division's encouraging the publication of periodic anthologies of Antarctic writing from the bases. We don't have these things because our educational system has brought us to a point where there is no-one capable of writing down what they think or experience any more. And if they did there are few who would or could read it."

I'm often grumpy at breakfast, and my friends don't take me too seriously. But to my surprise Paul Butler, the 1985 Davis oic who was eating with us, quietly said: "You're quite right."

LATER

It has been an eventful afternoon. First, we had a patriotic social function on the rear deck. I sent off a message to the *Australian* about it:

> Surely Australia's most unusual national day barbecue has just been held on board this ship in a driving north-west snowstorm and sub-zero temperatures. We are in a latitude just north of the Antarctic Circle, and in a longitude which runs through Bombay.
>
> Steak and sausages were cooked on the open poop deck of this Antarctic vessel, and gnawed in shivering jaws by expeditioners in full polar rig. Australian tomato sauce, a rarity on this ship and frozen solid inside the bottles, was also produced. Cape pigeons fluttered in our wake, and through gaps in the blizzard icebergs could be glimpsed.
>
> Among remarks overheard at the party were "Watch out for the blowies" and "Good weather for the farmers". Less barbed observations included, from a government architect on board, "Thank God there are no flowering gums—I left Australia to get away from the hay fever," and from Sir Russel Madigan, at sixty-five the Father of the Ship, "It's good to be reminded of home." Snow lay deep on his shoulders.
>
> Sir Russel was inspired, not only by the Australian beer and champagne freely circulating, but also by the eucalyptus scent of the fire, on which someone had thrown pellets of "Australian Bush Incense" strong enough to reach our nostrils and flavor the meat before it was blown away in the snow to the continent below us.
>
> There were no late stayers.

I was up on the bridge, having fed this message via Inmarsat into the *Australian*'s computer in Sydney, when Graeme Manning came out of the radio room looking troubled. The fast ice at Davis, through which we had carved a channel before we left for home, has broken right out. What on earth were we to do? On the one hand here we were 250 miles north of Antarctica, with a complement amongst others of winterers from 1985 who have spent fifteen months away from their families, and many of whom hope never to see the continent again. On the other hand we still have a shipful of essential cargo for Davis.

Alistair is very much in favor of turning back, and says it will be impossible to get all Voyage 7 cargo on board next trip if we don't. This was discussed at length with the logistics officer in Hobart, Geoff, who rejected it. (Ewald: "Quick, make up your minds. It's costing you $5000 an hour in ship's time to talk it over." What Ewald means is that the *Icebird* is going to be off charter before this summer's work is over, and will then be on an hourly rate, a rate which, so far as I can gather, is more like $1300 than $5000.) After four hours' discussion the helm was put over and we headed south again.

In recent weeks the first few major changes of plan were accepted by those on board. There was recognition of the difficulty of Graeme's job as voyage leader, even if we did laugh at the increasing use of the word 'flexibility'. Later, with more changes of plan, came resignation. Now there is real anger. Morale is low. Several experienced people have said they will now never return to Antarctica. The matter has been made worse by a highly specific telex from Jim Bleasel, posted on the ship's noticeboard two days ago in response to unrest on board, pointing out in six numbered paragraphs the imperative reasons for the return of the *Icebird* to Hobart forthwith.

And now so many post-mortems! Why, people ask, for instance, when we started breaking out the ice at Davis as soon as we arrived, did we not finish the job then, instead of abandoning it until the last day? The normal chore, people say, is to break out ice first and unload later. Was this a mistake? If so, the cost was high: perhaps a week's time lost, morale dissipated, salaries wasted.

Some of the ship's officers go further than this. They claim that they're the ones who know more about working the ship in the ice than anyone else, and the ones with the real incentive to ensure that the ship is not placed in a dangerous situation, yet their advice is never asked. If they *were* asked they would tell the Antarctic Division to turn the first voyages of the year, the ice-edge voyages which simply transfer personnel and mail ashore by helicopter, into proper cargo-landing voyages. "We could get the cargo ashore on sledges, if ANARE had the right equipment, and take it right up to where it has to go, without double handling. In fact we did a bit of that this year, and the ANARE people were amazed how rapidly we unloaded. That would be the way to do it." But others say that the sea-ice, even early in the season, is not reliable enough to be able to count on doing this. Others, again, deny the right of the *Icebird* officers to be consulted or to be informed at all: "We employ them as ferry-drivers. The less they know about the details the less they can exploit circumstances in their own interests." The only way out of this kind of mess is to own a ship ourselves, or to lease one rather than charter one. This will probably never happen.

Graeme seems rattled by the flak he's getting. I've had a growing feeling of sympathy with him on this voyage, with his special passengers each wanting something different from the voyage, with the unprecedented ice conditions, with the unpleasantness at Casey. Pressures coming at him three ways—from the bases, from his passengers, from Hobart. He's the meat in the sandwich all right. On top of that he was also voyage leader on the previous voyage, simply turning round in Hobart and coming south again, which would place an unfair strain on men less sensitive than Graeme.

Anyway, he's made it clear over the bing-bong that the decision to return to Davis was not his. For all that I think it is the right decision, taking all the many factors in the equation into account. For me it's more experience of the A-factor, and I have plenty of good books, including Phyllis Rose's splendid discussion of Victorian marriages, *Parallel Lives*. But it has created havoc on board.

77

I am reminded of the story of the clergyman who prayed, only too successfully, for rain: "We thank Thee, O Lord, but this is ridiculous." The MS *Icebird*, already 250 nautical miles homeward to Hobart on the last leg of this extended Antarctic voyage, and after one decision not to turn back to Davis had already been made, finally changed course 180 degrees at 5.30 yesterday evening. We shall arrive back in Davis, which we left two days ago, in two hours time.

The fast ice in Davis harbor, part of which we broke out by assault before we left, has now—Davis base informs us—completely disappeared to sea. We can now unload by barge and land the 90 per cent of Davis plant and stores we could not get ashore during last week's stay.

So far as I am competent to judge, trying to master the vast range of variables the planners in Hobart have to take into account in such matters as this, the decision to turn back is justified. However, its effects on board have been unfortunate, coming as it does on top of numerous changes of plan announced over the ship's PA system in the past couple of weeks, sometimes following and contradicting one another within hours.

It may be unjust, but to many these "in again, out again, Finnegan" moves are demoralising. Antarctic morale is an important component of the overall logistics picture which, it seems to me, does not always receive the priority in planning which it should. The pool of applicants for Antarctic postings is said to be diminishing year by year. Inflexible public service rules play some part in this: for instance, the most important person on all bases, by common consent of all expeditioners, is the cook—who also happens to be the worst paid. [Salaries offered in 1987 at top of range included chefs ($39,500), diesel mechanics ($48,400), scientists ($48,800), carpenters $39,700), officers-in-charge ($55,200) and medical practitioners ($69,300). These salaries are taxable.] Certainly the belief in being 'mucked about' by people not on the spot is widespread. As change of plan has followed change of plan on this voyage some attempts have been made to post official explanations, but when actions subsequently contradict these explanations, cynicism mounts.

I have even received what may be called a 'deputation to the press' on this matter from some on board, representing in particular those winter expeditioners who have already spent fifteen months in Antarctica, who are regarded as the core of our commitment here, and who are bitterly resentful at turning back from the hoped-for reunion with their families.

More humorous expressions of dissent include the renaming of this ship the HMS *Meander*, and a posting on the noticeboard of the destination odds: "Davis, evens. Hobart, 400/1. Mawson, 2/1. Perth, evens. Molodezhnaya, 3/2. Capetown, evens. Cocos Islands, 100/1."

These matters may be thought trivial, but they do highlight some real problems. The first of these is communications. As work is the ruin of the drinking classes, so communications can be thought of as a major problem in Antarctica. They say that the communications room in the Antarctic Division headquarters in Hobart handles some million words a month. The radio room at our base in Casey, which is the transmission point for all messages from Australian bases here, as well as for some French and Soviet messages, would not disgrace Cape Canaveral.

As every ambassador knows, communications have undercut traditional diplomacy. Similarly, there is no doubt that modern communications have cut back the authority and responsibility of all in the field down here, including the authority and responsibility of the voyage leader on such missions as ours, who is now reduced to relatively trivial 'on-ship' decision-making. The cost of the Inmarsat phonecalls to and from decision-making points in Australia must, on this ship and on this voyage alone, have run into many tens of thousands of dollars. It is as though Captain Scott had to phone the Admiralty in London before he could send a dog-team to lay a depot. In short, communications, as they have developed in Antarctica, can clog the decision-making process as well as advance it. In a recent book, *The Mask of Command*, the military historian John Keegan points out that modern communications create the dangerous illusion for distant strategists that they have the direct vision of battlefield tacticians, thus tempting them to act as though they had the insights of the tacticians.

Communications also affect morale in other ways. The volume of official traffic from our bases places messages from expeditioners to their families well down the priority line. Few can afford direct phone calls by satellite, which cost over $16 a minute, or even by radio phone—a tedious process involving booking a day ahead and standing in a queue—at $2.50 a minute. Telex messages, though free, are rationed. In any case they sometimes meet with serious delays—three weeks has been mentioned—in onward transmission from Hobart to the home destination. These issues are a major gripe among those who live on our stations.

The 'A-factor' I have often mentioned, the so-called 'Antarctic factor', is accepted with good humor by all in Antarctica as a major factor in the 'ganging aglie' of human aspirations here. And there is no doubt that this has been a particularly difficult summer for the Antarctic Division, starting with the seven-week besetment of the *Nella Dan*, which has necessitated major logistical reallocations. Those of us who are observers on this Voyage 6 are profoundly grateful for the courtesies and opportunities presented to us in difficult circumstances.

At the same time the best way we can say "Thank you" is by offering our honest opinions, based on fair evidence. I think marvels have been performed by immensely dedicated men and women on this voyage. I am very proud of our Antarctic operations. I realise the difficulties. I know that truth in this region, no less extreme in opinion and counter-opinion than in climate, is hard to come by. But one truth I *can* identify is that the impression created, however misleading this may be, is of indecision and—as one foreign observer has put it—of "whimsicality". I am also sorry to report the remark of another, vastly experienced in Antarctic logistics and in working with Australians: "Australians are good at many things, but they are not good at this."

'Flexibility' has become a much-mocked word in Australian Antarctica at the moment. To restore its true meaning we have to consider the issues I have raised in previous despatches. We need to reduce the emphasis on lines of communication, and we need also to transfer more operational responsibility to our forward bases and our ships. Individuals will respond to being invested with a real dignity of function.

(*Australian*, 28 January 1986)

In Antarctica, incidentally, telex messages from loved ones are called *wyssas*, pronounced *whizzers*. Messages may be sent in code to save transmission time, and WYSSA is code for *All my (our) love darling*. So—"Did you get a wyssa today?". Another word to have passed into the Antarctic language from the code book is YIKLA, *This is the life!* Returning expeditioners have been heard to exclaim "*yikla p. a.*", a well understood phrase meaning *this is the life, pig's arse*.

78

Diary, Davis, 28 January 1986

We got back to Davis about midday yesterday. It was strange to see the harbor free of ice, and the barges were working almost before the ship anchored. Vast quantities of cargo have now gone ashore, the whole new operations building for a start. Although I'm used to seeing the oddities that go ashore—again, very like Erith Island—I *was* surprised to see bargeload after bargeload of large concrete U-drains, and had to remind myself that almost everything is now prefabricated for Antarctica. Better, in any case, than making them on the spot and having clouds of cement dust flying about.

I decided to keep out of the way, and spent a profitable day on the bridge, reading Lyall Watson's marvellous book *Whales of the World*, full of fascinating 'incidentals': the dolphin calf which, when a man puffed smoke against an underwater window, went and got a mouthful of mother's milk and puffed back; the way dolphins can determine the sex of men and women in the water; the fact that killer whales never attack humans, even when the humans are in seal-like wetsuits. I wish I had known this when the pod of killer whales swam into our cove on Erith Island a few years back.

And I had a very profitable time talking to Wayne, back from traverse at Casey, who gave me the 'view from below', so to speak, of what happened at Casey during this last year, not excusing the collapse of control at the station, but certainly telling me detailed stories which made it more plausible. And last night, over what is nearly the last of my Black Label, several hours with a couple of my cronies on this ship discussing the lessons to be learnt from our experiences.

Today a very useful day ashore. A delightful morning in the sun, perfectly comfortable in cords and a jumper. A most pleasant lunch in the living quarters with Rob Easther, a man I should like to stay in touch with. A talk to Gillian Deakin about the base library, which she is in charge of. We were rather at cross purposes, in fact. I was very critical of the library, as I was of the library at Casey, though at least Casey had some books on Antarctica. (To be fair, books on Antarctica tend to be stolen, and such valuable ones as remain on the bases, Mawson's *The Home of the Blizzard*, for instance, are kept under lock and key.) The Davis library mainly consists of paperbacks discarded by previous expeditioners. It would seem to me to be the simplest thing in the world for the Antarctic Division to ask a small committee of qualified people to nominate, say, the ten best Australian novels of the year, the ten best Australian non-fiction books, and the ten most suitable overseas books, sets of each to be sent to our four permanent bases. But this would entail attention to the People Principle I have talked about. There is no regular or substantial subsidy, books arrive from the Antarctic Division on a hit-or-miss basis and, above all, there is no basic library of Antarcticana, locked up or not, on any station. Australian mindlessness in action.

Gillian was defensive, and kept insisting on the right of people to read what they wanted to read at the same time as she emphasised the wide literary tastes to be met with among expeditioners. I couldn't make her see that I believed in both. No

doubt she already saw me, though she's only been here a few months herself, as an interfering outsider. Fair enough, I suppose, but I'd been asked to look at the 'cultural' facilities on the bases, and I still think the libraries a disgrace. Odd to think of the amount of money spent on the buildings, and the contemptuous attitude to the cultural artefacts within them.

There's more to all this than meets the eye. I shall write a special piece on it later.

The article I wrote when the ship turned about has appeared in the *Australian* and has caused something of a stir. Jim Bleasel was asked to appear on television, and rang Graeme Manning in some dudgeon. Graeme says he told Jim that he thought the article was a fair and balanced one; and I must say that Graeme, who has read all my press articles before transmission, has never once raised any other objection than a factual one. There wouldn't be many in his position of whom one could say as much. One result of this was that Bob Beale and I were called in for a briefing on the logic and the success of the most recent changes. As far as I am concerned this was never in question. One thing is certain: the more unpopular I am in Kingston, the more popular I am in the Antarctic. I have had a number of congratulations on the ship and at the base, and a number of requests for copies of what I wrote.

I rang Deal Island as soon as I got back on the ship. Nita and Joanna and the party arrived back at Port Albert a couple of hours ago: a fair trip, a bit 'jobbly' I gather, improving as they got in towards the coast. I've missed four weeks of happiness and incident on Erith Island with my family. And the trade-off, this trip? Many would think me mad even to consider the matter, but it hasn't been a bargain that's gone all my way. There have been many moments of interest; I've learnt a lot; it's been amusing to have the temporary powers of a journo; there's been a lot of boredom and near-boredom, and not enough of the happiness that can come to those on Erith: waves of contentment and delight simply in being who you are, being where you are and doing what you're doing, from sharing the lives of those you love. No, it hasn't been all one way. But Nita, Jo and Ray, from what I hear, are full of the flush of Erith sea, air and sky.

8 p.m.
We have passed through the icebergs of Davis for the fourth time, now truly homeward bound, we hope, and I blush to say that even that stupendous spectacle now rates hardly a glance. I'm a little depressed. Brendan says it's because we're leaving Antarctica. Perhaps, but I suspect a number of reasons, one being the contrast between the untouched world here and the unthinking motives behind our presence. Antarctica is too nice a place to have people in it.

Yet such is perversity and the spirit of aggression in man that it pleased me to see the great girders and culverts and crates going ashore over this last day or so, and to see them, after years of meticulous design and fabrication and test-erection being fitted into place by decent, likeable fellows, happily working within the great concrete footings of the new operations building, and cheered to think they may have the building up by the time, in four weeks, they are lifted out.

Nor has Phyllis Rose's *Parallel Lives* helped. In its examination of the lives of the illustrious of a century ago, the book suggests something sinister in the strategies of marriage and family. So, does the consciousness I have of achievements here—including my own achievement, whatever that may be—hide the dishonesties and exploitations, predominantly male, so common in those Victorian marriages?

Axel the Funker, the man who finds a problem in everything and who is certainly the most humorless character on board, has astonished everyone by making a joke. He has announced on the bing bong that a message has just been received directing us to Heard Island.

79

Every month our Antarctic stations exchange newsletters by teleprinter. Those from Mawson and Macquarie Island have just been posted. Here are extracts.

Mawson.

MAWSON

January's newsletter is brought to you by your friendly met department, where irrelevant information is available at any hour and accurate forecasts are almost as common as polar bears in the Simpson Desert.

The New Year began with a field party to the North Masson Ranges. The magnificent scenery around Fearn Peak was not lost on the group, who spent the first day of 1986 climbing various peaks.

Back at Mawson New Year's Eve began with a banquet and a pig on a spit, prepared by our chef Bernie Sorenson and his team. This was followed by a fancy-dress party in the club. [Oic Jim Hasick went as a gangster, and other costumes included pirates, a designer garbage bag and a 'beetle in drag'.]

From the met standpoint operations have certainly been much safer and easier, thanks to the efforts of those who helped in moving the helicopter to a new location. Thanks chaps.

At cosray [the cosmic radiation laboratory] Jim Cooper and Jim Milne have been busy replacing the cosray telescope.

In the bar one night some people, whom I shall not embarrass by naming, namely Garry Anderson, Ross Weeks and Harry

Hudson, under the guidance of medic Kevin Donovan, were seen to be conducting complicated experiments in co-ordination, such as patting their heads with one hand and rubbing their tummies with the other. Seems the field of medical research knows no bounds.

January was a bit of a rest month for the huskies. Apart from one trip of several days to Rumdoodle, and a few short trips behind the station, the boys have been able to relax. Christmas Eve saw the birth of three new pups. After some imaginative suggestions they were named Gunner, Sam and Choofer. It won't be long before they're running around the station, playing 'steal the expeditioners' hats and gloves' like pups always do. Meanwhile our previous litter, dubbed "the ratpack", have gone on the line, and are always overjoyed to get off for a walk. With the first boat (almost) in the harbor, there will be no shortage of visitors to keep them well catered for in the patting and playing department.

Field training continued in earnest during the month to make the most of Warwick Williams' remaining few weeks at Mawson. One trip with a difference, which included oic Jim Hasick, chef Bernie Sorenson, Dave Gillies, carpenter Jim Milne and diesel mechanic Brian Baxter, set off for the central Massons on the polar plateau with all the usual tents and safety gear, plus a portable gas

barbie and ample supplies of steaks and sausages. Also a portable generator to recharge Bernie's video batteries. Unfortunately a huge snow storm compelled the intrepids to cook inside their polar pyramid tents. However, Bernie got some excellent video film.

Amongst other field trips a party dropped off supplies for the dog trippers at Rumdoodle, on the way to North Massons. This group also built an igloo and renovated a snow cave.

A Russian plane flying over Mawson at 2.30 a.m. on the 14th caused a few revellers in the Mawson Club to look twice. During the next few days arguments for and against believing the story were heated. A subsequent enquiry to Molodezhnaya confirmed that it was flying to Beaver Lake, about 400 km inland from Mawson, where the Russians have fifty summer expeditioners doing work on a geological and geophysical survey.

Cold fronts have abounded this summer and strong winds with below average temperatures have kept the ice in the harbor much longer than normal. A low temperature of −9° was recorded on the 29th, equal to the lowest on record for January.

A book has been made on the first ship into Horseshoe Harbor:

4/6	*Icebird* (scratched)
2/1	*Nella Dan* (followed by *Shirase*)
15/1	*Australia II*
150/1	*Titanic*
250/1	*General Belgrano*
500/1	Davis Hagglund.

[A couple of hidden cracks there. The *Shirase* of course was the Japanese ice-breaker that went to the rescue of the *Nella Dan*. The "Davis Hagglund" was the vehicle the Davis people put through the ice.]

MACQUARIE ISLAND

After our busy first month on the island establishing ourselves we let off a bit of steam in January with outdoor work and quite a few field trips. The *Southern Quest* arrived here on New Year's Eve but, because of high winds and heavy seas, we couldn't welcome them ashore until the next morning. It was very sad to hear of the loss of the *Southern Quest* shortly after she left us, but fortunately we learnt that all escaped without harm.

The usual habit of giving nicknames has begun in earnest. "The Boss" is of course the oic, Bob Lachal, who also likes to be referred to as "The Man". He is usually found around the station with boots, stetson and whip in hand, encouraging us to take part in station work duties every Saturday on his plantation. "The Man" takes his name from Roy Orbison's song "Working for the Man" which he is frequently heard to hum as he cracks the whip over our shoulders.

We have seen people such as Dion, Dusty (Dale), Rosco (Ross), the Pom (Bruce) and Radio Rob (Thomas) beaten into submission over such tasks as stripping and painting the field store and the plumber's workshop, enclosing the new Inmarsat antenna behind a log fence, erecting a new log fence around the western side of the station and installing a new stove in the kitchen.

The met team is 40 per cent of the station's population and spend much of their time occupied with their gases and rubber balloons. Whenever they are asked for daily weather reports they tell us the usual: "Strong winds and rains, with scattered hail, snow and sunshine."

Megan and Lightning (Trevor) are perpetually soggy due to their exploits in the briny depths investigating the sexual life of seaweed, which you can now include in the list of things that children should not be exposed to. While we are kicking scientists let's not forget Pythagoras (Michael) who, despite his photographic output, still manages to do whatever he does with aurorae and the ionosphere at night-time, and Dave, who is on first-name terms with all those electrons and pi-particles that the rest of us take for granted whenever we turn on a tape cassette or a switch.

The dam and the station tank have both been drained and cleaned, and both have refilled to overflowing. Roofs have been put onto two of the old buildings, the surgery and the Garden Cove dongas. The northern giant petrel banding program has almost been completed, and the sooty albatrosses are almost completely banded.

Many island trips have been undertaken, combining work and

pleasure. Huts have been checked for their electrical status, recladding or rebuilding, and to check the food stores. It has been an enjoyable and exciting month.

80

Diary, 29 January 1986

Well, I'm to be a grandfather. Nita told me when I rang her this morning. I wasn't expecting the news, and soon spread it round the ship—after sending congratulations to Cleeve and Michael, tacked on to the end of a despatch to the *Australian*, asking Piers Akerman there to pass it on.

We are heading due north, rather than on our proper course to Hobart, which would be north-east, in order to get out of the iceberg region as soon as possible, in view of the lengthening nights. One disappointment, though, is that the almost-twenty-four-hour days have prevented our seeing any auroras, though a rare phenomenon called a 'solar pillar' did manifest itself the other night. Our course will also enable us to escape the easterly Antarctic current and weather and to replace them with westerlies, which will blow us home.

Despite Antarctic conditions and amateur labor, our cargo was unloaded at Casey and Davis in 46 per cent of the time it took to load it in Hobart. I'm not sure how significant this statistic is. In Bass Strait, at least, unloading is always easier, for there's no worry about stowage.

81

Diary, 30 January 1986

Well, we got what we wanted and we're out now into the real Southern Ocean. There was little sleep for anyone on board last night. The cabin floor is strewn with books, papers, pens, bottles. They stay there because it is just too hard to pick them up and stow them, and if we did they would soon be back. Lee Ranford has just put his head in the door to say the ship's rolling 28° each way. The last couple must have been more than that.

At the moment it's even worse than usual, because we're turning in circles. It's Axel the Funker adjusting his aerials. Owing to the position of the satellite, and the rolling of the ship, he tells me it's impossible to transmit messages.

All the same, I've been trying to get through to Rod Ledingham, at the Bunger Hills summer station, now christened Edgeworth-David. The largest ice-free area in Antarctica, they were first sighted by members of Mawson's expedition in 1912, and first visited when a Lieutenant Commander Bunger of the U.S. Navy landed a seaplane on one of the lakes in 1947. After a lot of trouble with non-satellite radio I managed to have a talk to Rod and get a message written for the paper.

82

The newest Australian Antarctic base, Edgeworth-David, has been successfully set up in the Bunger Hills area, 230 nautical miles west of the existing base of Casey, and is in full and effective operation.

I was informed of this today by Rod Ledingham, of Hobart, who is officer-in-charge at Edgeworth-David, and was formerly in charge of the Macquarie Island station. Ledingham's wife, Jeanette, is the doctor at Edgeworth-David.

I spoke to Ledingham from the MS *Icebird*, 600 miles off the Antarctic coast on its return journey to Hobart. The Edgeworth-David party of twenty-two landed from the *Nella Dan* a fortnight ago. As the Bunger Hills area is screened by the Shackleton Ice Shelf, extending some forty kilometres offshore, the party were flown in to the site chosen for the new station by three helicopters.

They took with them their own accommodation, slung under the helicopters, three prefabricated 'apple' huts and two 'melon' huts. (The 'apples' look like apples and are designed and built in Tasmania. 'Melons' are extended 'apples'.)

One 'apple', specially fitted to be the darkroom for the extended photo-mapping program of the Bunger Hills area, which is now almost completed, was dropped by accident from the helicopter onto a glacier, from a height of 1300 feet. It is no longer dark. The Antarctic Division people say that it "failed the drop test."

The Bunger Hills, of some 900 square kilometres, comprise one of the remarkable ice-free areas which make up about three per cent of the Antarctic continent, and which excite scientists because their secrets are accessible and not secluded under a couple of kilometres of ice. These areas, "dry valleys" as they used to be called, were first investigated by the Australian Griffith Taylor in the Ross Sea area during Scott's expedition of 1911–12, and first written of at length in his book *The Silver Lining*, one of the rarest and most interesting items of Antarcticana. There are several ice-free areas in Australian Antarctic Territory, the best known of which is the Vestfold Hills area around Davis.

Rod Ledingham reports that his base is established in a valley forty nautical miles inland, fifty metres one way from the shore of an inland sea, fifty metres the other way from a lake. This lake will be among a number the biologists in the party will be investigating. Great interest has been aroused by the recent discovery of one of the world's most unusual organisms, apparently capable of living without oxygen, in lakes in the Vestfold Hills.

Three field parties have been deployed from Edgeworth-David, the furthest being twenty nautical miles inland. During this first summer the concentration is on broad scientific survey work, which will enable more detailed studies to be carried out in subsequent years. The teams include geologists from the Bureau of Mineral Resources and the Universities of Melbourne and Adelaide, biologists from the University of New England and geomorphologists—who have the special task of looking closely at the ice/land margin—from Macquarie University and the University of Tasmania. There are also specialists from National Mapping.

The Edgeworth-David party will return on the *Icebird* early in March.

The former Soviet base of Oasis, later the Polish base of Dobrowolski, is nearby, in good order and was complete even to a bottle of vodka left on the table when an Australian party visited the base last year. (We left a bottle of whisky in return.) The Antarctic Division decided not to use the former Soviet/Polish base, although the Antarctic Treaty approves such transfers, and on principle to establish a new Australian base.

This is because Edgeworth-David will be the model for a new—or, rather, a revived—concept of Australian Antarctic operations. The lively new director of the Antarctic Division of the Department of Science, Jim Bleasel, who spoke to me about these matters before I came south, is firm in his determination to break away from the vicious circle of heavy investment in our all-too-fixed assets in Antarctica—the position where we build stations to support scientific work which end up in administration and maintenance so costly that the ratio of scientists to support staff can be as low as one to ten, or less.

"We don't need the best of everything," Bleasel has said, and he has pinned his strategy of Antarctic deployment on these light-weight, cost-effective summer stations, where there will be some twenty scientists to five support staff, which will stay in operation as long as they are needed, but which may be abandoned without concern. Nevertheless some, such as the proposed new summer station at Commonwealth Bay in the eastern sector of Australian Antarctic Territory—where, to our chagrin, there is the Soviet base of Leningradskaya but no Australian base—may eventually become permanent. During this voyage we surveyed a site for such a station near Sir Douglas Mawson's old base.

Other summer stations are planned for Heard Island, Enderby Land (near our western border), the Prince Charles Mountains near Mawson, the icecap on the way from Casey to the inland Soviet base of Vostok, and Larsemann Hills, eighty nautical miles west of Davis, which is also an ice-free area.

It is a spirited and promising development. It will certainly inject new morale into Australian expeditioning, and new achievement into our scientific work down here.

If Edgeworth-David shows the way, as indications are that it will, it will be a fitting tribute to a great Australian scientist.

Edgeworth David apologised when he had to call Mawson out of a tent to pull him from a crevasse. No apologies are needed for the base which carries Edgeworth David's name.

(*Australian*, 3 February 1986)

83

POSTSCRIPT

In the summer of 1986–87 attempts to reactivate Edgeworth-David were frustrated by the besetment of the *Nella Dan*. Summer stations were, however, instituted at Commonwealth Bay, Heard Island and Law (Larsemann Hills).

For the 1987–88 summer it is planned to extend the station at Commonwealth Bay, and again to occupy Law and Heard Island. In addition a series of small field camps will operate between Davis and the Amery ice-shelf, some 200 kilometres to the west, into which runs the Lambert glacier, the world's largest.

For the moment it is impossible to reoccupy the Edgeworth-David station. A grounded iceberg, 100 kilometres by fifty kilometres, lies off the Shackleton Ice Shelf and effectively precludes the approach of any ship by holding fast the sea-ice. It is under continuous observation by satellite.

84

Diary, 1 February 1986

Feeling unwell, with a bad cold, sure to develop into bronchitis. Spending half the days being tossed about on my bunk. Fed up with the ship, and in particular with the communications problems. Sometimes a day's struggle against human and physical factors to get a story through to Sydney, by which time I've missed the deadline.

Still, I roused myself, Alistair Baillie very decently lent me the owner's cabin which he occupies, and I got my piece on women in Antarctica written. It owes a lot to Gillian Deakin's calm and intelligent observations at Davis.

85

"Young woman—go south. It's a ball. But don't come down here for romance."

This is Gillian Deakin's message to her sisters back home in Australia. Gillian, who is twenty-eight, is the station doctor at Davis, the second woman to hold that post and the sixth woman doctor at an Australian Antarctic station. She is small, self-assured, cool. She has thought through her position carefully in the four months since she has arrived. As she did for some time before that. She does fitness exercises on the landing outside her surgery every morning, and takes part in most activities on the base. She resents the fact that, though men grow flowers in the hydroponics shack, it is regarded as her role to put them on the mess tables. Her decision to drive a concrete truck raised some eyebrows at first. It has now become an accepted part of station life. Gillian is, she says, post-feminist, though conscious of the ground won for her by others.

For all her many interests, and her determination not to be typed, Gillian Deakin's main aims down south are medical. "I don't like the direction medicine is going in Australia—down here you can be the traditional doctor, which is wonderful." She has, as she says, only healthy young people to look after and, with the encouragement of the Antarctic Division, she has drawn up four research programs for the year. She is proud of the being the first to introduce computerised medical research into Australian Antarctica, and will carry out a synoptic review of physiological records from all stations over the past ten years. She will study the effects of exercise on cardiovascular status—in other words, when is enough exercise enough. And she will conduct two alcohol studies, for which there is no shortage of volunteers. One will test whether a certain fish-oil extract will lower cholesterol and triglyceride levels raised by drinking, and the other is a "binge study" of the effects of acute alcohol intake at parties on the blood-pressure system.

This is a great place for such tests—there are no booze buses on the way home.

There are a number of women down here for the summer at our three Antarctic bases—meteorologists, radio operators, scientists, technicians—but only three (four less than last year) will be spending the winter.

Apart from Gillian Deakin, there are two women winterers at Casey, Sheryl White, twenty-five, from Rockhampton, who is a radio operator and the cheerful postmistress there, and Kim Harrington, twenty-seven, a radio technical officer from Launceston.

The women I have spoken to at our base, including the summer expeditioners, who have been here four months, have all come down with a high sense of expectation which has not been blunted since arrival, despite minor irritations. If they share characteristics, these are that they are small, active, cheerful and articulate. The big cities aren't represented, and there is usually some background in service life or outdoor activities which has led to a self-possessed outlook: "I knew what I was in for before I came down."

As expeditioners they are at least as adaptable and effective as the men. Jim Bleasel, the director of the Antarctic Division, has, semi-seriously, talked of a base run mainly by women. No-one I have talked to here regards such an idea as undesirable or impracticable.

The motivation of these women seems in most cases to be a version of the typical young Australian's desire to "see as much as possible before I settle down". They refer, time and again, to the constant renewal they get from the physical beauties of Antarctica, and to the delights of being able to choose from a variety of spare-time activities: seal counts, blizzards when out at a camp, skiing across the sea-ice to the penguin rookeries. "Every morning when I look out," Sheryl White says, "I think there's no other place in the world like it."

The women share such feelings with the men on the stations. But another motivation they have all to themselves: that they have to establish that women have a place in Antarctica.

The first woman to winter at any Australian Antarctic station was Louise Holliday, the doctor at Davis in 1981. Since then there have been about twenty. But, says Gillian Deakin, "We are still very much on trial. There are plenty of people around who think we're more trouble than we're worth. If a man makes a mistake down here, it's because of his personality and the circumstances. If a woman makes a mistake, it's because she's a woman."

Given the Australian male ego, the quite false image of Antarctica as a he-man frontier of the Yukon type that Robert Service wrote his poems about (an image many wish to protect), *and* the problem of female toilets (I have heard this seriously mentioned), it is surprising that women were ever allowed south of the Antarctic convergence.

Anti-feminine prejudice as such seems rare, though it exists. Gillian Deakin believes that the men are asked if they will accept a woman doctor and, if they will not, are sent to a base without one. Offensive behavior towards women is also rare, though it does happen. "When things look like getting a bit rough in the club, we just get out of the way," say the women at Casey. At least one of the women doctors who have served down here is acknowledged to have had a very rough time.

Unease about women there certainly is. "Some men," says Gillian Deakin, "only know women as mothers, sisters or girlfriends." The concept of the sentient, independent career woman can be strange and unsettling to these men, demanding adaptations they cannot make. Gillian Deakin again: "We've all got to feel good about ourselves in some way. If men want to feel good about their masculinity, I can accept it." On the credit side, though, Dr Deakin is impressed by the way Antarctica teaches people to tune into each other's feelings: "You can get finely adjusted sensitivities here."

The real problem is that, as at present constituted, life at our bases is a monastic life. As such, it is psychologically demanding. Violent tendencies have to be suppressed by self-control, for otherwise there is no knowing where they may lead. The tendency of isolation, as Gillian Deakin says, and as Shackleton said before her, is for people to live more intensely, but at a simpler level. With the natural environment, this can be profoundly uplifting. Gillian talks of the sense of peace that comes from standing on a hill looking at the icecap. But, in other ways, especially in relationships with a small group you have had no choice in assembling, there can be a lot of individual suffering—suffering which does not always lead to new understanding.

The presence of women on a base makes a difficult situation more complex, more volatile, more reactive. A married couple on one station was criticised for holding hands at the pictures. The perfume and clothes a woman wears can disturb men more than she realises. Recently, on one station, two men who criticised the work of a woman were physically attacked by her self-appointed defender.

Of course it's not easy for the woman. One I have spoken to says, "It's like living under a microscope—ten minutes' talk with a man and the rest think the worst." Gillian Deakin says: "Men can be buddies and do everything together, including going out into the field. If I want to do something with a bloke I have to worry about the consequences. Pat one, pat them all, of course, and I've made a firm intellectual decision not to get involved with anyone down here. But emotionally I shall be interested to see how I handle this as the year goes by."

It's all very well to say, as one male observer does, "The problem is not with the women, but with the men and their hangups," but that solves nothing. The cultural tensions remain. In earlier times one enthusiastic woman doctor had to be talked out of giving therapeutic body massage to all the men on her station. There have been several compulsory repatriations of women, for pregnancy or alleged inappropriate behavior.

Such treatment may seem discriminatory and unjust, but it does reflect a real situation, which is that until there are enough women on the bases to make their presence there less remarkable, less 'unsettling', then they are in danger of being seen as a complication of questionable worth. And not only by the unthinking and prejudiced. Intelligent, compassionate and pro-female men say: "The novelty value is too high."

The outgoing officer-in-charge at Davis, Paul Butler, who is with us on this ship, has a seventeen-month-old son he has not seen for fourteen months. The new officer-in-charge at Davis, Rob Easther, has a two-month-old daughter he has not seen at all. Sensible people are beginning to ask why the wives of such men as these, if they so wish, are not on the stations with them. A few kids around the place would have a marvellous effect on morale and, after all, Dangerous Dan McGrew had the lady who was known as Lou.

This is more than whimsy. It is part of the whole necessary process of getting away from the fortress concept of station life in Antarctica. The bases are here, as intimidatingly permanent as Ayers Rock. They have to become more human, more ordinary places, places that are on the way to somewhere, not places at the end of the line.

The British, French and Germans bar women in Antarctica. So, I am told, do the Russians. The Americans welcome them, and even find ways to solve the lavatory problem. All have good reasons. But these nations do not regard Antarctica as an extension of their homeland, as we are beginning to do.

Australia has to move as rapidly as possible towards the position where women in Antarctica stop being curiosities and become part of the scenery. We need common or garden Adélies, rather than empress penguins.

(*Australian*, 12 February 1986)

86

Even if I hadn't been feeling ill, the journey home, I am sure, would have been one of desultory feelings of anticlimax. The contrast with the voyage south, all high hopes and grand excitement, was strong. The picking up of loose ends is less compelling than watching the tapestry being woven. And we continued to be knocked about by the sea, the only consolation being that those on the little *Nella Dan* have a much worse time.

Still, there were things to do. Graeme Manning, for instance, allowed me to have a twenty-minute talk to Jim Hasick, the oic at Mawson, on Inmarsat. He sounded a good chap. Talking to him made me even more sorry we hadn't got to Mawson, which Jim Bleasel told me, when he boarded the ship with the pilot as we went back up the Derwent, was the most impressive of our Antarctic stations—no doubt as a counter to what I had written about Casey and Davis. Well, at least Mawson's the oldest and most traditional of our stations, and it has the huskies—magnificent stories from Paul Butler, who wintered at Mawson ten years ago, and remembers well all their individual personalities and eccentricities. Wonderful dogs, Paul says, describing a thousand-mile trek from base, along the coast with a thousand-pound sledge. The men, to the dogs' delight, do a great deal of the work, especially in soft snow.

Jim Hasick's most interesting news was that the *Nella* had breezed into Horseshoe Harbor after only twenty-four hours of ice-breaking, a task for which the *Nella* has little capacity in any case. Hasick says the *Icebird* could have got in even more easily, and that he had implored the Antarctic Division and the ship to do this. More evidence of the low priority given to the views of the man on the spot? Or, as Jim Bleasel would claim, superior knowledge back in Hobart, with the advantage of satellite pictures? Anyway, not a word of Hasick's views were passed on to the ship's officers in the *Icebird*, who have renewed their bitter complaints that whether or not they get an important situation report, or personal or official message concerning them, is merely a matter of luck if the Antarctic Division is involved. Even the *Icebird*'s own messages to its offices in Hobart were not being passed on by the Antarctic Division, so the ship now communicates directly via Inmarsat.

Then some evenings we had 'lantern lectures' by the eggheads and boffins on board. Anders Karlqvist talked on Swedish polar research—he has, incidentally, a horrifying story of tourists on Spitzbergen, their camp raided by a polar bear, sitting on a hillside watching a companion being eaten alive—and Ron Lewis-Smith on British work in the Weddell Sea area. I produced my slides on Tristan da Cunha and had an overflow audience in the mess: many questions, and pleas to continue the show another night, which I did.

These talks were an excellent idea. They proved that nearly all on board, including and even especially the so-called 'hard cases', were hungry for information and ideas, and that they were more than willing to trade drinking time for things to think about. The talks also helped to dispel the puzzle, for many, of what the 'joy-boys' on board were on about. There should have been an organised program of this kind of thing throughout the whole voyage. The fact that there wasn't is part of the 'people problem', the inability of our Antarctic planners to understand that attention to people is not a separate issue from logistics, but intimately bound up with it.

As the seas quietened down a bit, and we got closer to Hobart, I got out my little Olivetti and made some notes on this.

87

'Happy is the country that has no history' might be a slogan coined for Australian Antarctica. After six weeks in Antarctica and three separate landfalls my most pervasive impression is that we Australians are the ultimate existentialists. Each year here begins anew with the breakup of the winter ice.

I have heard young people in Germany describe themselves as being of the "fatherless generation". Australians could be called a fatherless (and motherless) nation. There is little consciousness that we live in a continuum of past, present, future. (The supposedly 'educated' have no advantage here over the underclass.) Many of the people on this ship can only account for the interest of the Project Blizzard people in Mawson's hut at Commonwealth Bay by saying that "they must be making something out of it".

A young Argentinian friend, recently migrated to Australia, asks me searching questions about Antarctica. He knows a lot about its history, back to the days of Scott and Shackleton.

"Where the hell did you learn all that, Jorge?" – "In primary school." Australian schoolkids shown over the *Icebird* are flummoxed: "*What's* Antarctica? *Where* is it?" "They know more about the Maoris in New Zealand than they know of Antarctica", I was told.

To ask over breakfast when and how and why Mawson base started, or Casey, or Davis, is to receive blank stares, even from those who work for the Antarctic Division. "What's this man on about now?" The bases started when we saw them. Why should anyone want to know more?

The single indication I have had here that Australian Antarctica has a history is the framed photograph of John King Davis, that curmudgeonly Antarctic seadog whom I once met, above the notice boards in the living quarters at Davis. Apart, of course, from the sad neglect of Mawson's hut.

Seek on the bases for some outline history of each station, to interest, to instruct, perhaps even to inspire those carrying on the work down here today, and you will look in vain. Surely we can't understand the tasks that lie before us without knowing what they are the end product of?

At Davis I was given a map of the Vestfold Hills. Up the coast a few miles from the base there's a notation: SIR HUBERT WILKINS CAIRN (1939). CANISTER SURMOUNTED BY ROCK CAIRN. Rob Easther, the Davis oic, actually has a copy of the message in the canister in his files, though he hasn't yet visited the site. It reads:

TO WHOM IT MAY CONCERN

RECOGNIZING THE RIGHTS OF THE COMMONWEALTH OF AUSTRALIA TO ADMINISTRATE THE AREA REFERRED TO IN AN ORDER IN COUNCIL DATED 7TH FEBRUARY, 1933, WHEREIN IT IS ORDERED AS FOLLOWS: –

"THAT PART OF HIS MAJESTY'S DOMINIONS IN THE ANTARCTIC SEAS WHICH COMPRISES ALL THE ISLANDS AND TERRITORIES OTHER THAN ADELIE LAND WHICH ARE SITUATED SOUTH OF THE 60TH DEGREE OF SOUTH LATITUDE AND LYING BETWEEN THE 160TH DEGREE OF EAST LONGITUDE AND THE 45TH DEGREE OF EAST LONGITUDE IS HEREBY PLACED UNDER THE AUTHORITY OF THE COMMONWEALTH OF AUSTRALIA."

I PLACE THIS DOCUMENT AS A RECORD OF HAVING PUT FOOT ON THE ANTARCTIC MAINLAND IN SEVERAL PLACES AND UPON SEVERAL OF THE ISLANDS IN THE VICINITY BETWEEN LATITUDES 68 SOUTH AND LATITUDE 69 SOUTH AND BETWEEN LONGITUDES 77 EAST AND 79 EAST AND HAVING FLOWN THE FLAG OF AUSTRALIA, LEAVE IT WITH THIS RECORD ON THE LAND BORDERING THE PRESENT CONTINENTAL GLACIER SURFACE AT APPROXIMATELY LATITUDE 68.30 SOUTH AND 79 DEGREES EAST LONGITUDE.

DATE JANUARY 11TH. 1939. HUBERT WILKINS

At the bottom of this document three members of ANARE noted their visit on 10 May 1957.

So here's a piece of local history, and of Antarctic history as well. The background is interesting, even amusing. Wilkins shipped with the American explorer and aviator, Lincoln Ellsworth, on the *Wyatt Earp* in October 1938, as adviser and expedition manager. Wilkins had been south with Ellsworth several times before, and had been his companion on the epic flight from Graham Land to Little America in 1935. On their way south, Ellsworth informed Wilkins of his intention to claim sections of Australian Antarctic Territory for the United States. As a result Wilkins quietly rowed ashore at several points along the coastline and made his claims for Australia. In this canister there was—and presumably still is—both Wilkins territorial claim *and* a copy of the travel magazine *Walkabout.* The area is now officially known as Walkabout Rocks.

I'd be rather surprised if anyone at Davis, with the exception of Rob, knows that a copy of the document is there. Wilkins is the chap, incidentally, who said of his fellow Australians: "Most Australians are well off in regard to creature comforts, and many of them soon reach independent means; yet the absence of the expressed desire for culture and for higher things, and their contentedness with the mediocre, make them perhaps the poorest rich people in the world today."

With Mawson station we at least now have Phil Law's *Antarctic Odyssey*, which tells us how Mawson was selected as the first Australian base in 1954, how it was reconnoitred, how it was settled. It's an absorbing story, which he doesn't take much further than this, and to me it helped to put our whole Antarctic story into perspective. I doubt if there's a copy of that book on any of our Antarctic bases. After what I have seen, and more to the point felt, down here, I'm sure that Phil wrote that book out of some kind of despair that the Antarctic present badly needs contact with the Antarctic past.

One could go further, and point to the self-evident lack of interest of the Antarctic Division in the educational and cultural life and the entertainment of the expeditioners down here. These men and women have minds which many are eager to expand, and they have the opportunity to do so. Only some *ten* videos a year are being sent to our stations, which is about one a month for the period of isolation. At the moment no films are being sent, though there is a strong demand for classics and for contemporary films. (There are residual collections on the bases from times past, quite valuable now, they say.) No real effort is being made to send down, on a firm annual basis, the best books of the year to each station. The excuse is always the same: "We don't have the money left over after we've done other things." The answer to that is: "You'd soon find the money if you thought it important." Just another aspect of the lack of attention to Antarctic morale.

The most serious immediate impact of the poverty of history in Antarctica, of the poverty of the Antarctic Division's historical imagination, is that working data are lacking for every aspect of our Antarctic operations. Should an officer-in-charge of a station need to know urgently the records of fast ice in the bay for the past ten years, he has no source, except some fallible memories if he's lucky. Should a scientist wish information about the ground covered by field parties in earlier years, he has no readily accessible key to open the door. Should a plumber need to know the age of a building, he can only guess.

Until last year there was at least the officer-in-charge's daily log, the originals in Hobart and a duplicate set from the beginning on each station. They run to many feet of shelf space in the cluttered cubbies which serve oics for offices, but they are there. Perhaps the ultimate expression of the lack of interest in our history here is that the oics have been told that the logs are no longer officially required. The reason is believed to be fear of the Freedom of Information Act.

These log-books, in any case, are largely a wasted resource. In them, and even more in files in Hobart, lies the wisdom of thirty or forty years' experience, not to speak of the record of a vast expenditure of treasure. Every malfunction, every crisis, every human drama; every unexpected crevasse, every treacherous whim of the seasons, every curious discovery which may some day lead somewhere, is, or should be, recorded. But, at the start of every year, this accumulation of knowledge begins anew. There is no key to the storehouse. There is no abstraction under headings, loose-leafed and added to year by year, to act as a ready-reckoner and a *vade mecum* to new expeditioners. What has been done where? What are the problems of walking overland to this hut? Who did first climb that peak? Where is the sea-ice in Long Fiord most dangerous? What day of late summer do the elephant seals haul out on the beach? When was the fast ice as thick and long-lasting as it is this year?

Some of these questions are vital, some merely of long-range interest. All will go unanswered, unless an outgoing expeditioner passes on some folk-wisdom, or someone returns from an earlier year. And I have heard such questions asked, unavailingly, many times in recent weeks.

The absence of codified operational data is detrimental, dangerous and a very expensive economy. Far more serious are the broader intellectual questions. While there have been academic studies in the broader legal and political implications of our Antarctic responsibilities, there have been no searching historical analyses of the directions our technology, our science and our politics have taken us, *in Antarctica itself*, in the past fifteen years or so—or, for that matter, since the establishment of Mawson in 1954.

What is needed is the writing of real, 'professional' history about Australia's involvement in Antarctica. This is not something that can be handed over to a superannuated public servant, or to a desk clerk with time on his hands. It is something that calls for as much skill as turning a difficult job on the lathe, administering a complex organisation or navigating a ship through the ice. It involves sensitivity, interest, hard work in archives, the ability to find the right people and to know how to ask them the right questions. It involves the ability to ask the right questions of one's material and of oneself. It involves the courage to identify and espouse an argument, a standpoint.

History is not a luxury. We shall lack the essential tool to our understanding of Australian Antarctica until those with the interest and capacity to write its history are found. And not just one history. Preferably several, or at least a history that will provoke a debate.

It would be pleasant to think that the intellectual horizons of the Antarctic Division were wide enough to see this investment as imperative.

88

There are also other ways of approaching the truth. "Art," says Oscar Wilde, "is our spirited protest, our gallant attempt to teach Nature her proper place." Before Australians can begin to understand Antarctica, they will need poets there, painters, writers of all kinds, sculptors and musicians too. Designers, and craftsmen and women. Lots of them, feeding new perceptions into our national consciousness of the territory we have the impertinence to claim. This will be more important to the future than organising the birth of a baby at Casey, or performing a wedding ceremony at the top of the Scullin Monolith, or conning someone into paying us royalties for minerals.

89

Diary, 6 February 1986. Our wedding anniversary.

Feeling very much happier. The sea is down and the ride more comfortable. The sound of the ABC news fanfare down the corridor reminds me that we shall soon be home. There's a shout outside the cabin: "Only one more day to go! It seems yesterday that it was four hundred!"

We shall see Tasmania at sunrise tomorrow.

There's been an informal get-together, a spontaneous party, down on the foredeck, awash with an Australian summer sun and steady enough to wander about from group to group, all with tinnies in their hands. Now that the helicopter deck is clear of most of the deck cargo we brought down it's pleasant to have a little space to perambulate, a reminder that we've not been able to do this before. The occasion brought most of us together in a mutuality of affection cemented by the realisation that we should soon part for ever. Anders Karlqvist was made to take part in a mammoth Vegemite-sandwich eating contest, and inducted as an Australian to a great ovation.

As I came back from the party up those steep external companionways on the outside of the module, steps I have climbed up and down so many times, heavily accoutred and weighed down, I felt a flash of sentiment for what I have been

The *Icebird* in Horseshoe Harbour, Mawson.

through on this ship, for how much I have seen and done in six weeks, how much learnt, how many first impressions modified and corrected. In particular I've learnt respect for most or even all of the ones called "hard cases", even "animals", by others. As these fellows keep on telling me, their mates are wonderful people to work with; they all give what is asked of them, and more; they resent foolish and thoughtless leadership; they shrewdly note who is not with us at the little rage they're having. I was in the army as a private soldier, and I know how they feel. No doubt they can't fully accept me as one of them, but I won't stand above them now.

This has been a Dante-esqe voyage to unimagined regions. The experiences came so fast on top of each other that overload delayed effective response. I had to adapt to climate, but to find my latitude in other ways also. I came to detest the ship and the predictability of life aboard it. But I have come increasingly to like those with whom I travel. Different people, and different *kinds* of people, certainly; different degrees of Antarctic experience, different ways of amusing ourselves. But the passing around of the tinnies on the foredeck seemed to say that we had learnt from each other as well as from the South.

90

And as for the *pensieri segreti*?

On the way up the Derwent I asked my Italian friends for their secret thoughts, as so many weeks before I had told them I would.

"Perhaps if you claimed less of Antarctica you would be in less trouble," said one.

The other said: "Why don't you say to us Italians: 'You've got enough troubles in Italy already—why try to make more for yourselves in Antarctica?'"

And from Jaime the Spaniard: "You're killing a gnat with a sledgehammer. Only rich countries can afford to do that."

The remarks are all true, and all deserved. They have the insights of the detached observer. But I'm not that detached. To echo Vance Palmer, those are my people down there.

AFTERWORD

The Director of the Antarctic Division, Jim Bleasel, kindly commented on this manuscript before it went to press. As I pointed out in my Author's Note, the book is essentially intended to be a record of events and impressions as they happened or were conveyed to me on my visit to Antarctica. In fairness to Jim Bleasel and the Antarctic Division, however, the following observations on my text are here recorded. Others have been incorporated into the text itself.

Section 1 Customs procedures for returning expeditioners have now been changed, and inspections are now carried out as the ships come up the Derwent, allowing the immediate reunion of families at the wharf on docking.

Section 5 The Antarctic Division has since insisted on a reduction of the charges made for liquor on the *Icebird*, and on the provision of Australian as well as German beer. Australian food (Section 45) is also now supplied.

Section 16 The ANARE huts and the Project Blizzard markers, the presence of which I criticise at Commonwealth Bay, are—together with all other intrusive material—to be removed from the vicinity of Mawson's hut and placed over the ridge at the site of the new summer base.

Section 29 Jim Bleasel argues that money has not been *diverted* from Australian science in Antarctica to other purposes, but that it has suffered *relative* to the building and support programs; programs which have, at least to some extent, been designed to make it safer and easier to conduct science in Antarctica. He adds that the development of the lightly-mounted summer bases is not as a result of the scientists' complaints, but because science can more effectively be promoted this way.

Section 43 The portraits of the Queen and Lord Casey, damaged during ructions at Casey station that year, are now again in place at the station, as are similar pictures at other stations.

Section 73 The issue of Australian radio licences to the Soviet stations within Australian Antarctic Territory was routinely announced in the *Commonwealth Gazette* until 1985. Since then the relevant Act has been changed, and the procedure discontinued, though it will probably be reinstated.

Section 75 Jim Bleasel informs me that newsletters and 'annuals' are produced on our stations. The ones I have seen, though, are largely photographic and have little literary interest.

Section 76 Jim Bleasel firmly defends the increasing use of centralised communications in Antarctic affairs, especially when they enable a sophisticated analysis of ice conditions, and hence the direction of shipping movements, on the basis of satellite information. He says that the 1985 besetment of the *Nella Dan*, costing between $20,000 and $30,000 a day over 54 days, was due to the fact that satellite communications were not at that time available. "Effective communications remove emotions from the scene and keep voyages on schedule." He also states that the delays in forwarding messages through Hobart to expeditioners' families have now been overcome, and that private telex messages from stations are only rationed in the sense that station business must take priority. Bleasel does not agree that more operational responsibility should be transferred to ships and bases.

Section 86 Jim Bleasel states that a copy of Phillip Law's book would have been sent to all bases. On the question of station logs, these had been discontinued without Bleasel's knowledge and were reinstituted following my report to the Minister on my return. The question of 'sector logs' for each base, in which data relating to specific areas will be codified, is (1988) under consideration.

More generally, Jim Bleasel draws attention to a considerable development of scientific work in Antarctica in the past two seasons, with 131 scientists in the field in the 1987–88 season working in nine different areas. He claims that Australia has retrieved its position in the Antarctic science stakes to now lie third or fourth in the field; though at the same time he holds that our international prestige in the Antarctic Treaty area lies primarily in our capacity to develop well-argued policies, drawing of course on relevant science where necessary.

No garbage, says Bleasel, is now left in Antarctica. It is either incinerated in a closed system or brought back to Australia. Each station now has an environmental officer, and all tips have been closed. (This still leaves, of course, the problems of the past to be dealt with.)

Morale—the 'people problem'—is now receiving professional attention from psychologists, at considerable expense. (I don't much like the sound of this—I would have thought that what was primarily needed was thought, common sense, adequate debriefings, listening to people—and attention to some of the small, human issues I have mentioned in this book. The 'people problem' will not respond to being diverted to 'professionals.' The debriefing problem may in part be solved by a new system whereby 'station managers' at head office in Hobart will be responsible for all that happens at specific stations, and will visit Antarctica yearly to conduct debriefing sessions at their stations.)

Increased attention is, Bleasel says, being paid to Antarctic libraries, and especially to the supply of Antarctic books. I remain unconvinced, however, that enough attention and money is being devoted to the provision of general books, let alone to quality fiction and the like, which remains ignored.

APPENDIX: MV *ICEBIRD*, VOYAGE 6, 1985–86

Crew List

Ewald Brune, master.
Norbert Sickert, first mate.
Jörg Thielheim, second mate.
Alistair Baillie, supercargo.
Axel Feurer, radio officer.
Harald Watenphul, chief engineer.
Martin Uhlig, second engineer.
Maciej Tomcyk, electrician.
Klaus Jannssen, AB.
Michael Zylau, OS.
Andreas Adolphi, OS.
Peta Bragg, OS.
Manfred Mischke, AB.
Uwe Johannssen, chief cook.
Horst Herrmann, second cook.
Ernst Klein, chief steward.
Andrea Philippen, stewardess.
Ulricke Feddern, stewardess.
Matthias Matz, greaser.
Richard Kintrup, greaser.

Passenger List

Jan Adolph, works supervisor.
Maurice Afafaci, upper atmosphere physics engineer.
Trevor Bailey, laboratory manager.
* Joe Banhidy, DHC civil officer.
* Ian Bayly, biologist.
Bob Beale, *Sydney Morning Herald.*
* William Blunt, Project Blizzard.
* Manfred Boelter, ecologist (Germany).
Keith Bolton, technician.
* Steven Bunton, Project Blizzard.
Gary Burns, physicist.
* Paul Butler, officer in charge, Davis 1985.
Robert Cervellati, observer (Italian).

* Jonathan Chester, Project Blizzard.
* William Couch, DHC plumber.
  Graham Courtney, corporal, Larc Detachment.
* Gregory Crispo, Project Blizzard.
  Paul Croton, surveyor.
  Brendan Doran, Department of Foreign Affairs.
* Earl Dorney, Project Blizzard.
* Hayden Drysdale, surveyor.
* Steve Dulfer, DHC plant operator.
* Wayne Eastley, maintenance plumber.
* Danny Eslake, seal researcher.
  Warren Farmer, corporal, Larc Detachment.
* Brian Fitzgerald, surveyor.
  Tony Foran, DHC construction engineer.
  Phil Gard, Antarctic Division, cargo-master.
* Michael Gatehouse, Project Blizzard.
  Alan Gibson, crane operator.
  Peter Gormly, medical officer.
* Darryl Grove, DHC plumber.
  Judy Hall, Antarctic Division, typist.
  John Hannaker, project manager, DHC.
  Alex Harris, engineer.
* Glen Hay, DHC foreman.
  Bill Hazelton, glaciologist.
* Greg Hodge, field training officer.
* Bob Hollingshead, meteorological observer.
  Rodney Hutchinson, geophysicist.
  Ross Jongejans, electrician.
  Steven Jukes, Australian Maritime College student.
* Ludger Kappen, ecologist (Germany).
  Anders Karlqvist, director, Swedish Polar Research Secretariat.
* Kevin Kazazes, DHC project officer.
  Peter Kerr, DHC maintenance officer.
  Helmut Kopp, surveyor.
* Glen Kowalik, field training officer.
* Andreas Kühn, ecologist (Germany).
* Ron Lewis-Smith, botanist, British Antarctic Survey.
  Soren Linneman, Antarctic Division.
* Gerry Love, diesel mechanic.
  Michael Madigan, surgeon, observer.
  Russel Madigan, Polar Names Committee.
  Brian Malcolm, DHC business manager.
  Graeme Manning, Antarctic Division, voyage leader.
* Eric McGibbon, National Mapping.
* Shaughan McGovern, electrician.
* Angela McGowan, Project Blizzard.
  Linda Millard, DHC administration officer.

Stephen Murray-Smith, ministerial observer.
Geraldine Nash, Antarctic Division, deputy voyage leader.
Greg Newman, captain, Larc Detachment.
* Martin Nowell, DHC senior technical officer.
David O'Neill, plant operator.
Malcolm Parnell, National Mapping.
Leigh Perkins, private, Larc Detachment.
Don Petersen, DHC training officer.
* David Phillips, DHC carpenter.
Patrick Quilty, assistant director, science, Antarctic Division.
Lee Ranford, Antarctic Scientific Advisory Committee.
Jamie Ribes-Lorda, major, observer (Spain).
Gabriel Riccardi, observer (Italy).
* Reg Sheridan, National Mapping.
Matt Sherlock, Antarctic Division, engineer, ionospheric prediction.
James Shevlin, Antarctic Division.
* Wayne Smith, DHC.
* Peter Sprunk, diesel mechanic.
John Stanhope, secretariat, Antarctic Scientific Advisory Committee.
* David Steele, radio technical officer.
Leslie Stonach, DHC personnel officer.
Greg Stuart, private, Larc Detachment.
* Gary Sugrue, meteorological observer.
Ian Swan, private, Larc Detachment.
* John Tanusoski, DHC.
Ivan Taylor, plant supervisor.
* John Tibbits, radio technical officer.
Greg Tucker, surveyor.
Brian Turnbull, Antarctic Division, project manager.
* Alistair Urie, upper atmosphere physics engineer.
* John van den Hoff, biologist.
* Colin Walker, DHC plumber.
John Walling, surveyor.
William Ware, meteorological inspection officer.
* Don Waugh, diesel mechanic.
Paul Wright, *Sydney Morning Herald*.
Peter Yates, physicist.
Anthony Young, Antarctic Division.

* signifies homeward bound only.

INDEX

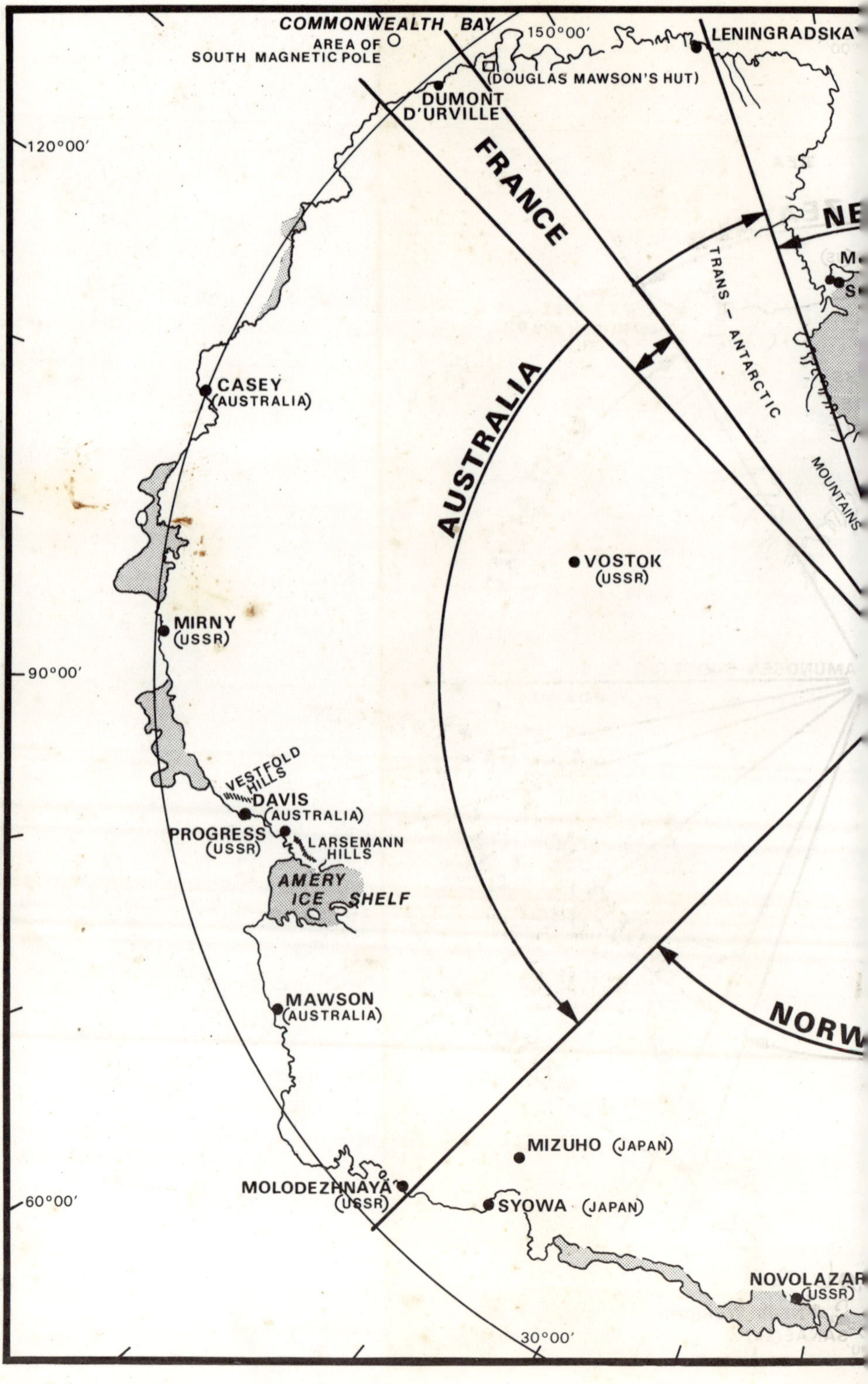

COMMONWEALTH BAY
AREA OF SOUTH MAGNETIC POLE
150°00′
LENINGRADSKAYA
(DOUGLAS MAWSON'S HUT)
DUMONT D'URVILLE
120°00′
FRANCE
TRANS – ANTARCTIC
MOUNTAINS
AUSTRALIA
CASEY (AUSTRALIA)
VOSTOK (USSR)
MIRNY (USSR)
90°00′
VESTFOLD HILLS
DAVIS (AUSTRALIA)
PROGRESS (USSR)
LARSEMANN HILLS
AMERY ICE SHELF
MAWSON (AUSTRALIA)
NORW
MIZUHO (JAPAN)
MOLODEZHNAYA (USSR)
60°00′
SYOWA (JAPAN)
NOVOLAZAR (USSR)
30°00′